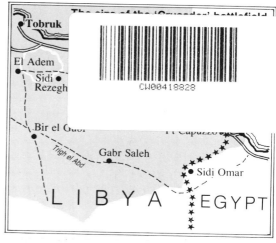

The size of the 'Crusader' battlefield

Tobruk
El Adem
Sidi Rezegh
Bir el Gubi
Ft Capuzzo
Gabr Saleh
Trigh el Abd
Sidi Omar
L I B Y A   EGYPT

M E   A N

Tobruk
El Duda   Belhamed
El Adem   Zaafran
di   Sidi Rezegh
uftah
Bir el Gubi   Gabr Saleh
Gas
Main battle area
18 November -
7 December
Fc

Mersa
Matruh   Maaten
Baggush
Kenayis
El Alamein

I C A

~EX~
LIBRIS

J.C. Clark

G. M. HOUGH

Oasis Force

Jarabut

T

Siwa

CRUSADER

CRUSADER

Eighth Army's forgotten victory,
November 1941 – January 1942

RICHARD HUMBLE

Leo Cooper

First published 1987 by Leo Cooper Ltd
Leo Cooper is an independent imprint of
the Heinemann Group of Publishers,
10 Upper Grosvenor Street,
London W1X 9PA.
LONDON   MELBOURNE   JOHANNESBURG   AUCKLAND

ISBN: 0-85052-2846

Printed by Redwood Burn Ltd
Trowbridge, Wiltshire

CONTENTS

ILLUSTRATIONS

The author and publishers are grateful to the Imperial War Museum for permission to reproduce illustrations nos. 6, 7, 8 and 9. All the other photographs are reproduced by kind permission of the Robert Hunt Library.

MAPS

INTRODUCTION

When Winston Churchill coined the phrase 'Before Alamein we never had a victory' he was being grossly unjust. Amid all the British triumphs and setbacks of the North African 'Desert War' of 1940–43, the epic of Alamein had been preceded a year before by the British Eighth Army's first victory. This was Operation CRUSADER, Eighth Army's first desert offensive, launched on 18 November, 1941, by General Sir Claude Auchinleck, Commander-in-Chief, Middle East. CRUSADER not only cracked the myth of the German 'Desert Fox', Rommel, and the invincibility of his *Afrika Korps*: it was the first clear-cut defeat suffered by the German Army since the outbreak of the Second World War, after over two years of unbroken triumph on all fronts.

Admittedly the fruits of CRUSADER were snatched away before they could be gathered, because German reinforcements arrived while the Eighth Army was still gasping at the end of an over-extended supply line. A well-timed counter-attack by Rommel in late January, 1942, sent the Eighth Army reeling back, on the first stage of its bitter road through Gazala and Tobruk to Alamein. But the fact that the CRUSADER victory was wasted does not alter the way it had been won; and in many ways CRUSADER still ranks as the most fascinating encounter of the entire Desert War.

CRUSADER was the mobile battle incarnate. It was not dominated – as were Gazala, Tobruk, Alamein, or the last battles in Tunisia – by attempts to breach or turn a fortified line. Minefields and fixed defences played little or no part. CRUSADER was nearly all pure manoeuvre in the virtually featureless open desert, governed by each side's efforts to locate and destroy the enemy's armoured forces: the battle squadrons of the desert.

Major-General von Mellenthin, at the time a Major and Rommel's chief Intelligence officer, has paid his own tribute to the CRUSADER fighting:

> Between 19 and 23 November, 1941, the Eighth Army and the *Panzergruppe Afrika* were engaged in an armoured battle which has a unique place in the history of war. There has never been a battle fought at such an extreme pace and with such bewildering vicissitudes of fortune. More than a thousand tanks, supported by large numbers of aircraft and guns, were committed to a whirlwind battle fought on ground which allowed complete freedom of manoeuvre and were handled by commanders who were prepared to throw in their last reserves to achieve victory. The situation changed with such rapidity that it was difficult to keep track of the movements of one's own troops, let alone those of the enemy. The dust clouds raised by charging men and tanks and moving columns added to the obscurity, and, as Auchinleck says, "at times the fog of war literally descended on the battlefield".
>
> This battle made tremendous demands on generalship and staff work, and for this reason I believe it deserves very careful study today. We are likely to learn far more from these great "manoeuvre battles" of the desert than from the later campaigns of the war in which the issue was decided by weight of numbers and weapons.[1]

German expertise in mobile warfare had been humiliatingly demonstrated in every desert encounter since Rommel's first panzer units had crossed to North Africa in February, 1941. Until the American Grant and Sherman tanks arrived in the Middle East in the summer of 1942, German tanks consistently outranged the best machines the Eighth Army could field. The tanks of the two panzer divisions of the *Afrika Korps* were also more reliable mechanically and better handled tactically, and they were closely backed by superior anti-tank guns – most notably the notorious '88', the 88mm anti-aircraft gun used with devastating effect against Allied armour.

Against this formidable opposition, unbeaten in the open field since its arrival in North Africa, the newly-formed Eighth Army nevertheless advanced, engaged – and won.

I have tried to make this the first in-depth account of this unique battle as it unfolded from day to day, drawing on personal and official accounts from both Axis and Allied sources. From these it would appear that, though glaring errors of judgment were made on both sides, the Germans made most. If Rommel ever put his thoughts on his defeat in writing, they have not survived; Sir David Hunt (then G3 Intelligence in XIII Corps) has commented that Rommel 'seems to have adopted the motto of the sundial, "I only count my sunny hours"'. But it is certain that none of Rommel's mistakes handed the Eighth Army the gift of a freak or opportunist victory.

Seventeen days of non-stop fighting – six more than it took Montgomery to break through at Alamein in 1942 – separated the opening of Eighth Army's offensive and the gaining of CRUSADER's main objective, the relief of Tobruk. Another exhausting fortnight of pursuit and hard-fought rearguard actions was required to gain the second objective: the expulsion of all Axis forces from Cyrenaica. Though torrential rains turned the desert into a quagmire and prevented the third phase – 'ACROBAT', the advance on Tripoli – from getting under way, Eighth Army had by mid-January, 1942, recovered all the ground lost to Rommel in the previous spring. Such was the victory of CRUSADER.

CHAPTER 1

THE BATTLEFIELD

On 10 June, 1940, Italy's declaration of war on France and Britain marked the first major extension of the Second World War outside the confines of Europe. Within twenty-four hours, on the border between Italian Libya and British Egypt, the first shots were fired in the North African theatre of war. The British possessions in the Middle East, above all Egypt, with the vital maritime artery of the Suez Canal, now lay exposed to attack from Italy's territories in both North and East Africa: Libya to the west and Ethiopia to the south-east.

The alignment of Fascist Italy and Nazi Germany had been established with the proclamation of the Berlin–Rome 'Axis' of October, 1936, and confirmed by the signing of the Italo–German 'Pact of Steel' on 22 May, 1939. In the last months of peace – both before the outbreak of European war in September, 1939, and Italy's participation ten months later – the prospect of Italy going to war in alliance with Germany had not unduly worried the Franco-British alliance. With Italy and Libya contained by French Morocco, Algeria and Tunisia to the west, and British Egypt to the east, Allied control of the Mediterranean seemed secure enough. But the total collapse of France in June, 1940, transformed the strategic position in the Mediterranean. With Vichy France maintained, after the surrender of June 22, as an Axis vassal state, French North Africa was no longer a check on Mussolini's expansionist plans. The Duce thereupon prepared to advance his 'New Roman Empire' with the conquest of British Egypt and the seizure of the Suez Canal.

Though convenient and brief, the term 'British Egypt' requires

1

qualification; the status of the British in Egypt was very different to that of the Italians in Libya. The Italian tenure of Libya derived from outright conquest in 1911–13, followed by colonial rule. Egypt, however, was technically an independent kingdom prepared to grant Britain military and naval base facilities by treaty, the last of which in 1940 still had sixteen years to run. Egypt's young King Farouk (aged twenty in 1940) had no intention of sacrificing himself or his country by fanatical adherence to the British cause, which after the fall of France in June, 1940, seemed parlous in the extreme. Until the tide turned permanently against the Axis in the autumn of 1942, high-pressure British diplomacy was required to discourage pro-Axis sympathies on the part of Farouk, his ministers and his army officers. These sympathies, naturally, waxed and waned with the changing fortunes of war in the Western Desert. But the real prospect of a pro-Axis rising in Egypt represented a constant weakness from which the Axis forces in North Africa never suffered.

'This lunar land'

Alexandria in Egypt, Tripoli in Libya – for all but the last six months (December, 1942–May, 1943) of the war in North Africa, these were the rival ultimate objectives of the Axis and British armies. Between the two cities lay a vast irregular arc of desert terrain some 1400 miles long, dominated in the centre by the prominent northward bulge of Libya's eastern province, Cyrenaica.

This coastal bulge is formed by Cyrenaica's dominant natural feature: the range of the 'Green Mountains' or Jebel Akhdar. Some 50 miles wide and 150 miles in length, the Jebel Akhdar was in 1940 the deepest sector of the ribbonlike coastal strip which contained some 95 per cent of Libya's Italian colonists and occupation troops. This coastal strip also contained the only tarmac road in Libya: the Via Balbia, hugging the coast and threading the Jebel Akhdar from Tripoli all the way to the Egyptian Frontier 20 miles south of Bardia.

South of the coastal strip lies an interminable belt of flat and stony desert, broken only by occasional low ridges or watercourses (*wadis*), the latter dry throughout the year except when converted to torrents by highly infrequent cloudbursts. The dreary reaches of this desert belt finally vanish, on average about 150–200 miles inland from the coast, into the shifting expanses of the Libyan 'sand sea'.

Along the northern extremity of the sand sea (the 'real' desert of popular imagination, with giant dunes and little or no hard going) are dotted the infrequent oases of the eastern Sahara: Murzuq, Marada,

2

Aujila, Jalo and Jarabub in Libya, and Siwa 40 miles across the frontier in Egypt. South of this line, in the sand sea, only the Beduin Arabs and the light patrols of the British Long Range Desert Group (formed July, 1940) moved at will. In general the oasis line marked the southernmost boundary of the North African battle zone, which was restricted to the coastal strip with the Via Balbia and the inland belt of 'hard' desert, where tracked and wheeled vehicles could operate.

'This land', wrote British war poet Jocelyn Brooke,[1]

> was made for War. As glass
> Resists the bite of vitriol, so this hard
> And calcined earth rejects
> The battle's hot, corrosive hand, no green
> And virginal countryside for War
> To violate. This land is hard,
> Inviolable; the battle's aftermath
> Presents no ravaged and emotive scene,
> No landscape à la Goya. Here are no trees
> Uprooted, gutted farms; the unsalvaged scrap –
> The scattered petrol-cans, the upturned
> And abandoned truck, the fallen Heinkel; all
> The rusted and angular detritus
> Of war, seem scarcely to impinge
> Upon the hard, resistant surface of
> This lunar land.

A poet or philosopher could well argue that the wastes of the Western Desert were the ideal environment for the destructiveness of twentieth-century warfare. Put in terms of hard military reality, a more intensely difficult theatre in which to deploy and supply armies – especially motorized and armoured forces – could hardly be imagined. It was a theatre about 1100 miles long and 50 miles deep, containing only one metalled road threading its length, with a northern flank closed by the Mediterranean coast and a southern flank wide open as far as the sand seas of the interior. Food, fuel, spares, workshops – there were none of these in the Desert, where the ancient ideal of 'living off the country' was impossible. (In the Western campaign of May–June, 1940, for example, even mechanized forces had been able to refuel from wayside garages and petrol pumps in the Low Countries and France.)

The one exception – water, the most vital commodity of all in the Desert – only pointed the rule. An army's effectiveness in Desert warfare was largely measured by its ability to survive, when outrunning or being cut off from its own lines of communication, on the infrequent wells of local water. The natural properties of this local water varied widely in taste and mineral content, often verging on the undrinkable. At Jarabub Oasis on the southern flank, for instance, the water was stiff with magnesium salts, guaranteeing instant diarrhoea with all its debilitating effects. Salinity was the usual problem. Just enough salt in the water was a positive advantage, compensating for body salt lost by sweating; but too much salt in the water made it impossible to brew drinkable tea or coffee, and the intense temperature drop during the night made hot drinks an essential in the Desert.

Though both sides in the Desert War shrank from the atrocity of poisoning wells when abandoning terrain, it was considered legitimate to contaminate wells with non-poisonous but nauseating substances. (The British, when abandoning Cyrenaica in March–April, 1941, put bone oil down every well between Tobruk and the Egyptian Frontier and regretted it heartily when they came back eight months later in CRUSADER.) On the whole the Axis forces in Libya had the worst of it with the natural water resources in Cyrenaica, nearly all of them salty. The British in western Egypt could draw on the copious wells of comparatively sweet water at Buq Buq and Mersa Matruh. As every can of water which had to be transported meant one less can of fuel, this was a considerable supply advantage when added to that of the railway running west to Matruh from Alexandria.

The Italian Army in Libya was logistically anchored to the coastal strip: to the road lifeline of the Via Balbia, and the coastline sealane running east from Tripoli. In 1940 the hills of the Jebel Akhdar separated the only two ports in Cyrenaica – Benghazi and Tobruk – capable of feeding an army with seaborne supplies. Because of the threat posed by the British Mediterranean Fleet based on Malta and Alexandria, Benghazi was the most eastern port in Libya to which it was prudent to ship supplies direct from Italy. But Tripoli, only 300 miles south of Sicily, always remained the main supply terminus for convoys and single-ship sailings from Italy. From Tripoli, coast-hugging ships could run supplies 400 miles east to Benghazi; and from Benghazi another 280 miles around the bulge of the Cyrenaican coast to Tobruk, only 80 miles west of the Egyptian Frontier, and the only sheltered anchorage between Benghazi and Alexandria. The latter facility gave Tobruk a unique importance throughout the Desert War.

The overland supply-route east from Tripoli was not only restricted to the lone artery of the Via Balbia but was far longer than the sea route, skirting first the southward meander of the Gulf of Sirte and then the northward bulge formed by the Jebel Akhdar. From Tripoli the Via

Balbia ran 450 miles through Misurata, Buerat, Sirte and Nofilia to El Agheila, where the provincial boundary was marked by a grandiose triumphal arch known to the Italians as the *Arco dei Fileni* and to the British as 'Marble Arch'.

El Agheila was to the Axis in Libya what El Alamein was to the British in Egypt: the only place where the lie of the land provided a natural bottleneck which could be held with reasonable confidence in the southern flank. Though seven times further from Tripoli than Alamein was from Alexandria, and nowhere near as formidable a natural obstacle as the Qattara Depression south of Alamein, the salt marshes of the Sebcha el Chebira nevertheless protected the El Agheila position from any rapid flanking move to the south. Deepened and widened by abnormally heavy winter rains, the Sebcha el Chebira was destined to play a decisive role in the last act of CRUSADER in January, 1942.

From El Agheila the Via Balbia followed the sharp northward swing of the coast 160 miles through Mersa Brega, Agedabia and Ghemines to Benghazi, the second port of Libya and administrative centre of Cyrenaica. Benghazi ties with Alamein and Tobruk as the most-remembered place-names of the Desert War; it was always a favourite with journalists (not to mention postwar film-makers), most probably because of its vaguely dramatic-sounding name. In 1940 Benghazi had about 65,000 inhabitants, roughly one-third of them Italians. Though geographically set aside from the mainstream of the Desert campaigns, up on the western side of the Cyrenaican bulge, Benghazi was a logistic prize of the highest importance to both sides because of its port facilities. But to desert-weary troops of all nationalities, Benghazi always exercised a particular fascination; it was, after all, the only 'European-style' *town* between Tripoli and Alexandria, with hotels, bars, cinema and shops, desirable beyond compare after weeks of heat, sand and iron rations 'out in the blue'.

From Benghazi two modest railway lines served the Italian settlers in the western Jebel Akhdar: one running 30 miles south-south-east to Soluq and the other, via Er Regima, 65 miles north-east to Barce. Skirting the inland rise of the Jebel Akhdar 2500 feet (760 metres) above sea level, the Via Balbia hugged the coast on the 45-mile stretch from Benghazi to Tocra before heading inland, climbing steeply towards Barce 20 miles east. At Barce, Libya's road link forked for the only sector between Tripoli and the Egyptian frontier. Before the two branches rejoined 85 miles east of Barce at Giovanni Berta they were connected by a third road running south from Apollonia on the coast via Cirene, crossing the Via Balbia 8 miles east of Beda Littoria (Sidi Rafaa) and connecting 10 miles further on with the southern branch at El Faidia.

5

Reunited at Giovanni Berta, the Via Balbia continued east for 25 miles, leaving the eastern Jebel Akhdar to return briefly to the coast at Derna. It then swung south-east via Martuba and Tmimi to cut off the Ras el Tin peninsula, which forms the Gulf of Bomba at the eastern end of the Cyrenaican bulge, resuming an easterly course at Gazala, 60 miles from Derna. From Gazala the Via Balbia ran slightly south of east 40 miles to Tobruk, on again 75 miles to Bardia, and finally south 10 miles to Fort Capuzzo on the Egyptian frontier. Once landed at Tripoli, therefore, all troops bound for eastern Cyrenaica and the invasion of Egypt faced a journey of some 970 miles before they even reached the Frontier.

The Frontier zone

The Frontier between Libya and Egypt was delineated by three dominant features, two artificial, one natural: the Wire, the Road and the Escarpment.

The Wire was the triple fence of staked barbed wire which the Italians had strung along the Libyan side of the Frontier, from the coast 7 miles south of Bardia to Jarabub Oasis, 150 miles to the south. By its very nature, this fatuous creation spoke volumes for the Fascist regime's preference for outward display at the expense of military practicality. The Wire connected no natural gradients and linked up no natural strongpoints. It was of little use in its original function, to control Arab movements across the Frontier; as a military obstacle it was negligible, being easily gapped or merely pushed aside by vehicles. Far too long to be converted into a genuine barrier by reinforcement with belts of mines, it was erratically studded with a handful of blockhouses, none of which was within sight of its neighbours. Events soon proved that a whole army could pass the Wire without being detected. And yet, as Alan Moorehead has commented, 'that absurd fence, like many another absurd Italian device in the desert, seemed to give the Fascist soldier a sense of security, and he patrolled it with the persistence of a goldfish edging along the confines of his glass jar'.[2]

Two miles east of the Frontier blockhouse of Fort Capuzzo, the Road crossed the Wire into Egypt, snaking down the coastward plunge of the Escarpment to the toylike Frontier village of Sollum with its modest barracks for the Frontier guard, thence eastward hugging the coast past Buq Buq, Sidi Barrani and Maktila towards Mersa Matruh. From the railhead at Matruh, 135 miles east of Sollum, road and rail ran side by side for the last 175 miles past Maaten Baggush, El Daba and El Alamein to Alexandria and the Nile Delta. To concentrate in the Sollum

6

area, British forces based in the Delta therefore had to travel some 310 miles – 175 miles of which could be assisted by rail as far as Mersa Matruh – compared with the 970 miles demanded of Italian forces moving east to the Frontier from Tripoli.

The third and easily the most dramatic feature dominating the Frontier zone was the Escarpment, where the inland plateau takes a breathtaking plunge to the level of the coastal strip. The effect of the Escarpment was to divide the terrain at the Frontier into two levels: that of the plateau above and the road beneath. But the Escarpment was not an impenetrable barrier. By the vital defile of Halfaya ('Hellfire') Pass, 10 miles east of the Wire, it was possible for attackers, whether bound east for Egypt or west to Libya, to outflank defenders trying to block the road or to reach the inland plateau, without having to restrict their activities to the coastal trip. Command of Halfaya Pass therefore became an essential prerequisite for successful operations on either side of the Wire. West of Halfaya the Escarpment curves north, frowning straight down over both Sollum and Bardia to the east, and in the other direction levelling out to merge with the plateau extending westward to Tobruk.

The tremendous effect of the Escarpment in the Frontier zone has been vividly captured by Sir David Hunt:

> . . . for a parallel to the Escarpment at Sollum you must think of Beachy Head. The Escarpment was in fact a steep, precipitous cliff on land. Halfaya is not a pass like the Brenner or the Khyber; it is a place where a steep spur slopes down to the coastal plain looking like a ladder placed against a wall, up which a track zigzags to the top (There is a second Halfaya some 30 miles further east at a place called Halfway-House.) To see the escarpment at dawn or at sunset when the air was clear and cool enough and the low sun cast an oblique shadow was to see one of the great works of nature. It sharply divided, by a sheer plunge of some 300 feet, the coastal plain at its foot, sandy, and near the sea marshy, from the plain which ran back level with its crest, bare limestone covered with gravel and a thin crust of sand, tilting away southwards to Jarabub and the Sand Sea.[3]

Such were the natural lie of the land spanning the Libyan–Egyptian Frontier and the meagre artificial aids to mobility and defence which had been created there by June, 1940. The natural challenge to orthodox military operations, particularly those with long-range objectives stretching lines of communication, was great. But so was the opportunity presented by the ever-open desert flank to the south. When Italy's declaration of war extended the European conflict to North Africa, it remained to be seen which army would prove the most adept at exploiting that opportunity.

Hit and run on the Frontier, June–September, 1940

In June, 1940, the Italians had two armies in Libya, the Fifth and the Tenth, facing respectively towards French Tunisia and British Egypt. The French collapse enabled Marshal Italo Balbo, commanding in Libya, to concentrate his formidable resources against Egypt. But in Cairo the British Commander-in-Chief, Middle East – General Sir Archibald Wavell – had no such advantage. His vast command area included not only Egypt but the Sudan, Palestine and Transjordan, and Cyprus. He was expected to provide forces to assist in the defence of British Somaliland, Aden and Kenya, and if necessary to support operations in Iraq and the shores of the Persian Gulf. The collapse of France created a potentially hostile 'northern front' in the form of French Syria, which remained fully garrisoned under the Vichy régime. To fulfil all these tasks, Wavell had some 86,000 men in the 'Army of the Nile'. He could afford to deploy no more than 36,000 in the Western Desert – against the 250,000 contained by the two Italian armies in Libya.

As with the Army of the Nile as a whole, none of Wavell's 36,000 troops in Egypt included units at full strength. The 7th Armoured Division's two armoured brigades were supposed to have three regiments each; instead they had two, and incompletely equipped at that. The 4th Indian Division had two brigades instead of three, with most of its artillery still to arrive. The New Zealand Division was at an even more rudimentary stage of preparation, with a single infantry brigade, an incomplete cavalry regiment, a machine-gun battalion, and one field artillery regiment. The other troops in Egypt consisted of fourteen British infantry battalions and a couple of artillery regiments. Under his hand in Egypt, Wavell in June, 1940, therefore had the equivalent of two under-strength divisions to pit against an estimated fifteen Italian divisions in Libya, backed by additional Italian Army, Corps and colonial troops.

These certainly appeared hopeless odds on paper, but Wavell diagnosed several factors working to his advantage. The first was that Italian Tenth Army was not fully concentrated in eastern Cyrenaica – the 'Marmarica', as the Axis called the region between the Jebel Akhdar and the frontier. No invasion of Egypt was imminent; indeed, several weeks were likely to pass before such an invasion could be attempted. The second advantage was the issue of quality versus quantity. Incomplete and outnumbered though they were, Wavell's units did not consist of raw colonial recruits and conscripts. Two of Tenth Army's six divisions were native Libyan troops; another two were 'Blackshirt' divisions, supposedly manned by enthusiastic crusaders of the Fascist régime but of indeterminate training and combat value. In Tenth Army there were in fact only two metropolitan (regular) Italian Army divisions, of which slightly more than half were reckoned to be volunteers who had undergone adequate training; the rest were conscripts.

The third British advantage was Italy's chronic unreadiness for war, as reflected by known and suspected deficiencies in Italian weaponry and equipment. Italian tanks were certainly in no way superior to the obsolescent models in British service. The Italian Army was also deficient in artillery, especially medium artillery, which was in short supply. Not only did the Italian Army lack any equivalent to the excellent British 25-pounder gun howitzer, but its standard infantry rifle and light machine-guns soon proved inferior to the British Lee–Enfield rifle and Bren. The only serious miscalculation of Italian potential by British Intelligence was the believed lack of motor transport. (In fact the Italian Army in 1940 had more motor transport than the German Army, which still relied extensively on horsed transport. Without the vast numbers of captured Italian trucks the British, in their first desert offensive, would never have been able to push on further west than Tobruk.)

These question-marks over the combat worthiness of the Italian 'big battalions' gave definite grounds for reasonable confidence in Cairo, though the taciturn Wavell could never be accused of succumbing to euphoria. He was, however, as confident as he could be that the Italians had nothing to match the best of his units. This was 7th Armoured Division, which had been formed and trained in Egypt as the 'Mobile Division' after the Munich Crisis of autumn, 1938. It had been moulded by its first commander, Major-General Percy Hobart ('Hobo'), the most controversial advocate of modern tank theory in the British Army. Hobart had created a superb fighting unit, wise in the desert and its ways, a self-supporting team of armoured cars, tanks, artillery and motorized infantry. The divisional emblem of 7th Armoured was that fast-moving survivor of the desert wastes, the jerboa or 'desert rat'. By June, 1940, the 'Desert Rats' of 7th Armoured Division were familiar with every inch of terrain between Base Area in the Delta and the Libyan frontier. Their commander was Hobart's successor, Major-General Michael O'Moore Creagh.

In 7th Armoured Division Wavell therefore had the perfect instrument for his planned course of action against the Italian Frontier Forces as soon as war broke out. This could be described as a mix of intelligence-gathering and instruction, the latter to the Italians' cost. Wavell urgently needed to know how ready the Italian Army might be to cut loose from its bases, strongpoints and lines of communication, and operate as freely in the open desert as the British were learning to do. At the same time he was determined to demonstrate that the British *were* masters of the desert, and that in consequence Italian forces could nowhere consider themselves safe from sudden and damaging attacks.

Such was the brief given by Wavell to Major-General Richard O'Connor, appointed on 7 June, 1940, to command 'Western Desert Force', the core of the future XIII Corps, and ultimately of the Eighth Army. O'Connor was a desert-wise commander who enjoyed Wavell's complete confidence, and who in turn had complete confidence in the ability and potential of 7th Armoured Division. When O'Connor commanded 8th Infantry Division in 1939 he had worked closely with Hobart's 'Mobile Division' and described it as 'the best-trained division I have ever seen'.

It therefore fell to O'Connor to make the first combat test of the British Army's mechanized cavalry regiments, which had been merged with the Royal Tank Corps to form the Royal Armoured Corps on 1 April, 1939. The first mechanized cavalry regiment to draw blood was the 11th Hussars. This famous regiment had ridden in the first line of the Light Brigade at Balaclava, but its performance in the first ten days of the Desert War could hardly have been in greater contrast to that headlong charge to destruction. On the night of 11/12 June the 11th Hussars, in their Morris and Rolls-Royce armoured cars, pushed through the Wire on a broad front and fell on the Italian Frontier outpost at Sidi Omar, 20 miles south-west of Sollum. Surprise was complete because no news, either of the imminence or of the outbreak of war, had been passed to the Italian Frontier forces. Sustained vigorous patrolling by the 11th Hussars took seventy prisoners by nightfall on 12 June.

This success was promptly reinforced by Creagh's 4th Armoured Brigade and the motorized infantry of 7th Armoured Division's Support Group, pushed west from Buq Buq, the 7th Queen's Own Hussars, in light and cruiser tanks, and a company of 1st Battalion, King's Royal Rifle Corps. The aim was now to keep up the pressure along the Frontier line and push north-west to beat up Italian forces moving up the Via Balbia from Tobruk. Hit-and-run was the order of the day, striking at objectives which were as widely dispersed as possible. On 14 June, while the 7th Hussars captured Fort Capuzzo, the 11th Hussars raced south to take the Frontier strongpoint at Maddalena 60 miles away. By nightfall on the 15th the 11th Hussars were lying in ambush on the Via Balbia west of Bardia which on the 16th yielded a 'bag' of twenty-one Italians killed and eighty-eight captured. The latter included General Lastucci, the Tenth Army's Engineer-in-Chief. The news of Lastucci's capture enraged Mussolini, who had been comforting himself with the thought that the initial losses had been suffered by Libyan and not Italian troops. 'It is the material that I lack. Even Michelangelo had need of marble to make statues. If he had had only clay he would have been nothing more than a potter. A people who for sixteen centuries have been an anvil cannot become a hammer within a few years.'[4]

The Duce was being grossly unfair to his own troops, who were trying to counter the fluid tactics of the British with the static defensive tactics in which, always unimaginatively and as often as not sketchily, they had been trained. This static mentality enabled a squadron of 11th Hussars to locate a powerful Italian force at Nezuet Ghirba, 30 miles west of Sidi Omar, on 15 June. The aggressive movements of this handful of armoured cars froze the Italians into immobility until 4th Armoured Brigade sent forward a squadron of cruiser tanks from the 7th Hussars and a troop from J Battery, Royal Horse Artillery. With these reinforcements the British promptly attacked and routed the Italians, killing or capturing over 100 of their 400 infantry, capturing all seventeen of their light tanks, all four of their guns and several trucks. British casualties from this spirited action were nil.

The efforts of Western Desert Force on the ground were ably supported by the Royal Air Force, whose commander in the Middle East theatre was Air Chief Marshal Sir Arthur Longmore. As with Wavell's ground forces, the RAF in Egypt and Palestine faced heavy odds: 205 aircraft of all types – fighters, bombers, reconnaissance and transport – against an estimated 425 Italian (in fact an over-estimation of 112). The RAF's obsolete Gloster Gladiator biplane fighter was reckoned a match for the Italian Fiat CR42, also a biplane design; but in bombers the Italians had a definite edge over the British, in quality as well as quantity. Unable to reach as far west as Benghazi with a full bombing load, the RAF's twin-engined Bristol Blenheim Mk 1s were forced to concentrate on targets in eastern Cyrenaica. But the Italian three-engined Savoia–Marchetti SM79 could not only reach western Egypt from airfields in the Benghazi region, it could range deep into Egypt from forward airfields such as El Adem, south of Tobruk.

For all that, Air Commodore Collishaw's No 202 Group, RAF, supporting Western Desert Force from its HQ area at Maaten Baggush, matched the ground forces in seizing a decisive moral advantage in the first week of the Desert War. The Blenheims struck first at El Adem, destroying or damaging eighteen aircraft caught undispersed on the ground. They then turned their attentions to Tobruk, damaging the old Italian cruiser *San Giorgio*, oil tanks and other shipping in three days of attacks by day and night. Apart from these attacks the RAF supported Western Desert Force's capture of Fort Capuzzo on the 14th as well as providing regular reconnaissance flights for the ground forces. Nightly 'nuisance raids' on Tobruk by lone aircraft left the Italians so jumpy that on 29 June trigger-happy gunners in *San Giorgio*, serving as a floating battery at Tobruk, shot down the aircraft in which Marshal Balbo was preparing to land. Balbo's loss was a considerable blow to Italian morale; no ordinary Italian general, he was an aviation hero who had personally led the first formation flight across the Atlantic in the 1930s. It is pleasant to record that the RAF saluted Balbo's passing by dropping a letter of condolence.

The death of Balbo coincided with a resumption of the defensive by O'Connor and Collishaw, before any serious rise in British casualties could be suffered. But O'Connor and Collishaw had achieved the basic aim envisaged by Wavell: to snatch the moral initiative on the Libyan Frontier and, by early and aggressive action, instil a healthy defensive-mindedness on the Italian side. This they had certainly done. Only nine days before his death Balbo had written to Marshal Pietro Badoglio, the Italian Chief of General Staff:

> Our light tanks, already old and armed only with machine-guns, are completely outclassed. The machine-guns of the British armoured cars pepper them with bullets which pierce their armour easily. We have no armoured cars. Our anti-tank defences are largely a matter of make-do; our modern weapons lack adequate ammunition. Thus the conflict has taken on the character of steel against flesh, which only too easily explains certain episodes which are luckily of little importance.[5]

This 'steel against flesh' state of mind was not the best of omens for the early invasion of Egypt which Mussolini demanded, and it was inherited by Balbo's successor, Marshal Rodolfo Graziani. In his former post as Army Chief of Staff, Graziani had passed on Mussolini's urgings to Balbo; now, as the man on the spot in Libya, he found that the situation looked very different from the way it looked in Rome. When Graziani took over, 15 July had been fixed as the date for the invasion of Egypt, but he wasted no time in scrapping the idea and pressing for an autumn invasion instead. In preparing for the first Desert offensive of the war, Graziani became the first of many generals (of whom most were to be British) forced to resist political urging for a premature advance in North Africa.

Though Graziani was later to protest that he was obliged to 'wage the war of the flea against the elephant', and to lament that 'one cannot break steel armour with fingernails alone', he was not at first deterred by fear of superior British numbers or matériel. Though usually maligned as the worst of the Desert generals, Graziani was entirely correct in his choice of first priority: the supply problem, without a solution to which no offensive could be sustained and no gains secured.

As his foremost reason for delaying the invasion of Egypt, Graziani pleaded insufficient motor transport, especially water tankers. Indeed, nothing more perfectly illustrates the Italians' military reluctance to adapt to Desert conditions than the fuss they made over the water problem. No other country would have dreamed of wasting priceless cargo tonnage in shipping thousands of tons of bottled spa water to North Africa, as the Italians did. Instead of concentrating on bulk water supplies and local water purification for all ranks, the luxury of bottled drinking water for officers was a symptom of a serious flaw in the Italian Army. The 'gap-osis' between the pampered officer caste and the troops was real, and it was destined to have disastrous results in battle.

Apart from the drinking-water obsession, Graziani showed good sense in demanding time to build an adequate supply-line for an invasion intended to arrive in Egypt to stay. He also judged, again with perfect correctness, that motorized infantry pushed forward without tank protection would be merely inviting disaster. Graziani refused to send the Libyan and Blackshirt divisions of Tenth Army into Egypt without the protection of an armoured group (light and medium tanks) to beat off the pestilential British armoured cars. But this armoured group, whose first units landed in Libya in July, had no tank more formidable than the 11-ton M-11 medium tank – easy meat for the British 2-pounder anti-tank gun. The armoured group was never intended to manoeuvre and fight in the open desert, where British combat superiority was taken for granted by Tenth Army Intelligence: 'As is well known, the enemy has units more manoeuvrable in the desert than ours.' This glum assumption had been implanted by sustained British raiding throughout July and August, which by 9 September had inflicted admitted Italian casualties of 3500 since 11 June. British casualties for the same period had been 150.

The Italian Invasion of Egypt, September, 1940

If Graziani had had his way, he would have deferred invading Egypt until the cooler weather of October; but Mussolini would have none of it. The Duce was desperately eager for a military exploit to set beside

Germany's conquest of the West in May and June, particularly after the abject failure of the Italian Army in the last week of the French campaign. By the second half of August, as the German air bombardment of southern England intensified, it seemed that all Italy would have to compare with the German conquest of Denmark, Norway, the Netherlands, Belgium, Luxembourg and France – and soon, apparently, of the British Isles too – would be the occupation of British Somaliland. This comparatively insignificant feat had been accomplished between 3 and 19 August. The Italians had invaded from Ethiopia in overwhelming strength, only to suffer a bloody nose in a four-day battle at Tug Argan (11–15 August). The British General Godwin-Austen then successfully disengaged and evacuated his tiny force from the port of Berbera, having suffered only 260 casualties and inflicted 2052 casualties on the invaders.

The Italian losses in Libya since 11 June had been inflicted by British mobile forces. Italy's conquest of British Somaliland, as costly as it was empty, had revealed what the British could do – with no mobile forces, let alone adequate artillery support – when denying a single road to a massive Italian frontal assault. Put together, the two experiences did nothing to enhance Graziani's prospects in Egypt, where the Italian divisions would be trying to push down the single coast road with their desert flank wide open to the British mobile forces. None of these considerations made the least impression on Mussolini. By the end of August, 1940, the Duce had one overriding obsession: for honour's sake, to save his face with Hitler, the Italian invasion of Egypt must coincide with the German invasion of England.

The air battle over southern England was still hanging in the balance when the first Italian troops crossed into Egypt in the early morning of 13 September. Wavell had perfectly judged his opponent, for Graziani had no intention of advancing further east than Sidi Barrani. If he had shown any signs of doing so, Wavell's defence plan provided for stiffening resistance culminating in a full-strength counter-attack by 7th Armoured Division at Mersa Matruh. Energetically harassed by rearguard forces, the Italian forces which advanced on the head of Halfaya Pass showed no inclination to attempt any ambitious manoeuvring in the southern flank. The Italian advance, as predicted, concentrated on the coastal strip, advancing painfully along the extensively demolished rough road. The effect of these demolitions was increased by the mounting weight of Italian traffic.

By nightfall on 16 September Graziani was able to report that Tenth Army's leading division, 1st Blackshirt, had occupied Sidi Barrani. With this feat Tenth Army had covered 60 of the 315 miles between

14

the Frontier and Alexandria. Even though there had been no British resistance worthy of the name, Italian casualties nevertheless numbered 120 dead and 410 wounded. (Graziani would have been considerably more depressed if he could have known that the British losses were only fifty.) The discovery that the British had rendered all local well-water undrinkable before abandoning Sidi Barrani was the last straw. Graziani therefore ordered General Francesco Berti, Tenth Army's commander, to dig in at Sidi Barrani. The next bound of 75 miles further east to Mersa Matruh could be considered only when a heavy-traffic road surface had been extended from the Frontier to Sidi Barrani, together with a water pipeline. Graziani expected the logistic build-up for the advance on Mersa Matruh to take at least two months.

Mussolini's reaction was predictable. According to his Foreign Minister, Count Ciano, the news of Sidi Barrani's fall left the Duce 'radiant with joy. He has taken the entire responsibility of the offensive on his shoulders, and he is proud that he was right'. This euphoria alternated with rages and sulks when realization dawned that Graziani would not advance further. Visiting Rome on 2 October, Graziani spelled out his reasons to Ciano: 'Graziani feels that we must still wait for some time, at least all of November, to complete our logistic preparation, which is the only real guarantee of success. He is afraid that the English may resist for a long time at Mersa Matruh. If our supply lines do not function well we would have to retreat. And [prophetic words indeed] in the desert a retreat is equivalent to a rout.'[6]

Graziani's prudence was both welcome and frustrating to Wavell. It was welcome because in London, even though the likelihood of an attempted German invasion was looming large, Churchill and the War Cabinet had bravely despatched substantial reinforcements to the Middle East. With other much-needed matériel, these reinforcements consisted mainly of three tank battalions (154 light, cruiser, and heavy 'infantry' tanks), forty-eight 2-pounder anti-tank guns and forty-eight 25-pounder gun/howitzers. They sailed from the United Kingdom on 22 August and were already approaching the Red Sea and Suez when the Italians marched on Sidi Barrani. If Graziani's caution granted enough time for the new troops, tanks and guns to be rendered desert-worthy, Wavell's eventual counterstroke would be all the stronger.

On the other hand the Italian halt at Sidi Barrani, though not wholly unexpected, prevented Wavell from inflicting the punishing early counter-attack with which he had hoped to drive the Italians back from Mersa Matruh. Now they would have to be dug out from their positions at Sidi Barrani. But Wavell's thinking was never limited to evicting Tenth

Army from Egypt and repossessing the Frontier; he intended to exploit the Italian retreat to the last attainable inch, pushing on from the Frontier to take Bardia for certain, probably Tobruk, and if possible Derna as well. The eventual depth of his hoped-for advance into Libya would depend on how much transport and fuel could be captured from the Italians. This in turn would depend on how the Italian machine would stand up to a sudden, unforeseen defeat. Wavell did not believe that the Italians would be able to execute a similar well-judged retreat to that carried out by Western Desert Force between 13 and 16 September (which incidentally made at least partial nonsense of Graziani's prophecy that 'in the desert a retreat is equivalent to a rout').

The 'COMPASS' plan, September–December, 1940

Such was Wavell's confidence that on 21 September, only five days after the arrival of the Italians at Sidi Barrani, he gave his Chief of Staff, General Smith, the first draft outline for Western Desert Force's counter-attack. By this date Wavell knew that the Italians were showing every sign of digging in for a long stay at Sidi Barrani, and that the convoy bringing his tank reinforcements had escaped any last-minute disaster on its voyage up the Red Sea. As he soon discovered, the price he had to pay for those reinforcements was constant urging from Churchill that they should be sent into action, and the sooner the better. By October, 1940, Wavell and Graziani were in the same boat; both generals were fighting off pressure from their political masters to get on with the war. And this pressure, again on both generals, increased with the approach of Mussolini's next military gamble: the Italian invasion of Greece.

The Greek campaign, opened from Italian-held Albania on 28 October, 1940, weighed far more heavily on Wavell than on Graziani. Wavell already had to parcel his military resources between the Western Desert and East Africa. Once the Italians invaded Greece, he was obliged to send all assistance he could to Britain's last ally on the European mainland. Though willing to send a modicum of air support to Greece, Wavell could not send any sizeable expeditionary force of troops without staying on the defensive both in the Western Desert and in East Africa. To fend off any potentially disastrous orders to that effect from Whitehall, Wavell informed Foreign Secretary Anthony Eden (during the latter's visit to the Middle East in mid-October) of his plan to attack Tenth Army in its positions at Sidi Barrani. As Wavell had hoped, Churchill 'purred like six cats' when he got the news on 8 November, after Eden's return to Britain. Inevitably, Wavell was bombarded with requests for precise details from Churchill – details which Wavell

16

declined to give. For COMPASS, the Sidi Barrani attack, silence and security were vital; on Wavell's orders, the men of 7th Armoured Division and 4th Indian Division were only let into the secret 48 hours before the attack.

During November, the last month of lull in the Western Desert, two resounding Allied successes simultaneously 'cleared the decks' for the COMPASS attack and ensured that Graziani would be left to fight with what he had. The first was the series of Greek counter-attacks (2 November–5 December) which hurled the Italians back into Albania with immense suffering and loss. The second was the British Fleet Air Arm attack on the Italian battle fleet at Taranto (11 November), which gave the British Mediterranean Fleet a decisive superiority in battleship strength until the summer of 1941. The next result was to focus the attention of the Italian High Command on the latest fiasco in Albania, and to ensure that no massive reinforcements could be shipped to Libya in time to stem the effects of the British attack.

By the first week of December Wavell had all the information he needed to order the COMPASS attack on Sidi Barrani with reasonable confidence of success. The five forward divisions of Tenth Army were now firmly anchored on ten fortified camps, designed to provide immunity from damaging raids of the type launched by the British back in June and July. Six of these camps were grouped on the coastal strip, south and east of Sidi Barrani; the other four, some 20 miles away to the south-west, were apparently intended to block the eastern approach to the Escarpment and Halfaya Pass on the desert flank. Viewed in its simplest terms, Wavell envisaged COMPASS as a concentrated blow against one or more of these camps, sustained for a minimum of four to five days; subsequent operations would depend on the effectiveness of the Italian response.

One of the thousands of Italian letters, captured when it was all over, summed up the basic errors of the Italian deployment:

We are trying to fight this war as though it is a colonial war in Africa. But it is a European war in Africa fought with European weapons against a European enemy. We take too little account of this in building our stone forts and equipping ourselves with such luxury. We are not fighting the Abyssinians now.[7]

It was General O'Connor, charged with the execution of COMPASS, who noted that the Italian camps were sited purely with a view to beating off a frontal assault from the east. Reconnaissance patrols had discovered a 15-mile gap in the centre of the Italians' defensive arc, between Nibeiwa camp 15 miles south of Sidi Barrani and Rabia camp to the south-west. O'Connor proposed to pass the COMPASS strike force – 7th Armoured Division and 4th Indian Division – through this gap. He would then take out the four central camps – Nibeiwa, Tummar West, Tummar East, and Point 90 – with 4th Indian Division attacking from the *west*, releasing 7th Armoured towards Buq Buq to raise havoc on the main Italian line of communications. The Navy would meanwhile bombard the two coastal camps: Sidi Barrani and Maktila, 12 miles further east. 'Selby Force', a motorized column some 1800 strong under Brigadier A. R. Selby, was to attack west along the coast road and interdict any attempt by the Sidi Barrani and Maktila garrisons to assist the Nibeiwa and Tummar camps.

As COMPASS would stand or fall on the speed of Italian reaction everything was done to give the impression of a large-scale desert training exercise south-west of Mersa Matruh. How long this could be sustained was questionable, for the final jumping-off point of 'Piccadilly', 15 miles south-east of Nibeiwa, was to be reached by a march of 60 miles across the open desert on D −1 (December 8). As it happened, the approaching COMPASS forces were spotted by an Italian aircraft at about noon on the 8th and their position (30–40 miles south-east of Nibeiwa) was accurately reported. But no further reconnaissance sorties were ordered to amplify this lone sighting, which was interpreted by Italian Intelligence as being consistent with the British patrolling of past weeks. After nightfall on 8 December 4th Indian Division made its final 13-mile march into the Rabia/Nibeiwa gap, and lay poised to launch its attack on Nibeiwa at first light.

COMPASS: the Battle of Sidi Barrani, 9–11 December, 1940

The keynote of the attack on the Sidi Barrani camps was a triple chord: surprise, well-directed bombardment programmes by concentrated artillery, and the shattering moral effect of the massive Infantry ('I') tanks. These weapons were being used for the first time in the desert. As their name implied, they were designed not for fluid tank-versus-tank engagements but for the anachronistic role of infantry support in the attack. The 'I' tanks were perfectly suited to the task set them at Sidi Barrani, their slow speed (little more than 6mph cross-country) and 2-pounder gun being more than offset by their maximum armour thickness of 78mm. This was impenetrable to every Axis anti-tank gun in service in 1940–1 apart from the German 88mm. The 'I' tanks were easily the most terrifying 'secret weapon' hurled at the Italians at Sidi Barrani; the only way of stopping them was by anti-tank minefields of a density surpassing anything achieved by Italian Tenth Army since September. Nor were the perimeter defences of the Italian camps continuous. Expecting attacks from the south-east, the Italians had left the north-west sectors weak – and it was from the north-west that 4th Indian Division fell upon Nibeiwa and the Tummars on the morning of 9 December, 1940.

Given the adverse effects of the matériel and moral factors outlined above, the Italian garrisons deserve more credit for the fight they put up on 9 December than they usually receive. At Nibeiwa General Maletti, his outclassed medium and light tanks overrun outside the perimeter, died trying to rally his men, who tried with great gallantry but utter futility to stop the 'I' tanks with grenades; the Tummar East garrison launched a sortie in a vain attempt to beat off the attack on Tummar West. Nothing, however, could stop the determination and energy of 4th Indian Division's attacks. By nightfall on 9 December Nibeiwa and Tummar West had fallen and the 'I' tanks had already fought their way inside the perimeter of Tummar East.

In the 7th Armoured Division's sector, the Support Group covered 4th Indian Division's southern flank and stood ready to block any aggressive moves from the Rabia/Sofafi camps. Passing west of Nibeiwa, 4th Armoured Brigade surprised an Italian garrison of 400 at Azziziya, captured it and moved on to straddle the Sidi Barrani–Buq Buq road. Out to the east, on the coastal sector, Selby Force did not hear of the fall of Nibeiwa until it was too late to prevent the withdrawal of 1st Libyan Division from Maktila. Within twenty-four hours, however, 4th Indian Division had cleared Tummar East and driven north to trap 1st Libyan Division, and the remnants of 2nd Libyan Division escaping from the Tummars and Point 90, east of Sidi Barrani. Also in the trap were the eastermost units of 4th Blackshirt Division, which had been battered in half by the northward push of 4th Indian Division.

The destruction of the two Italian corps in Egypt was completed on 10–11 December: 4th Blackshirt, 1st and 2nd Libyan Divisions of General Gallina's Libyan Corps, and 64th 'Catanzaro' Division of General Dalmazzo's XXI Corps. The utter brittleness of the Italian formations, once they had been forced off balance and cracked out of their carefully-prepared defensive positions, came as a total surprise to the British. In this, the first outright British victory of the Second World War, the victors were all but swamped by the floods of prisoners. From the first attack on Nibeiwa on 9 December to the destruction of the 'Catanzaro' Division on the Buq Buq road forty-eight hours later,

Western Desert Force captured 38,300 prisoners, in exchange for 624 killed, wounded, and missing.

The unique nature of COMPASS was that only the initial attack on the camps was planned in any detail; all that followed was, in effect, improvisation, all within the basic concept of a maximum five-day operation. This improvisation usually took the form of a hastily-detailed column of tanks and motorized infantry, ordered amid the swirl and confusion of battle to tackle a specific objective. This was a new technique and Western Desert Force lacked the signalling resources to make it work properly. (Fortunately, the Italian signalling was much worse.) As a result, there were many instances of columns being sent off 'into the blue', beyond effective signals control, on faulty information. A new word entered the vocabulary of British desert warfare: 'swan'. To 'go on a swan', or 'to go swanning', was taken to mean 'cruising aimlessly about with your neck sticking out'. In COMPASS, orders directing 4th Armoured Brigade and the Support Group to the south-west arrived too late to prevent the 63rd 'Cirene' Division from abandoning the Rabia and Sofafi camps and escaping westward along the Escarpment towards Halfaya. The escape of 'Cirene' was the only flaw in the development of COMPASS, which remains one of the most brilliant victories in the history of the British Army.

COMPASS and its no less brilliant aftermath could never have been achieved *without* this improvisation and dispersal of force, once the initial attack-in-force had gone in. The technique was ideal for exploiting the weaknesses, guessed and proven, which plagued the Italian forces in the winter of 1940–1. Kept off balance by relentless British pressure, under the inert command of generals more concerned with saving what they could from the wreck than improvising a counter-attack, the Italians never tried the same technique themselves. Yet it was a game which two could play, and, moreover, an intensely dangerous game when countered with equal energy and more attention to the concentration of force. On the British side, the most unfortunate legacy of COMPASS was a tendency to rely too much on ad hoc, mixed-arms columns rather than the concentration of the various arms – above all tanks and artillery – in full unit strength.

The breathtaking sequel to the Battle of Sidi Barrani, so fully deserving of a book in itself, must be briefly described here. It began with Wavell's courageous decision (11 December) to pull the superb 4th Indian Division out of the line and transfer it to the Ethiopian front. Its replacement was 6th Australian Division (Major-General I.G. Mackay), which took until 18 December to reach the front in full strength. The pursuit was meanwhile kept up by the two armoured brigades of 7th

Armoured Division, one thrusting along the Buq Buq–Sollum road and the other up on the Escarpment. By 14 December 4th Armoured Brigade was through the Wire and menacing the original Italian strongpoints along the frontier. But without infantry support in divisional strength 7th Armoured Division could do little to prevent the withdrawal of the Italians at Sollum and Capuzzo.

Still obsessed with holding positions no matter what the cost, Mussolini and Graziani were heartened by the lull caused by the replacement of 4th Indian Division. They pinned their faith on the prolonged defence of Bardia by XXIII Corps under the fork-bearded General Annibale Bergonzoli – 'barba elettrica' to the Italians, 'electric whiskers' to the derisive British. Hauling in the last Italian troops at Capuzzo and Sollum, Bergonzoli packed Bardia with some 45,000 troops and over 400 guns, a force which British Intelligence underestimated by over 50 per cent. While 7th Armoured Division pushed north to cut off Bardia from Tobruk, O'Connor and Mackay carefully planned the assault on Bardia's 17-mile perimeter – a continuous anti-tank ditch and wire entanglement studded with concrete blockhouses which would have to be gapped and bridged to let in the 'I' tanks.

On 1 January, 1941, Western Desert Force was re-styled 'XIII Corps', forty-eight hours before the attack on Bardia went in. Mackay and O'Connor had decided to assault not the southern but the western perimeter, where the lie of the land made observation and spotting for the guns easiest. Supported by battleship fire from the Fleet, the attack was launched early on 3 January, the break-in of the 'I' tanks producing another spectacular collapse after initial fierce resistance. Australian casualties came to 456 in the three-day fight for Bardia (3–5 January) – but the Italians lost over 40,000 killed and captured, together with 425 heavy, field, anti-aircraft and anti-tank guns, 120 tanks and over 700 transport vehicles. Only a handful of battle-worthy troops emulated Bergonzoli and broke out to Tobruk, where Graziani could concentrate only 25,000 men for another attempt at a stand.

O'Connor's men had now destroyed no less than eight Italian divisions in under a month; but as the numerical odds decreased with each advance, the supply problem became enormous. Though the use of mobile 'Field Supply Depots' (FSDs) eased the position, the capture of Bardia did nothing to assist the landing of supplies by sea. Only the comparative nearness of Tobruk, 75 miles from Bardia, permitted its early investment by 7th Armoured Division. But the day Bardia fell saw Churchill coming to a momentous decision in London. Fears of the Italians receiving decisive German aid against Greece prompted Churchill to press for the sending of a Middle East Expeditionary Force to Greece as soon as Egypt had been thoroughly secured by the expulsion of the Italians from Cyrenaica. After 5 January, therefore, the strategic objective of XIII Corps was defined as the clearance of Cyrenaica, not the conquest of all Libya; Benghazi, not Tripoli, was to be O'Connor's last big prize.

Six days later an equally momentous decision was taken by Hitler. 11 January, 1941, saw the issuing of Führer Directive No.22: 'German support for battles in the Mediterranean area'. In addition to prescribing help for the Italians in Albania (thus confirming all Churchill's fears), the Directive ordered:

> Commander-in-Chief Army will provide covering forces sufficient to render valuable service to our allies in the defence of Tripolitania, particularly against British armoured divisions. Special orders for the composition of this force will follow.
>
> Measures will be so timed that this formation can be transported to Libya in conjunction with the movement now in progress of one Italian armoured and one motorized division (from about 20 February).[8]

This has been decribed as the birth certificate of the German 'Army Special Detachment, Africa', destined for immortality as the *DAK*, or *Deutsches Afrika Korps*. The codeword for its transfer to Libya was *Sonnenblume* ('Sunflower') and its original *raison d'être* was purely defensive – to help the Italians hold Tripoli.

Nothing could be done to avert the fall of Cyrenaica once the Italians had lost so many men and resources at Bardia. This was an error of major dimensions, given the supreme importance of Tobruk as the only natural harbour between Tripoli and Alexandria. To XIII Corps Tobruk was a vital aid in sustaining the conquest of Cyrenaica, a harbour where one 6000-ton merchant ship could unload the freightage which would otherwise require 1000 trucks and lorries. In an attempt to make Tobruk self-sufficient in water, the Italians had drawn an enormous, 40-mile defensive perimeter, which was neither complete in January, 1941, nor anything like as easy to defend as the Bardia complex. Tobruk's Achilles' heel lay at the south-east corner of the perimeter, where the defences were overlooked by the low but distinctive elevations of Sidi Rezegh and Belhamed outside. It was on this sector that O'Connor launched his attack at 0540 on 21 January.

It was the mixture as before: 7th Armoured Division masking the western perimeter while 6th Australian Division launched the main assault. Again the 'I' tanks (only eighteen of them now) acted as 'can-openers' for the infantry, assisted by a squadron of Australian cavalry mounted in captured M-13 Italian tanks. The attack of 21 January was notable for the speed and depth of the penetration, with the attackers rapidly fanning out to overrun the inner strongpoints. Though stubborn resistance was encountered in several sectors, nearly half the perimeter had been overrun by nightfall on the 21st and the remainder collapsed when the advance was resumed next morning. The 'bag' of Italian prisoners topped 25,000, with eighty-seven tanks and 208 guns and over 200 trucks. Best of all, the speed of the attack prevented the beaten garrison from carrying out extensive demolitions to the port facilities, power station (captured intact with 4000 tons of coal), distilling plant and bulk petrol tanks. After the Navy had swept mines from the harrour approaches, Tobruk stood ready to receive shipping within forty-eight hours of the Italian surrender.

The transport, fuel and supplies captured at Tobruk gave O'Connor's forces the vital transfusion they needed to accomplish his master-stroke. This was nothing less than the envelopment of all remaining Italian forces in Cyrenaica. By the last week of January these consisted of General Cona's XX Corps, which included Tenth Army's last intact division: 60th 'Sabratha' at Derna. Further back in the Jebel Akhdar were units of 27th 'Brescia' and 17th 'Pavia' Divisions, while south of the Jebel, blocking the cross-desert route via Mechili, Msus, Agedabia and El Agheila, was General Babini's armoured brigade.

The objective set for XIII Corps after the fall of Tobruk was the capture of Benghazi as quickly as possible, so that troops could be withdrawn from Cyrenaica for the expeditionary force to Greece. While seeking to comply with the early capture of Benghazi, O'Connor had his sights set on Tripoli. He hoped that a last crushing victory in western Cyrenaica would convince Churchill and the Chiefs of Staff that the conquest of Libya could and should be completed before large-scale troop shipments to Greece began. To this end O'Connor planned to flush Graziani's last troops out of the Jebel Akhdar, like putting a ferret down a rabbit hole, by sending 6th Australian Division along the Via Balbia (Derna–Giovanni Berta–Barce–Benghazi). At the same time 7th Armoured Division was to strike south-west through Mechili and Msus with every tank and truck still able to run, cutting off the southward retreat of the Italians from Benghazi.

For six confused days (24–9 January) it seemed that the Italians might contrive at least to delay XIII Corps on the Derna–Mechili line. On 24 January there occurred the first genuine tank-versus-tank battle of the campaign – a spirited clash between General Babini's armoured brigade and the 4th Armoured Brigade, north of Mechili. The Italians withdrew after losing nine tanks to the British seven, an exchange ratio which 7th Armoured Division could certainly not sustain for long, in view of its attenuated tank strength. Though hotly pursued and attacked from the air, Babini's armour successfully disengaged and escaped northward to Slonta, apparently to bolster the Italian defence of Derna, where the Australians advancing from Gazala and Bomba encountered stiff initial resistance.

Yet the Mechili tank battle was the catalyst which brought on the final Italian collapse. Graziani drew no consolation from the escape of Babini's tanks to fight again. Instead he viewed the Mechili fight as the final warning that Tenth Army must evacuate western Cyrenaica without further delay. The retreat began on the night of the 29th, with the Australians entering Derna unopposed on the 30th; Barce fell on 5 February, and the first patrols entered Benghazi on the 6th. O'Connor had meanwhile unleashed 7th Armoured Division on its epic cross-desert drive to Msus, unopposed but forced to contend with wickedly hard going. By dawn on 5 February, 7th Armoured had advanced just to the east where it split, the Support Group pushing west to take Sceleidima fort, and 4th Armoured Brigade pushing on south-west through Antelat to reach Beda Fomm and the Via Balbia, just in time to close the coast road as the retreating Italians pushed south with the Australians hard on their heels.

'This is not an offensive,' Wavell had told the war correspondents in Cairo on the exciting morning of 9 December, 'and I do not think you ought to decribe it an offensive as yet. You might call it an important raid . . . I cannot tell you at this moment how far we are going to go.'[9] Now, two months and 560 miles further on, Wavell's 'important raid' was ending with the remnants of Italian Tenth Army desperately trying to break out of a steel trap. Once again Italian morale was staggered by the speed and range of the British advance. Throughout 6 and 7 February the Battle of Beda Fomm rested on a knife-edge as the Italian columns tried in vain to batter their way through 4th Armoured Brigade. General Tellera, commanding Tenth Army, was mortally wounded. The last Italian breakout attempt, at first light on the 7th, came closest to success, but when this supreme effort failed the white flags began to blossom. The final count for Beda Fomm, the battle which destroyed the rump of Tenth Army, came to 25,000 prisoners, over 100 tanks, 216 guns and 1500 vehicles.

Set down on paper, the achievement of O'Connor's forces since 9 December was almost too great to take in. With never more than two divisions, they had completely destroyed an Italian field army of four corps and nine divisions. Total Italian losses from 9 December to 7

February came to 130,000 prisoners, over 380 tanks and 845 guns; British losses were only 500 killed, 1373 wounded, and 55 missing. But, even if the Greek expedition and the opening of the Ethiopian campaign had not forced a halt, XIII Corps was a spent force. It had been an exhausting campaign for man and machine, and as Wavell set about organizing Cyrenaica for defence he had no choice but to pull 7th Armoured Division back to the Nile Delta for complete reorganization, rest and refit. The 2nd Armoured Division had arrived in Egypt from Britain at the beginning of January, but two of its regiments had been rushed west as reinforcements and were in much the same threadbare state as 7th Armoured. Wavell also wanted to make up an armoured brigade group to go to Greece, the ingredients for which could only come from 2nd Armoured Division. All that remained, to relieve 7th Armoured Division in Cyrenaica, was one under-strength armoured brigade, short on transport and field workshop facilities.

The desert front, February–March, 1941

Wavell's dispositions for the holding of Western Cyrenaica were dictated first and foremost by the very limited resources left to him by the demands of other war fronts. He was quite correct in believing that the remaining Italian forces in Tripolitania represented no immediate threat to the British in Cyrenaica. The urgent question was that of German reinforcement, which had begun with the arrival of General Geissler's X *Fliegerkorps* in Sicily at the end of December. By the time of Beda Fomm, the operations of X *Fliegerkorps* were dominating the Axis supply-route to Tripoli and had been extended to Cyrenaica, primarily against the port facilities at Tobruk and Benghazi. British Intelligence was, however, entirely correct in estimating that the German High Command could not spare sufficient forces to launch simultaneous offensives in North Africa and Greece. It is a matter of record that May, 1941, was the earliest vague date at which both Wavell and German Army High Command (*Oberkommando des Heeres*, or OKH) considered that a limited Axis offensive against Benghazi would be possible. The German plan was not to attempt such a move until two German armoured divisions had been shipped to Libya, the leading elements of which began to arrive at Tripoli the week after Beda Fomm.

Wavell was therefore confident that the rump of 2nd Armoured Division, working with another division, should be capable of holding Cyrenaica. The 6th Australian Division, whose losses in the recent campaign had been slight, was withdrawn to be sent to Greece. Its replacement was 9th Australian Division (Major-General L.J. Morshead) – less two of its brigades, also earmarked for Greece. The acute problems of supply, intensified by the inability to use Benghazi harbour in the face of German air attack, meant that the main deployment area of 9th Australian Division would have to be east of the Jebel Akhdar, effectively restricted to the triangle Derna/Mechili/Gazala. The low escarpment overlooking the Via Balbia south of Benghazi was to be held by 2nd Armoured Division (Major-General M.D. Gambier-Parry), with light patrols pushed west of Agedabia, Mersa Brega and El Agheila towards Mugtaa and Nofilia. With the nearest Italian outposts identified at Sirte, nearly 200 miles west of El Agheila, western Cyrenaica and Benghazi seemed safe enough.

Apart from severely weakening the British forces in Cyrenaica, the baleful effects of the Greek expedition included a command reshuffle destined to have the unhappiest of results. O'Connor went back to become General Officer Commanding British Troops in Egypt; to replace him in Cyrenaica, Wavell chose Lieutenant-General Philip Neame, VC. He did not know Neame, but respected him as a great friend of O'Connor. Wavell also judged (on his own admission) that Neame's Victoria Cross 'was a guarantee of his fighting qualities'. This misapprehension, a judgment of the military heart rather than the head, has bedevilled British military appointments ever since the institution of the Victoria Cross in the Crimean War. The supreme award for gallantry in battle is not, and never has been, an automatic certificate of the many qualities required for high command.

Perhaps the fairest verdict is that if Wavell can be excused for this error of judgment because of the crushing load on him in 1940–1, Neame deserves full credit for loyally trying to make bricks without straw in his new appointment. But Neame was not the right man for the job, and Wavell soon unhappily sensed this when he visited western Cyrenaica on 19 March. 'Just crazy,' was Wavell's private opinion of Neame's dispositions, and Wavell was also shocked to find that the escarpment north of Agedabia (a pale shadow of the precipitous Great Escarpment at Sollum) could easily be penetrated by mobile troops. But having seen these flaws, Wavell did nothing to put them to rights. Nor did he see that the most naturally strong defensive position was not the Benghazi–Agedabia line of high ground, but the bottleneck of El Agheila, between the coast and the Sebcha el Chebira marshes. Wavell claimed that as he returned to Cairo, 'I had forebodings and my confidence in Neame was shaken'. These forebodings Wavell chose to suppress, falling back on the easier belief that another month must surely pass before Neame was subjected to any serious attack. But nemesis was only six days away, it was German and its instrument was called Erwin Rommel.

Enter the Afrika Korps, *February–March, 1941*

Since January intensifying German air attacks in the Mediterranean had concentrated on suppressing the airfield and naval base facilities on Malta, on attacking the British Fleet at sea, and on interdicting the British coastal supply route from Alexandria along the Egyptian and Cyrenaican coast. Coinciding as it did with the severe weakening of the Desert Air Force (again because of the Greek venture), the effective new presence of the Luftwaffe also had the effect of preventing adequate British air reconnaissance of Tripoli. As a result, Wavell's information on the arrival of the first German land forces in Tripolitania was dangerously sketchy.

Mussolini's reluctance to accept German aid in Libya was dispelled by the fall of Tobruk and his Tenth Army's lurch to destruction at Beda Fomm. The German armoured forces earmarked by the *Sonnenblume* plan for despatch to Libya were strictly limited by the forthcoming Axis campaign against Greece, which was itself a distraction from the supreme *Barbarossa* plan for the conquest of the Soviet Union. The German OKH was only willing to spare one armoured (panzer) division for Libya – the 15th, scheduled to arrive in Libya by the end of May. As a stop-gap and eventual running mate, 15th Panzer Division would be preceded by one of those hybrid armoured units already obsolete and upgraded into regular panzer divisions in the rest of the German Army – a 'light division', the 5th. (Light divisions, a prewar concept which proved a failure in the 1939 Polish campaign, had only one tank regiment of two battalions with ninety tanks apiece – half the tank strength of a full-blown panzer division.) The 5th Light Division, with its simpler transport needs, would arrive in Tripoli in the second half of February. Its role was to assist the Italian 'Ariete' armoured division, 'Trento' motorized division, and the 'Pavia', 'Brescia', 'Bologna' and 'Savona' infantry divisions in the defence of Tripoli. Such was the briefing given to the designated commander of the German expeditionary force, Lieutenant-General Erwin Rommel, on 6 February.

The essential point is that the German forces earmarked as the vanguard of the *Afrika Korps* were hastily and grudgingly found, and that they had no experience of service in Africa whatsoever. The shattering effectiveness of the *Afrika Korps* in its first campaign led to inevitable stories in the British Press about hand-picked crack troops, 'desert-trained' in giant glasshouses complete with wind machines to simulate

27

sandstorms. All were false. Much the same applied to the British myths speedily woven around Rommel, who knew nothing of desert armoured warfare when he first arrived in Libya in February 1941. Rommel was not one of the founding fathers of the panzer arm. As far as his early career was concerned, Rommel was an infantryman rather than a tank man, and a mountain infantryman at that. It was his textbook on infantry tactics (*Infanterie Greift An*, 1937) which first earned him Hitler's admiration and appointment to command the Führer's escort battalion (*Führerbegleitbattaillon*) in October, 1938.

After commanding the *Führerbegleitbattaillon* through the German occupation of Czechoslovakia and the 1939 Polish campaign, Rommel asked Hitler for one of the coveted panzer commands and in February, 1940, was appointed to command the newly-formed 7th Panzer Division. Hitler's confidence was amply repaid during the Western campaign of May–June, 1940, in which Rommel proved himself a daring and resourceful 'front-line' commander of armoured troops. In the last week of the campaign Rommel's 7th Panzer set the all-time record for a single day's advance by any unit in modern warfare – 150 miles from south of Rouen to Cherbourg (19 June, 1940). This performance, plus Hitler's continuing favour (orthodox military thinking at OKH was less than enthused with Rommel's impetuosity) meant that Rommel was ripe for promotion to a panzer corps in the New Year of 1941.

But why Africa? There were scores of German generals better suited to the requirements of *Sonnenblume*, for which Rommel's press-on virtuosity was emphatically not needed. It was, remember, first a defensive, then a waiting brief. The defence of Tripoli was to be followed by a cautious build-up for a strictly limited offensive to re-take Benghazi. Moreover, Rommel had no experience of military liaison with the Italian Army which, as he would be operating under an Italian theatre commander, was of the highest importance. Indeed, there was almost black irony in that Rommel had won the *Pour le Mérite* (the Prussian supreme award for gallantry) when helping bring about the Italian collapse at Caporetto in 1917.

The many biographers of Hitler and Rommel have pointed out that both men had an acute *fingerspitzengefühl* – the German term for 'feeling in the fingertips', or intuition. It seems most likely that Hitler sensed that Rommel was the right man for the job, and when the time came would accomplish more in Africa than was envisaged by the plodding Army professionals at OKH whose opinions Hitler despised. Certainly the last thing either Hitler or OKH wanted in February, 1941, was the premature opening of an African offensive. The imminent campaign against Yugoslavia and Greece was quite sufficiently distracting from

28

the all-out *Barbarossa* assault on the Soviet Union with which Hitler intended to win the war in 1941. So far from being given a free hand in Libya, Rommel was sent out to make his initial reconnaissance accompanied by Hitler's chief adjutant, Colonel Rudolf Schmundt.

First contact, February–March, 1941

Receiving his assignment from Army C-in-C Brauchitsch and Hitler on 6 February, Rommel headed south via Rome and Sicily with Schmundt in company. On the morning of the 11th, Rommel reported to General Alfredo Guzzoni, *Comando Supremo* Chief of Staff in Rome. At this meeting, with Guzzoni's approval, he stated his view that the Tripoli defence front ought to be shifted south-east past Sirte towards El Agheila. The afternoon found Rommel at Catania in Sicily, conferring with General Geissler of X *Fliegerkorps*, barely able to believe that German air attacks on Benghazi, vital to impede the British advance westwards, had so far been vetoed by the Italians 'as many Italian officers and civil officials owned houses there. I had no patience with this,' noted Rommel testily, 'and so Colonel Schmundt communicated with the Führer's HQ that night and received authority to go ahead. A few hours later the first German bombers took off on their mission to cripple the British supply traffic to Benghazi.'[10] Thus, before he had even set foot in Africa, Rommel took the first step towards carrying the war back to the British in Cyrenaica.

Rommel landed at Tripoli on 12 February to learn that the hapless Graziani had been replaced by his former Chief of Staff, General Gariboldi. Reporting to Gariboldi, Rommel found that his new C-in-C had no enthusiasm for a move forward to the Gulf of Sirte; Gariboldi pointed out that Rommel had no idea of the terrain in eastern Tripolitania. Rommel's response was to take off on an immediate reconnaissance flight to Sirte. His aerial survey of the land approaches to Tripoli 'confirmed me in my plan to fortify Sirte and the country on either side of the coast road and to reserve the motorized forces for the mobile defence.'[11] Rommel returned to Tripoli that evening to find that Gariboldi had received Guzzoni's approval for the move to Sirte to reinforce the Italian regiment there. No time was wasted. On the 13th the Italian X Corps – 'Brescia' and 'Pavia' divisions – began the advance to Sirte. The 'Ariete' armoured division was to follow and take up position at Buerat, some 50 miles to the rear.

Rommel had little faith in the Italian armour, which he dismissed as 'tanks of completely obsolete design . . . far too light and had once been used to chase the natives round Abyssinia'.[12] Until his own 5th Light

29

Division arrived, however, they were all he had, and it was with heightened impatience that he awaited the unloading of the leading elements of the 5th Light Division on the 14th. These were the armoured cars of the 3rd Reconnaissance Battalion under Lieutenant-Colonel Baron von Wechmar, and an anti-tank battalion – the first *Afrika Korps* troops into Libya. Still believing that only *Luftwaffe* attacks stood in the way of a resumed British advance, Rommel insisted on a rushed disembarkation which continued through the night, accepting the risk of British air attack, heightened by the dockyard lights. No sooner had the men of 3rd Reconnaissance Battalion received their tropical kit, and staged a quick march-past to boost the morale of the Tripolitans, than they were packed off to the Sirte front, overtaking the labouring 'Brescia' and 'Pavia' Divisions on the way. By 17 February, with the first German troops already in the line at Sirte, Rommel was beginning to feel that the immediate crisis had passed. 'As far as I am concerned they [the British] can come now,' he wrote to his wife on the 17th.

But Rommel had no intention of staying on the defensive at Sirte until the 5th Light Division's *panzer* regiment arrived in Libya. Advancing the Axis front to Sirte was to be followed without delay by as aggressive a posture as could be put up: 'to appear as strong as possible and to induce the maximum caution in the British'. To this end, amid constant personal flying visits to the front, he urged Wechmar to push armoured car patrols further and further south-east, down the Via Balbia past Nofilia in the direction of El Agheila. This was in response to *Luftwaffe* detection of what seemed to be increased British activity between El Agheila and Agedabia. British air reconnaissance west of El Agheila was notably scant, even after one of Wechmar's big armoured cars was spotted west of El Agheila on 21 February. By this time, encouraged by the inertia displayed by the British, Rommel had already ordered Wechmar to move on to Nofilia, only 90 miles from El Agheila.

The first direct clash between German and British armoured car patrols occurred at El Agheila on the morning of 24 February. It was a mutually startled encounter, a sharp but brief fire-fight in which the lightweight British Marmon–Harrington armoured cars were completely outclassed by the 8.3-ton Sd.Kfz 232s with their 14mm armour plate and 20mm guns. The fight at El Agheila ended with the first prisoners taken by the *Afrika Korps*: Lieutenant Rowley, Lance-Corporal Allen and Driver White of the King's Dragoon Guards, which had replaced the 11th Hussars on the western frontier patrol. The Germans' booty consisted of two Marmon–Harringtons and a truck.

This archetrypal 'minor skirmish' had slow-burning but momentous consequences. On the British side the threadbare condition of 2nd Armoured Division not only ruled out any energetic counterstroke, but ruled out the courting of excessive casualties in minor actions. The result, inevitably, was the insidious growth of a sense of British inferiority in matériel akin to that previously suffered by the Italian Army. As expressed by Brigadier Desmond Young, Desert War veteran and one of Rommel's most perceptive biographers, 'Newcomers to the Desert and even a minority of the old "desert rats" were inclined to explain: "We bumped into Germans," as though that in itself was a sufficient excuse for failure.' And Young wryly commented, 'Perhaps those rather too easy victories over the Italians had not been very good for us after all.'[13]

But to Rommel's *fingerspitzengefühl* the evident British inertia on the frontier of Tripolitania appeared ripe for exploitation. The initial cost would be low – no more than an extension of his current redeployment further and further along the Sirte coast. In this redeployment the lack of Italian wheeled transport was being usefully countered by Rommel's chief quartermaster, Major Otto, who used small coastal ships on coast-hugging runs to deliver supplies to the front. During his constant flights to the front south-east of Sirte, Rommel had marked down the coastal bottleneck north of the Sebcha el Chebira, the value of which had obviously escaped the British. He impressed its importance on *Generalleutnant* Johannes Streich, commanding 5th Light Division, when the latter took over command at the front in the last week of February. On 4 March Streich advanced to the western exit from the Sebcha el Chebira bottleneck at Mugtaa, took it, and mined the whole defile. Tripolitania was now secure from any surprise British pounce from the Agedabia region.

Though Rommel was vastly encouraged by the British withdrawal towards Agedabia which the *Luftwaffe* detected after the German seizure of Mugtaa, 5th Light Division could achieve little more until its *panzer* regiment arrived. He also wanted to make an exhaustive test of German desert kit and equipment, against the time when he would attempt to use the open desert to out-manoeuvre the British in Cyrenaica. Rommel was able to kill two birds with one stone because the Italian High Command was unhappy over the apparent threat posed to the southern Libyan outposts by the 'Free French' garrisons in Chad, which had declared support for General de Gaulle in defiance of the Vichy régime. Rommel therefore planned a long-range desert route march down to Murzuq and the other major southern Libyan outposts. Commanded by Lieutenant-Colonel Graf von Schwerin, it was a mixed-arms mobile column of the type destined to be used by both sides in the desert over the coming months. The route march, known as the *Unternehmung* (undertaking) *Graf von Schwerin*, was a joint Italo–German venture which combined showing the flag with practical training. It was detected by the British and did nothing to lessen their defensive-mindedness in Cyrenaica. The *Unternehmung Graf von Schwerin*, despatched on 15 March, was the main active task of *Afrika Korps* between the arrival of 5th Panzer Regiment at Tripoli (11–15 March) and its advance to the front. As soon as the latter had been accomplished and Schwerin's column had re-joined, Rommel planned to take El Agheila, effectively moving 5th Light Division to the threshold of Cyrenaica.

During this necessary lull Rommel flew to Berlin (19 March) to receive the Oak Leaves (*Eichenlaube*) to his Knight's Cross. This was a retrospective award for his achievements with 7th Panzer Division in Belgium and France. He used the opportunity to report on the favourable opportunity which he saw in Cyrenaica to request reinforce-ments and the authority to launch an immediate attack. At OKH Brauchitsch and Army Chief of Staff Halder turned him down flat. *Afrika Korps* was to stay where it was until 15th Panzer Division arrived in Libya. Rommel was thus effectively forbidden to attack El Agheila until the end of May, and even then he was to look no further east than Benghazi. He protested in vain that even without the opporunity presented by the current British weakness, the lie of the land in Cyrenaica did not work that way. Merely to take Benghazi would not only be over-cautious, but positively dangerous. As the British had proved only two months before, a battle won in the open desert south of the Jebel Akhdar (at either end) meant the conquest of the whole Cyrenaican bulge. But Brauchitsch and Halder were adamant in their refusal, which made Rommel the only general ever to open a desert offensive in flat disobedience to the orders of his chiefs, instead of being nagged to do so before he was ready.

Prelude to conquest: El Agheila and Mersa Brega, 24 March–1 April, 1941

Though the British in western Cyrenaica were not massed in large garrisons within fixed defences, in one respect Rommel's first attack was nevertheless similar to Wavell's COMPASS attack of December, 1940. It was exploratory, capable of being followed either by rapid exploitation or a resumption of the defensive, as the reactions of the enemy dictated. Rommel's initial objective was to push 5th Light Division through the centre of the El Agheila coastal bottleneck to its eastern exit at Mersa Brega, thus forcing the British on to the defensive in south-western

Cyrenaica. He was confident that even if this move prompted a wholly unexpected British counter-move in force, he already had enough resources at the front to cope with it. These included the small but potent tactical air force, detached from X *Fliegerkorps* to support the Axis land effort in Libya. Under *Generalleutnant* Stefan Fröhlich as *Fliegerführer* (air officer commanding) *Afrika*, it included a reconnaissance squadron, plus about seventy dive-bombers and ME110 twin-engined fighters. For long-range bomber support Fröhlich could call on the JU88 and HE111 squadrons in Sicily.

On the ground Rommel's material assets were considerable. In the 5th Light Division he had a force untested as such in battle, but which was soundly contructed of combat-proven components: reconnaissance battalion, field artillery battery, anti-aircraft unit, motorized machine-gun regiment with armoured troop carriers and anti-tank guns, and two specialized *panzerjäger* ('tank-hunting') battalions whose anti-tank batteries advanced with the armour. The latter, 5th Panzer Regiment, consisted of about seventy light tanks (Pzkw. Mk II, armed with a 20mm cannon) and eighty mediums (Pzkw. Mk III with 50mm gun, Pzkw. Mk IV with 75mm gun). The division was sustained by mobile workshops and supply units. To the British one of the most disconcerting qualities of the German armour was its ability to engage at ranges at which the lighter British tank and anti-tank guns were useless, and with tank guns which could fire high explosive shells against infantry as well as solid shot against tanks. German armour was also much more mechanically reliable than the British, whose worst defect was the tendency to shed tracks in hard going or sharp manoeuvring. Rommel went into his first desert campaign with tanks which were basically better 'runners' than those of the opposition, a considerable advantage in the long distances and punishing terrain of the desert theatre.

Time would reveal other formidable German advantages, most notably the basic superiority of German tank design which permitted constant improvements to the basic marks, above all in armament. When it came to logistics, particularly the crucial subject of fuel supply on which victory or defeat ultimately depended, the Germans entered the Desert War with what almost amounted to a master-weapon. This was the tough, excellent liquid container which the envious British christened the 'jerry-can', took over whenever they could, and eventually copied. The jerry-can was formed of two stamped halves and every drop could be poured from it; it was free from the manifold vices of the wretched 4-gallon tin used to carry the British Army's fuel, most notably the tendency to leak copiously when stacked in motor transport and jolted over desert tracks. As the troops tended to counter the resultant fire hazard by jettisoning the whole tin, the fuel wastage between base and battle front was horrific – estimated, in 1941, at no less than 30 per cent. This twofold curse – large-scale fuel wastage, with a concurrent inevitable waste of transport – dogged the British through every major action of the Desert War. It was, moreover, self-inflicted: the abominable 4-gallon tins were not supplied from an immense prewar War Office stockpile but were manufactured on the spot in a factory outside Cairo. And it went far to offset Axis difficulties in shipping adequate fuel supplies from Italy to Libya, especially in 1941.

On 23 March 5th Panzer Regiment's arrival at the front from Tripoli coincided with Rommel's return from his frustrating trip to Berlin. Rommel wasted no time in ordering an advance to El Agheila which was occupied on the 24th. During a six-day build-up at El Agheila Rommel obtained Gariboldi's grudging permission to attack the British force at Mersa Brega. This was the Support Group of 2nd Armoured Division, with the tanks of the threadbare 3rd Armoured Brigade lying 5 miles behind its left flank.

The action at Mersa Brega – 31 March, 1941 – is one of the least-remembered clashes of the Desert War, yet it is memorable on several counts. It was, after all, the first 'set-piece' attack launched by the *Afrika Korps*. and if not a day of near-disaster for the Germans it certainly came close to justifiying the caution ordered by Rommel's superiors. The British position at Mersa Brega was strong, occupying 8 of the 13 miles between the coast and the inland marshes. The Support Group fought superbly, giving the *panzer* crews their first disconcerting taste of intense 25-pounder fire; though supported by Stuka attacks, Streich's opening frontal *panzer* attack failed. The Support Group held its ground until the late afternoon, when German infantry was pushed forward to work round the British left flank. Obsessed with the standing order that the meagre strength of British armour was not to be dissipated in minor actions, General Gambier-Parry of 2nd Armoured Division refused to counter-attack with the 3rd Armoured Brigade. As night fell the Support Group fell back on Agedabia, having been forced to abandon the only natural defensive position between El Agheila and El Alamein, 600 miles to the east on Alexandria's doorstep.

Once he had ejected the British from their lodgement at Mersa Brega, Rommel had no intention of granting them time to consolidate. As they withdrew they were not to be given a moment's respite, either on the Via Balbia–Jebel Akhdar coastal route or in the open desert south of the Jebel. He therefore ordered 5th Light Division forward to Agedabia, bringing up the 'Ariete' and 'Brescia' Divisions to provide the aggregate force he would need for a multiple advance. The plan taking shape in Rommel's mind seemed utter folly to the cautious Gariboldi, over whose head Rommel appealed direct to OKW. It involved abandoning the classic military precept against dividing one's force in the face of a still-intact enemy – the phrase for which, in the normal Rommel legend, is 'tearing up the textbook'. But this depends on which textbook is consulted. In the first week of April, 1941, Rommel sensed, as 'Stonewall' Jackson had urged on Robert E. Lee at Chancellorsville in May, 1863, that the last thing the enemy would expect was a simultaneous packet of threats by elements of a divided force.

Advance to Mechili, 1–8 April

Rommel's attack, a three-pronged advance converging at Mechili, was a brilliantly improvised reversal of O'Connor's master-stroke which had culminated at Beda Fomm eight weeks before. To disguise the dangerous weakness of each prong, Rommel used the ancient Mongol tactic of simulating overwhelming strength by raising dust:

> Rommel's order was: '*Panzers* to the head of all formations. Rear vehicles to raise dust, nothing but dust!' Who in the Desert could distinguish more than the leading vehicles of a column, if in the rear the dust clouds rose thick and turbulent?[14]

The right-hand column, commanded by Schwerin, included the tanks of the 'Ariete' Division and proceeded via Giof al-Matar–Maaten el Orara–Ben Gania-Tengeder. The centre column, under Olbrich, carried the main weight of 5th Light Division's advance (minus the *panzer* companies detached to strengthen the flanking columns) via Antelat and Msus. The left-hand column, advancing north up Via Balbia to Ghemines and Benghazi, then heading east via Er Regima and Charruba, was formed by Wechmar's 3rd Reconnaissance Unit and the 'Brescia' Division. Placed in overall command of the left-flank sector was Major-General Heinrich Kirchheim who visiting Libya on an inspection mission for OKH, found himself 'press-ganged' by Rommel and packed off to the front.

It is worth noting that Kirchheim's snap field appointment was the only improvised command change made by Rommel as his advance gathered momentum. It worked extremely well, with Kirchheim rapidly adjusting to his new surroundings and turning in a fine performance. This was in sad contrast to the confusion on the British side, which was not relieved by Wavell's flying visit to Neame's HQ (2–3 April). By the time Wavell arrived at Barce, 2nd Armoured Division was beginning to fall apart in its retreat, decimated by breakdown and acute fuel shortage. Rather than risk the total loss of the Support Group on the coast road, Wavell ordered the abandonment of Benghazi and an all-out effort to block the cross-desert route at Msus. He also ordered O'Connor to fly up from Cairo to advise Neame rather than replace him, thus introducing split command. But all Wavell's hopes were ruined by the furious pace at which Rommel hounded his columns forward, flying from column to column in his invaluable Storch aircraft, overriding protests about fuel shortages and continuing to deny the British the respite which they craved.

By 6 April, two days after Wechmar's column entered abandoned Benghazi, General Morshead's 9th Australian Division was fighting its way eastward out of the Jebel Akhdar. Schwerin's column was already hooking north towards Mechili, with its leading 8th Machine-Gun Battalion (Lieutenant-Colonel Gustav Ponath) pushing through the night under Rommel's personal command. On 6 April, as Schwerin closed up to Mechili, Rommel urged Ponath north-east towards the coast at Derna. Rommel had in mind a double envelopment: of 9th Australian Division (by Kirchheim and Ponath between Derna and Mechili) and of 2nd Armoured Division (by Schwerin and Olbrich at Mechili). Though Ponath lacked the force to prevent the fighting withdrawal of the 9th Australian Division, one of his patrols captured Generals Neame and O'Connor as they drove towards Derna, in the small hours of 7 April. The captured generals were joined next day by Gambier-Parry and other senior officers of 2nd Armoured Division, captured in an attempt to break out of their encirclement at Mechili. And it was at Mechili on 8 April, viewing prisoners and captured British equipment, that Rommel acquired his most celebrated trademark:

The command trucks of the captured British generals stood on a slight rise. They were large, angular vehicles on over-size tyres, equipped inside with wireless and facilities for paper work. We christened them "Mammoths" then, but I did not realize that these useful trucks would be used by Rommel and his staff and commanders right through the long struggle that was now beginning in the Desert.

Rommel inspected the vehicles with absorbed interest after a brief interview with the captured British generals. He watched them emptied of their British gear. Among the stuff turned out he spotted a pair of large sun-and-sand goggles. He took a fancy to them. He

36

grinned, and said 'Booty – permissible, I take it, even for a General.' He adjusted the goggles over the gold-braided rim of his cap peak.

Those goggles for ever after were to be the distinguishing insignia of the 'Desert Fox'.[15]

Yet Rommel's triumph at Mechili marked the first distinct peak in his fortunes, for there was a price to be paid for the furious pace at which he had driven his force since 31 March. By 8 April they were strung out in labouring columns, nearly all gasping for fuel and supplies. This ruled out any concentrated strike at Rommel's next objective: Tobruk. Moreover, the final dissolution of 2nd Armoured Division at Mechili had not been in vain. It won just enough time for Morshead's Australians to reach Tobruk and deploy for the defence of the perimeter, after an admirably conducted fighting retreat from the Jebel Akhdar. Though 2nd Armoured Division had been wiped out of existence, its last forty-eight hours – 6–8 April – determined the course of the Desert War for the ensuing ten months.

Tobruk holds out, April–May, 1941

Wavell's swift recovery from the total surprise of Rommel's attack was all the more admirable because the British commander could not concentrate on Cyrenaica only: the Axis assault on Yugoslavia and Greece opened while Rommel's forces were still closing in on Mechili (6 April). With no troops or armoured reserves with which to fight Rommel to a standstill, Wavell used geography. He ordered the defence of Tobruk, accepting that although the garrison would be totally isolated by land it could still be supplied by sea. As long as Tobruk held out it would be a constant thorn in Rommel's side. Nothing could be done to stop his advance forces from reaching and even crossing the Egyptian frontier, but Tobruk was an objective which Rommel would have to take if he was to re-group for an advance into Egypt in full strength.

Rommel's failure to do so in April–May, 1941, was directly caused by the magnificent defence of Tobruk by 9th Australian Division under the iron hand of Morshead – 'Ming the Merciless' as he was known to his men. Their fighting qualities at Tobruk so impressed Rommel that he called the Australians the élite troops of the British Empire. Nothing can detract from the achievement of Morshead's Australians. Even so, argues Sir David Hunt,

It was helped by Rommel displaying, not for the last time, the defects of his qualities. . . . Rommel was always at his best when handling small, fast-moving formations. When later on his command increased notably in size he could usually be relied on so to mishandle the opening phase of an operation as to reduce it to the optimum size for the appropriate display of his talents. In this opening campaign he started off with the right-sized command.

In Hunt's view Rommel's great mistake was not to take the time for a proper reconnaissance of the Tobruk perimeter. This would have revealed Tobruk's weak spot: the south-eastern corner of the perimeter, overlooked by the twin elevations of Sidi Rezegh and Belhamed:

It was at this point that we had broken into Tobruk when we took it from the Italians, at this point that our garrison broke out to make contact with the relieving force when the German siege was raised, and at this point again that the Germans broke in when they captured Tobruk in June, 1942. A glance at the map, or a single ride round the perimeter, would have been bound to reveal this weakness to General Rommel; but that was not his way. His line of march had brought him to the south-western corner and he decided to attack there at once. It seems scarcely credible, but it is vouched for by the Italian liaison officer with him at the time, that he was not aware before he launched his first attack that there was a system of permanent defences with concrete blockhouses, anti-tank ditches, minefields and wire entanglements. After this it scarcely seems surprising to add that he chose the very strongest sector of the whole of the defences for his point of attack . . . the place where nature most favoured the defenders was Ras el Madauar. Here the permanent defences had been built on top of a prominent ridge commanding the countryside for a good distance all round. Moreover the artificial defences were there at their strongest.[16]

Rommel's big mistake at Tobruk in April, 1941, was to try to save time by overrunning the defences from west to east, in another *coup de main* which could be channelled back into an eastward advance with minimal regrouping. His reconnaissance, largely carried out in person (often under heavy fire), *was* hasty, but it was not helped by the failure of the Italians to provide maps of their former stronghold. According to one of Rommel's staff officers, Schmidt, only two maps of the Tobruk defences were available, one going to Rommel himself and the other to Streich. Schmidt has painted a vivid picture of what it was like up in the front line at Rommel's side, with his C-in-C trying to relate his map to the wholly unfamiliar terrain in front of him.

To explain Rommel's snap decisions and ill-judged attacks, Schmidt loyally blames the 'huntsman's urge', but it was far more of a rush of blood to the head, the recklessness of the fox-hunter, not the cunning of the stalker. This was in effect the clouding impact of Rommel's frustration in realizing that after his first brilliant onrush he was, after all, to be denied a clear run east to the Nile. Rommel's impetuous orders before Tobruk were emphatically not those of a *panzer* virtuoso. In the morning attack which Rommel ordered on 14 April, Olbrich's 5th Panzer Regiment was hounded forward into a killing-zone of defensive fire, losing seventeen out of the thirty-eight tanks committed. The withdrawal of the surviving *panzers* left 8th Machine-Gun Battalion exposed to shredding attacks by the Australians, leaving it with only five officers and ninety-two men, a shocking 75 per cent casualty list. But Rommel's furious reaction was to heap the blame on Olbrich and Streich and sack the pair of them, a piece of gross injustice which remains one of the ugliest moments in Rommel's career.

By the last week of April Rommel was running out of subordinate generals. On 11 April Kirchheim was wounded when his car was strafed by a British fighter, and General von Prittwitz, driving up to the front far ahead of his 15th Panzer Division (whose leading elements were landing at Tripoli), ran head-on into the Australian rearguard west of Tobruk and was killed by an anti-tank projectile. Rommel's vendetta against Streich and Olbrich added to the impression at OKH that he was way out of his depth; Chief of Staff Halder went further and noted in his diary that Rommel had 'gone stark mad'. After the failure of Rommel's second attack (April 16–17), OKH sent out a formal emissary to obtain a clear picture of the prevailing situation and bring Rommel to heel, making him see that his scurrying activity must stop until the supply position had been properly sorted out. Even when this had been achieved, Rommel could not expect to receive substantial reinforcements.

The emissary sent out by OKH was Lieutenant-General Friedrich Paulus, destined, in 1942, to lead the German Sixth Army to disaster at Stalingrad, but in the spring of 1941 still regarded by German Army High Command as a coming man. Paulus reached Rommel's HQ on 27 April to find Rommel preparing a third assault on the Tobruk perimeter. Fulminating at the bad performance of the Italian divisions in the earlier attacks, Rommel was proposing to bring back the easternmost German troops – Colonel von Herff's 3rd Reconnaissance Battalion and 15th Motorized Battalion, which had pushed on to Bardia, Capuzzo and Sollum by 11 April – and fling them into his new attack at Tobruk. Paulus vetoed this idea, which would place responsibility for the eastern flank of *Afrika Korps* on the very Italian troops which Rommel was decrying. The Tobruk attack went in between 30 April and 4 May, when Rommel called it off after biting a 2-mile segment out of the south-western perimeter. His losses had been high – 650 Germans and about 500 Italians – and Paulus insisted that the time had now come to place the Axis defence of Cyrenaica on a sounder footing. *Afrika Korps* must be withdrawn from its assault role and held as a mobile striking force, ready to counter-attack either a British advance from Egypt or a breakout attempt by the Tobruk garrison.

The Frontier battles: BREVITY *and* BATTLEAXE, *May–June, 1941*

The intervention of Paulus had the timely effect of switching Rommel's attention from Tobruk to the Frontier sector, which became the focus of the Desert conflict for the rest of May and June. Here the British had been pushed east to the Buq Buq–Sofafi line by Herff's capture of Halfaya Pass on 26 April, but this time they did not maintain an inert defensive as they had done after Beda Fomm in February. In a spirited response to the collapse in Cyrenaica, Churchill and the War Cabinet had decided (21 April) to send an emergency supply convoy through the Mediterranean to Alexandria. This 'TIGER' convoy would give Wavell's Desert forces an injection of tank replacements, enabling him to take on Rommel's two *panzer* divisions in a second Libyan offensive. Pending the arrival of the TIGER convoy, Wavell ordered Brigadier Gott to continue the aggressive patrolling on the Frontier which he had been conducting since the last ten days of April. All available British armour was sent up to Gott to form the improvised '7th Armoured Brigade Group' and, in a limited offensive called 'BREVITY', dislodge Herff's forces from their Frontier positions.

Gott's BREVITY attack, a three-pronged drive at Sollum, Halfaya and Capuzzo, and inland to Sidi Azeiz, got under way on 15 May with promising intial success. Halfaya Pass was recovered by 22nd Guards Brigade Group which pushed on to take Capuzzo; further inland, 7th Armoured Brigade Group brushed aside Herff's light reconnaissance forces and advanced 30 miles to Sidi Azeiz. But BREVITY lacked the surprise which had been of such benefit to COMPASS back in December, 1940. Lax British radio security before the attack had alerted *Afrika Korps* Intelligence, and Rommel's counterstroke, though necessarily limited by his need to keep a tight hold on Tobruk, was swift. He sent Cramer's 8th Panzer Regiment to reinforce Herff, thus creating the scenario for the first encounter battle between British and German armour in the open desert.

That the clash never occurred was the result of 8th Panzer Regiment arriving at Sidi Azeiz one hour after Gott had given the order to withdraw, then promptly running out of petrol and being unable to pursue the retreating 7th Armoured Brigade. Gott had called off BREVITY because of setbacks encountered by the forces advancing on the Capuzzo and Sollum sectors. A brusque counter-attack by Herff's 2nd Battalion, 5th Panzer Regiment, had thrown the Durham Light Infantry out of Capuzzo, while the slow progress of 2nd Rifle Brigade on the coastal sector was a further discouragement. Apprehensive about further punishing attacks by German armour against his central forces, Gott therefore ordered a withdrawal at 0200 on 16 May, barely sixty minutes before Cramer's petrol-starved panzers reached Sidi Azeiz.

Wavell had hoped that BREVITY would leave the Western Desert forces firmly ensconced along the Libyan frontier, ready for an all-out offensive to relieve Tobruk as soon as his latest tank reinforcements were fit for action. Instead of this general clearing of the decks on the Frontier, BREVITY had achieved no more than the recovery of Halfaya Pass. It had, however, served to alert Rommel to the weakness of his Frontier flank, fully justifying the apprehension at OKH which Paulus had come out to represent. His immediate reaction was to strengthen the German frontier positions against frontal attack, while giving them enough supplies to hold out if besieged or bypassed by a flanking advance.

BREVITY had shown that the most dangerous British tank was the snail-paced Matilda 'I' tank, whose armoured carapace was proof against the Germans' standard 37mm anti-tank gun. Rommel therefore ordered the emplacement of the most dreaded German gun of the Desert War: the 88mm Flak 18. Batteries of '88s', mounted on wheeled carriages to keep pace with the advance, had followed 5th Light Division and 15th Panzer Division to Libya, being standard elements of panzer divisional strength. When used in the anti-tank role, they had proved devastatingly effective against the thickest armour, their biggest weakness being their angular height. After BREVITY Rommel ordered gun-pits to be dug for the accommodation of 88s, making the emplaced guns practically invisible to advancing British tanks until they blundered into the deadly field of fire. Battlefield emergencies in earlier campaigns – most notably the British counter-attack at Arras on 21 May, 1940, against Rommel's own 7th Panzer Division – had frequently seen the 88 pressed into service as an anti-tank gun. But Rommel was the first panzer general to use dug-in 88s as a static complement to his armoured striking force. In doing so Rommel noted that he 'had great hopes of the effectiveness of this arrangement'. Rommel was indeed about to teach the British a lesson which they were not to take fully to heart until the following summer – a lesson which he himself had learned from personal experience during the Western campaign of May–June, 1940:

> What is certain is that at Arras Rommel learned and never forgot that tanks are not expendable cavalry to be used in Balaclava charges against a gun line, but that in engagements between forces of a comparable size a modern general should lure his enemy's armour onto his own well-established artillery and then – and only then – put his panzers into a counter-attack on their broken opponents.[17]

British troops, left exposed to the long-range lash of the 88 with no comparable reply, raged at the refusal of the War Office to produce a dual-purpose variant of the 3.7-inch anti-aircraft gun. This would have rapidly cancelled the German monopoly in long-range anti-tank artillery; but the mental inflexibility of War Office 'experts' could not countenance the use of a proven anti-aircraft gun against tanks, much less authorize the emergency development of a mobile dual-purpose mounting for the 3.7-inch gun. It was therefore small wonder that British tank tactics continued to feature 'Balaclava charges against a gun line'. There was little alternative. With the popgun 2-pounder as their main anti-tank gun (and their *only* tank gun) British tank crews went into battle knowing that German gunners

> could knock us out at 3000 yards, whereas the maximum effective range of our 37-mm and 2-pounder guns was reckoned to be about 1200. (This turned out to be wildly optimistic.) The result, in simple arithmetic, was that we would have to be within range of their tanks and guns for 1,800 yards before we could hope to get close enough to do any damage. Eighteen hundred yards, in those circumstances, is a long way. It's sixty-four thousand eight hundred inches.
>
> My mind was occupied with two problems: how to get near enough to the enemy, and how to live long enough to get there. Obviously, armour-plating was not enough protection . . . The only answer lay in mobility, and pretty fast mobility at that.[18]

But when it came to the search for mobility, British tank crews had another cross to bear – the mechanical unreliability of their machines. The tragedy here was that 1941 actually saw British tank production outstrip that of Germany, whose war industries were nowhere near at full stretch. (Even in 1942, when Britain's military fortunes hit rock bottom, Britain still built 8611 tanks to Germany's 7200 – and that was

42

after an increase in German tank production to 600 per month.) But quantity was not matched by quality and Britain's wastage in tanks dolefully kept pace with her wastage of fuel due to the wretched 4-gallon tin. The British failure to come up with a fast, reliable cruiser tank was typified by the notorious Mk VI, the Crusader, which made its combat début in the summer of 1941:

In a powerful passage Sir Winston Churchill complains that the commanders in the Middle East seemed to want a 50 per cent margin of superiority in tanks over the enemy. His comment that 'Generals only enjoy such comforts in Heaven. And those who demand them do not always get there', may well seem majestically convincing. But if in order to arrive with 100 tanks at the end of a march of 20 miles it is necessary to start off with 150 to allow for mechanical casualties, the demand for such a margin may not seem unreasonable.

At a later stage of the war, just before the battle of El Alamein, I had an officer serving with me from the Gloucester Hussars. He had such a dislike for his Crusader that, with the full concurrence of his crew, he swopped it with a neighbouring armoured regiment, recently arrived from Britain, for a 3-ton lorry. His argument was that a 3-tonner could go anywhere a tank could, was not prone to break down and a hit from an anti-tank gun would only make a neat hole in it instead of burning it up with all the crew. His CO, though understanding, thought that this might spread a bad example and had him transferred in a friendly way to GHQ. There he found another subaltern from the Bays, also then working with me, who had had no less than nine Crusaders 'shot under him'. He was suffering from shell shock, not I think a very common complaint in this war, but fully justified in his case.[19]

Mechanical deficiences could certainly be offset by improved tank recovery for 'battlefield surgery', retrieving battle-damaged tanks for repair in mobile workshops and a swift return to action. But this was a game at which two could play, and in the summer of 1941 German tank recovery and field-repair techniques were still superior to the British.

A final British disadvantage was the 'one-purpose' tank gun: solid shot only. German armour could plaster dug-in infantry with high explosive shell; British armour could not, and would not be able to do so until the arrival of the American Grant and Sherman tanks in the summer of 1942. In the cut and thrust of the Desert War this was a major British weakness, as was demonstrated by the ease with which the Germans snatched back the sole prize of BREVITY: Halfaya Pass. This was accomplished on 26–7 May, with 3rd Coldstream Guards being driven out after losing 173 in troop casualties, five Matilda 'I' tanks, four field guns and eight anti-tank guns. The 8th Panzer Regiment's infantry commander in this well-judged attack, Captain the Rev. Wilhelm Bach (who was 50 years old and walked with a stick) took over as Rommel's new garrison commander at Halfaya. Over the following seven months Bach was to prove himself as redoubtable in defence as in attack.

Rommel now concentrated on incorporating Halfaya into the eastern-most of a chain of strongpoints, staked out in a 20-mile arc from the coast to 'Point 208', on the Hafid Ridge 5 miles west of Capuzzo. He ordered the thirteen 88mm guns available for the Frontier zone to be sited in two main concentrations, defending Halfaya and Point 208. The defensive zone thus created was entrusted to 15th Panzer Division under *Generalmajor* Walther Neumann-Silkow, who relieved Colonel von Herff on the Frontier on 8 June. The 5th Light Division, now commanded by *Generalmajor* Johann von Ravenstein, was pulled back for a well-earned rest (its first since February) south of Tobruk, where it would be available as a mobile reserve when the British made their first genuine attempt to relieve Tobruk by land.

Wavell was meanwhile doing his best to use the tanks delivered by the TIGER convoy to rebuild 7th Armoured Division *as* an armoured division, which condition it had not enjoyed since being worn threadbare during the advance to Beda Fomm back in January and early February. At the same time he tried in vain to get Churchill to accept that the 'Tiger Cubs' could not drive straight from the quayside into battle. TIGER had been an enormous gamble: 295 tanks and fifty-three cased Hurricane fighters entrusted to a single convoy. The gamble had paid off, only one ship being mined and sunk with its cargo of fifty-seven tanks and ten fighters; 238 'Tiger Cubs' had reached Egypt safely, and Churchill naturally wanted a swift return on his investment. But as far as quality was concerned, the 'Tiger Cubs' were a dubious litter. There were twenty-one of the prewar, rattletrap Light Mk VI, now wholly obsolete and outgunned even by the armoured cars of *Afrika Korps*; eight of these needed a complete overhaul. The eighty-two cruiser tanks, vital for swift penetration in depth, included fifteen A-13s (Cruiser Mk IVA), which had on average already completed 700 miles, half their mechanical life. Apart from being chronic offenders in the breaking and shedding of tracks, the A-13s were (in the words of one of their embittered commanders) 'ponderous square things, like mobile pre-fab houses and just about as flimsy'. At least, when abandoned on breaking down, 'They were of no help to the enemy; no other army would have contemplated using them.'[20] The sixty-seven Mk VI Crusaders reached Egypt in good order, but their manifold built-in defects would not be revealed before the test of battle.

As for the 135 'I' tanks delivered by TIGER, these were found to require so much extensive overhaul that Wavell abandoned his usual taciturnity and spelled it all out in a signal to Churchill on 30 May. By 28 May, Wavell reported, only sixty-nine of the 135 'I' tanks had been rendered desert-worthy, after an average of forty-eight man-hours per machine in the Delta workshops. 'Examples of heavier repair are: two gear boxes, cracked and faulty, required exchange, broken sprockets, rackham clutches slipping, unserviceable tracks, one left-hand engine seized, top rollers seized, two engines over-heating and lacking power require top overhaul.' And Wavell continued, 'Had Cubs only required to be fitted with desert equipment and camouflage painted, all would have been ready for operations by 31 May'. Putting these and other deficiencies to rights meant that the armoured formations could not be brought up to strength until 10 June. Despite Churchill's fulminations, Wavell insisted on a minimum five-day familiarization period before unleashing his second Desert offensive, BATTLEAXE, on 15 June.

Wavell's distraction by the demands of other theatres had been of immeasurable help to Rommel ever since February, and Rommel's luck in this respect still held good during the British build-up for BATTLEAXE in late May and early June. Indeed, the strategic overload on Wavell had never been greater. In the first week of May Wavell had had to send mobile forces from Transjordan into Iraq to help overthrow the pro-Axis régime of Rashid Ali, which had seized power in April. Then there was the Ethiopian campaign, with one of its toughest battles – the dislodgement of the Duke of Aosta's army from the heights of Amba Alagi – raging between 3 and 19 May. Within twenty-four hours of the Italian surrender at Amba Alagi, the Germans launched their greatest airborne attack of the war: the invasion of Crete. This culminated in the British evacuation of Crete (29–31 May), less than a month after the evacuation of Greece. The fact that the German airborne arm took such heavy losses on Crete that it could never again launch a similar operation was scant comfort. It was certainly no compensation for the martyrdom of the British Mediterranean Fleet, which in the struggle to support the garrison of Crete lost three cruisers and six destroyers sunk, and one aircraft-carrier, six cruisers and seven destroyers damaged.

On top of all this, prompted by the German snatch at Crete, came Churchill's additional demand for Wavell to invade Vichy French Syria, seen as a potential Axis bridgehead in the eastern Mediterranean and Middle East. Wavell tried in vain to persuade Churchill that Middle East Command simply lacked the resources to conduct simultaneous invasions of Libya and Syria; it was a textbook example of failing to concentrate on the most important aim. Moreover, Churchill insisted on Free French troops participating in the invasion of Syria (also despite Wavell's protests) in the fond belief that this would prompt a cheap and easy victory, by encouraging mass defections of Vichy forces from the Axis cause. But Wavell was right: the reverse proved the case. The Vichy troops put up a stubborn defence of Syria, the combat (8 June–14 July) being given extra viciousness by the overtones of civil war between Vichy and Gaullist units. The result was one of the saddest campaigns of the war, costing 6500 Vichy casualties and 4600 Allied, overlapping with and distracting from the opening of the BATTLEAXE offensive on the Libyan Frontier.

General Beresford-Peirse, who had been in command of 4th Indian Division during the first Sidi Barrani attack in December, 1940, had commanded Western Desert Force since the capture of O'Connor and Neame in February, 1941, and was Wavell's tactical commander for BATTLEAXE. The force at his disposal was a stiffened rehash of the original COMPASS partnership, only this time without the heartening eve-of-battle feeling that the enemy did not know the game. It consisted of the newly re-equipped 7th Armoured Division (Major-General O'Moore Creagh); the headquarters, artillery, and 11th Indian Infantry Brigade back from the Ethiopian campaign (Major-General Messervy); and 22nd Guards Brigade (Brigadier Erskine).

Wavell and Beresford-Peirse worked up the BATTLEAXE plan in the foreknowledge that the German defensive positions on the Frontier were going to prove a tougher nut to crack than the Italian camps at Sidi Barrani back in December, 1940. But Western Desert Force would have to take those positions, shielded from counter-attack by only one armoured divsion against at least one and probably two panzer divisions, and maybe even a third Axis armoured division if Rommel managed to bring 'Ariete' into play. The prospects for success in BATTLEAXE therefore depended on 7th Armoured and 4th Indian Divisions re-discovering their hammer-and-anvil form of December, 1940, and overwhelming the panzer division known to be screening the German Frontier defences. A quick victory on the Frontier would enable Western Desert Force to advance, either defeating or driving back Rommel's other panzer division, and tackle the Italian forces besieging Tobruk.

Quite apart from the matériel deficiencies of British armour and anti-tank artillery, the BATTLEAXE plan was a long shot. It envisaged the piecemeal destruction of Rommel's forces, hopefully exploiting the German commander's known tendency to keep them too dispersed. Given enough time, stealth and eve-of-battle security, this *might* have been achieved. But the near-perfect surprise achieved in COMPASS was never possible for BATTLEAXE. Churchill's peremptory demands for an 'instant battle' led to too many orders being passed by radio and intercepted, and too many units having to hasten west to their start-lines in daylight, under the eyes of Luftwaffe reconnaissance. When Western Desert Force attacked on the morning of 15 June, 1941, Rommel was ready and waiting with his forces at full alert.

The failure of BATTLEAXE (15–17 June) was, when reduced to essentials, the failure of an attacking force sent out to break its head against custom-built defences. It must be stressed that this was not the result of blind stupidity or the 'Balaclava syndrome'. It was the result of Western Desert Force having been denied the time in which to build up the wherewithal – fully trained and equipped armoured and motorized units, with adequate fuel and supplies – to tackle the *Afrika Korps* behind its screen of fixed defences. BATTLEAXE repeated the three-pronged drive which had served well enough in the opening phase of BREVITY, but the three prongs could only be formed by much splitting and parcelling of the two attacking divisions. On the right, the coastal sector, half of 4th Indian Division was to take Halfaya Pass with a detachment of Matilda tanks from the 4th Armoured Brigade of 7th Armoured Division. In the centre, the Capuzzo sector, the other half of 4th Indian was deployed to help 22nd Guards Brigade and the rest of 4th Armoured Brigade punch through the German centre. On the left, the Desert flank, 7th Armoured Brigade was to advance to the Hafid Ridge to screen the centre and right, but not with all the guns of the Support Group in close support of the tanks. The Support Group was also split, into a mobile column ('Jaxo Column') advancing with 7th Armoured Brigade, while the rest of the Support Group was pushed westwards towards Sidi Omar as a flank guard.

As in the case of BREVITY, the first day of BATTLEAXE was a day of mixed fortunes. Both above and below Halfaya, 4th Indian Division's attacks were snuffed out with a massacre of 'I' tanks (fifteen lost out of the eighteen engaged), inflicted by emplaced 88s and well-sited minefields. Pressing forward towards the Hafid Ridge and Point 208, 7th Armoured Brigade suffered woefully from its lack of high-explosive fire-power against the excellently dispersed and dug-in German infantry. The solitary troop of 25-pounders in 'Jaxo' Column proved inadequate to take out Point 208's four 88s and additional 50mm anti-tank guns, and though some German positions were overrun on the 15th, Point 208 held out. For 7th Armoured Brigade, however, mechanical failure proved as damaging as the marksmanship of the German gunners. By nightfall on the 15th, 7th Armoured Brigade had been reduced to forty-eight of the ninety cruisers which had set out that morning. It was true that many of the missing cruisers were field-repaired and subsequently returned to action, but this was still an appalling rate of attrition, particularly as 7th Armoured Brigade still had to make serious contact with the panzer regiments of *Afrika Korps*.

These setbacks on the flanks contrasted with Messervy's advance in the centre, where 4th Armoured Brigade won a heartening success. Messervy detached some twenty Matildas to tackle Point 206, but did not wait for the outcome of a sharp engagement with a battalion from 8th Panzer Regiment. He pressed on to Capuzzo with 7th Royal Tank Regiment's massed Matildas, eighty in all. The panzer battalion contesting the approaches to Point 206 fell back to the north-east, shaken by its inability to crack the Matildas' armour and leaving the valiant German gunners defending Point 206 to be overrun. By mid-afternoon the Matildas of 4th Armoured Brigade had taken Capuzzo as well, but were then forced to wait for the infantry of 22nd Guards Brigade to arrive and take over the ground thus won. During this enforced wait, 4th Armoured Brigade had the satisfaction of beating off repeated attempts by German armoured groups to counter-attack and recover Capuzzo. Nightfall on 15 June found General Neumann-Silkow a deeply worried man. Though the German flanks were holding out at Point 208 and Halfaya, the British armour had smashed clean through the central sector of 15th Panzer Division's front. If on the following day the British launched a concentrated drive towards Bardia, the result could well be the defeat of 15th Panzer Division before 5th Light Division could join the fray.

Rommel, however, was about to give one of the most impressive displays of generalship of his entire career – not, for once, in a brilliantly improvised lightning offensive, but in response to the very different requirements of a defensive battle. Since reaching general's rank, Rommel had only had to fight one defensive action, when commanding 7th Panzer Division at Arras on 21 May, 1940. In BATTLEAXE, however, Rommel had not been taken by surprise, as he had been at Arras; nor was he obliged to rush to the front and improvise a frantic defence, with field guns blazing away at the British tanks at point-blank range over open sights. With admirably cool judgment Rommel watched the British unfold their attack on 15 June, refraining from any rash or premature commitment of his own reserves. Painfully short of resources himself, especially in fuel, Rommel had no intention of feeding 5th Light Division into a costly battle of attrition. Instead he planned to 'see off' the British by exploiting the low speed of the most effective British armour, the Matildas, and using manoeuvre rather than mass. To accomplish this 15th Panzer Division was to continue with attention-fixing attacks on the Capuzzo/Sollum sector. Out on the Desert flank, 5th Light Division would meanwhile push south from Sidi Azeiz, outflank 7th Armoured Brigade and threaten the entire British rear area.

The beauty of Rommel's plan was its blend of simplicity, economy and versatility. If 4th Armoured Brigade and 4th Indian Division headed west to help 7th Armoured Brigade take out Point 208, which was indeed originally planned by Beresford-Peirse for the 16th, 5th Light Division would take the strain on the Hafid Ridge while 15th Panzer struck south-west at the British rear. As it turned out the main British efforts on the 16th (apart from repeated vain assaults on Halfaya Pass) were directed east towards Musaid and Sollum, not west towards the Hafid Ridge. The last British successes of BATTLEAXE were the capture of Sollum Barracks by 22nd Guards Brigade and the repulse of another attack by 8th Panzer Regiment from the north, sustaining the dis-comfiture of 15th Panzer Division. But the continued presence of 15th Panzer Division on his northern flank dissuaded Messervy from releasing 4th Armoured Brigade to join the depleted cruisers of 7th Armoured Brigade. This decision left 7th Armoured Brigade exposed, in greatly inferior tank strength, to the mounting pressure of 5th Light Division as it came south from Sidi Azeiz. By nightfall on 16 June a series of rapid German hooks at the inland front, extending ever further to the southward, had forced 7th Armoured Brigade to fall back 10 miles in order to join its Support Group north of Sidi Omar. In the process the Brigade was reduced to its last twenty-one battle-worthy cruiser tanks, an overall loss-rate in cruisers of more than 75 per cent, all in less than forty-eight hours of campaigning.

By dawn on 17 June the 'fog of war' had descended on the commanders of Western Desert Force. Beresford-Peirse still believed that, with 4th Indian Division and 22nd Guards Brigade now securely ensconced around Capuzzo, 4th Armoured Brigade could be detached and sent to concentrate 7th Armoured Division; he was hoping that this would lead to a decisive engagement with the German armour operating on the inland flank. Faulty communications prevented Beresford-Peirse from learning the true state of affairs from his front-line commanders until it was too late. For his part Rommel had sensed, from Creagh's anxious signals, that 7th Armoured Division was in deep trouble. First light on the 17th found Rommel ready to launch his decisive stroke, not preparing to make a fundamental regrouping of his own forces. Under his urging 5th Light Division swung east, heading for Halfaya and the main British line of communication. Wavell flew up to confer with Beresford-Peirse and Creagh, but by the time he arrived the crucial

49

decision had already been reached by Messervy. Forty-five minutes before Wavell landed, Messervy, acutely aware of the danger of encirclement posed by the latest German advance, had ordered a general withdrawl from the Capuzzo sector. Seeing at once that any attempt to retrieve the situation with surviving tank resources could only result in accelerating casualties and possible disaster, Wavell decided to cut his losses, approve Messervy's order to withdraw and abandon BATTLEAXE. Pausing only to order that as many crippled tanks as possible were to be retrieved and repaired, Wavell flew straight back to Cairo to concentrate on winning the Syrian campaign as quickly as possible.

As Western Desert Force began its painful retreat back into Egypt, it was saved by the surviving Matildas of 4th Armoured Brigade. Throughout the 17th they blocked Rommel's every attempt to drive 5th Light Division east and north to Halfaya: an 'end game' manoeuvre which would have completed the dissolution of 7th Armoured Division and cut off the retreat of 4th Indian Division. But, if Rommel had failed to destroy Western Desert Force in the field, he was well pleased at having achieved the next best thing. He had destroyed the British armoured resources for a resumed offensive into Axis-held Libya, leaving the Tobruk garrison completely isolated again without hope of any relief attempt being mounted in the foreseeable future. The balance-sheet for tanks lost during the three days of BATTLEAXE (destroyed, abandoned, and captured) reflected the dominance of German anti-tank artillery. On the British side, sixty-four out of 100 Matildas and twenty-seven out of ninety cruisers had been lost. (Over sixty cruisers, effectively lost to 7th Armoured Brigade during the battle because of breakdowns were subsequently field-repaired and recovered.) In troop losses the casualties of Western Desert Force came to 122 killed, 588 wounded and 259 missing.

Afrika Korps' tank losses in BATTLEAXE were recorded as twelve panzers destroyed outright, with ninety-three men killed and 350 wounded. Both in matériel and men, therefore, the German casualty list was notably lighter than that of the British. Yet 235 German troops were posted as missing, a total only twenty-four short of that admitted by the British. This virtual parity bore out the impression which the tank men of Western Desert Force took with them back into Egypt – that German technique in tank-for-tank action did not match the superiority of their machines. In June, 1941, panzer commanders were still learning basic Desert tactics, most notably the knack of quick coordination in a tank-versus-tank mêlée and the use of cover, exploiting even the most modest ground undulations to show as little of the tank as possible when firing. Though they had been defeated in BATTLEAXE, British tank crews did not feel beaten; they knew that the closer they could get to the panzers, inside the best effective range of the 2-pounder gun, the more chance they had of matching if not defeating the enemy.

But the problem was still how to get there, and in sufficient strength. The British were still chasing the ability to manoeuvre tank regiments in maximum strength over the distances managed with ease by Rommel's panzer regiments. And this ability would continue to elude the British for two reasons. Of these, the mechanical breakdown and fuel-wastage syndrome formed only one. The other was the hopeless imbalance of British armoured divisions caused by their equipment with two fundamentally incompatible types: slow but tough 'I' tanks and fast but unreliable cruisers. What was really needed was an all-purpose battle tank, shedding the outmoded concepts both of mechanized cavalry and infantry support weapon, able at least to match the panzers in speed while excelling them in protection and fire-power. But there was nothing in the pipeline of British tank production to promise any immediate improvement; to keep up deliveries, the 'I' tank concept was maintained in production. The new Valentine or 'Infantry Mark III', which began to replace the Matilda in the Desert after BATTLEAXE, had over twice the Matilda's speed but could still make no more than 15mph (24kph) in ideal going. The British infantry/cruiser tank imbalance, which has been compared with a grown man and a boy trying to run a three-legged race, would not be solved until the arrival of the American Shermans in the summer of 1942.

Churchill, however, never accepted the matériel problems faced by the tank forces which he had hounded into battle. To him a tank was a tank, and the generals who had been sent substantial tank reinforcements in the supreme gamble of the TIGER convoy had no excuse for losing what should have been a decisive battle. It smacked of the bad workman blaming his tools. (It must always remain a matter for regret that Churchill's son, Randolph, a tank man himself, failed to educate his father in the realities of armoured warfare.) No individual was more crushed by the failure of BATTLEAXE than Churchill. By June, 1941, he was desperate for a clear-cut victory over German troops by British forces, to cancel the apparently unending run of German victories endured since February – Cyrenaica, Yugoslavia, Greece, Crete. Unhappiness with Wavell's leadership, sharpened by Wavell's refusal to rush the 'Tiger Cubs' from the dockside straight into battle, had led Churchill to consider a change in command even before the launching of BATTLEAXE. Now the Prime Minister acted. On 21 June Churchill informed Wavell that he was to change places with the Commander-in-Chief, India. Churchill gave as his personal reason his belief that Wavell was 'tired out' and needed a change, but few who saw Wavell at the time believed it, or reacted with thorough-going relief at his departure.

I for one was deeply sorry when at the close of this hard year's fighting the papers came out with the announcement that Wavell was going.

The war correspondents went down to GHQ to say good-bye. The general was in his shirt-sleeves again. And for once he was full of words. 'We have had some setbacks, some successes,' he said, and he went on to sum it all up. It wasn't a particularly good summing-up. The theme was 'More equipment'. But I saw suddenly how sincere he was, how hard he had tried – tried, fought, organized, argued and held on. There went out of Cairo and the Middle East that afternoon one of the great men of the war.[21]

Wavell's abrupt removal from the Middle East theatre after the failure of BATTLEAXE was the biggest compliment Rommel had yet received for his impact on the course of the North African war. Yet Churchill's lament that 'Rommel has torn the new-won laurels from Wavell's brow and thrown them in the sand' was only partially true. Against all the odds which had confronted him in June, 1940, saddled throughout with a burden of clashing responsibilities which would have broken many a lesser man, Wavell had not only secured but enlarged British supremacy in the Middle East. Rommel's recovery of Cyrenaica had not prevented Wavell from wresting Iraq, Syria and Ethiopia from Axis control, while the continued sustenance of the Tobruk garrison (a strategic contrivance without precedent in modern military history) prevented Rommel from pressing on into Egypt. Thanks entirely to Wavell, the British Middle East Command was, by the second half of 1941, at last able to look forward to a concentration of its best resources against the Axis front in Libya, now the only point at which British and Imperial land forces were in actual contact with those of the Axis.

Wavell's departure, therefore, would have been momentous enough in its own right without the world-shattering event which coincided with it: the German invasion of the Soviet Union on 22 June, 1941. After a year of lone survival (apart from the gallant, brief-lived Greek alliance) this at least gave Britain a powerful continental ally at last. But the rapid advance of the German forces towards Moscow, Leningrad and Kiev created grave doubts as to the Red Army's ability to survive until the Russian winter could come to its aid. These doubts, added to Churchill's mounting obsession with the need to defeat Rommel, inevitably resulted in renewed pressure from Churchill for a new offensive in the Western Desert.

1. General Sir Claude Auchinleck pinning the ribbon of the Victoria Cross on the tunic of Brigadier Jock Campbell (see p. 114)

2. General Erwin Rommel (centre) on his arrival in Tripoli

3. General Ludwig Crüwell,
Commander of *Afrika Korps*

4. General Johann von Ravenstein,
Commander of 21st Panzer Division

But the necessary build-up for this new offensive was imperilled by Churchill's simultaneous pledge to send the Russians all British weapons and munitions that 'time, geography and our growing resources' would allow. Every tank shipped to Russia would be one less shipped to Egypt, while at the same time it was impossible to repeat the TIGER venture. The establishment of the Luftwaffe on Crete made the despatch of supply convoys through the Mediterranean too dangerous, leaving nothing for it but the enormous detour round the Cape of Good Hope. The first battle waged by Wavell's successor, General Sir Claude Auchinleck, was therefore with his own impatient political master. Despite the bitter disappointment of BATTLEAXE, Churchill had learned nothing of the need to improve training and amass sufficient resources to offset the material disadvantages under which the Desert forces laboured.

On the German 'side of the hill', the invasion of Russia led to an equally paradoxical attitude towards the North African theatre. The paramount needs of the new Eastern Front meant that Rommel would never receive the full reinforcements for which he continued to clamour. At the same time, his position on the Egyptian frontier offered immense strategic possibilities, if the German conquest of southern Russia could be achieved according to plan. There could be no ignoring the potential of converging German forces striking south across the Caucasus and north-east out of a conquered Egypt: they would place the entire Mediterranean and Middle East under Axis control. Rommel must therefore be sent whatever troops and equipment could be found for the essential preliminary to any move against Egypt: the capture of Tobruk and the long-overdue clearing of his supply-line back to Tripoli.

So things stood as the late summer of 1941 drew on into autumn. BATTLEAXE had marked the end of the heyday of lightweight Desert forces probing the unknown. For both sides the terrain to be mastered and the objectives to be taken were clearly established. Though still minute in comparison with the scale of the Eastern Front, the North African war had ceased to be a theatre in which neither side operated in greater than corps strength, with more than a couple of divisions apiece. The forging of the Desert armies had begun, with Auchinleck gathering his resources for a full-strength offensive into Libya, while Rommel's attention was fixed on Tobruk. It remained to be seen which army would first be ready to go into action.

CHAPTER 2

THE ARMIES

The up-grading of the Desert forces from corps to army strength started with the Axis forces under Rommel's command in Libya, and the process began as a direct sequel to the fact-finding visit by Paulus back in April.

When Paulus made his report to OKH after witnessing the abortive attack on Tobruk in early May, it was decided that the first step towards tidying up the situation in Libya must be the strengthening of OKH's control over Rommel. In other words, Rommel's wasteful engine needed to be fitted with a governor. The outcome of BATTLEAXE did not change OKH's opinion, though it was appreciated that Rommel could hardly be brought abruptly to heel after winning a famous victory. It was nevertheless genuinely desirable to send out a proper staff, chosen and appointed by OKH, to help Rommel coordinate the tricky tasks of investing Tobruk while holding the Egyptian Frontier and at the same time improving the liaison with the Italian forces in Libya. The skeleton staff with which Rommel had conducted operations since his arrival in February was certainly inadequate for all three tasks. At OKH it was hoped that once Rommel was obliged to work 'correctly' with a proper staff, he could be painlessly educated out of excessive leading from the front and dissipation of resources. Only time would show that these hopes would, at best, be only partially fulfilled.

The creation of Panzergruppe Afrika

The German decision to attach an enlarged staff to Rommel's command – still, in late June, 1941, that of C-in-C, German Forces, Libya, or

Befehlshaber der Deutschen Truppen in Libyen – coincided with a remodelling of the Italian High Command. A distinct improvement, it shook the Italian chain of command more into line with its German counterpart, with the following result:

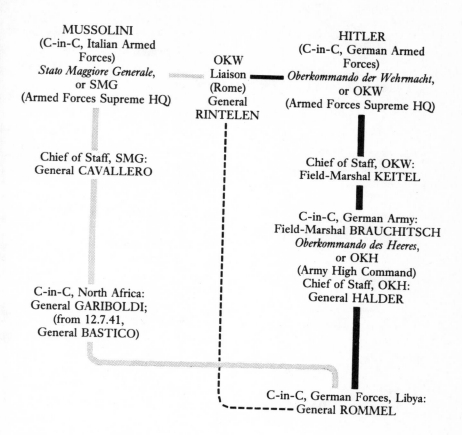

MUSSOLINI
(C-in-C, Italian Armed Forces)
Stato Maggiore Generale, or SMG
(Armed Forces Supreme HQ)

OKW Liaison (Rome) General RINTELEN

HITLER
(C-in-C, German Armed Forces)
Oberkommando der Wehrmacht, or OKW
(Armed Forces Supreme HQ)

Chief of Staff, SMG: General CAVALLERO

Chief of Staff, OKW: Field-Marshal KEITEL

C-in-C, German Army: Field-Marshal BRAUCHITSCH
Oberkommando des Heeres, or OKH
(Army High Command)
Chief of Staff, OKH: General HALDER

C-in-C, North Africa: General GARIBOLDI; (from 12.7.41, General BASTICO)

C-in-C, German Forces, Libya: General ROMMEL

Under the new command structure as under the old, Rommel was therefore kept nominally responsible to an Italian theatre commander. But he kept his invaluable direct 'hot line' to the top: the ability to communicate with OKW via Rintelen in Rome, rather than trace the convoluted, bi-national command chain via OKH and the Italian High Command. Though repeatedly bypassed by such communications, even the German Army High Command preferred this arrangement: anything was preferable to having German forces left subject to exclusively Italian Command, whose discomfiture was increased by the arrival of Rommel's new German staff at the end of June.

Italian resentment at this latest attempt by OKH to strengthen its grip on African operations might have been lessened if the Italian generals could have known that Rommel himself was equally distrustful. The archetypal fighting general, Rommel habitually professed scant respect for the 'Gentlemen of the Staff', the administrative career-officers who ran the Army from remote offices. Rommel can be excused for resenting OKH's attempts to restrict his operations in Africa since February, but behind this resentment lay an inability to see German grand strategy and its problems as they were, not as he wanted them to be. In the case of the 'ready-made' staff which *Generalmajor* Alfred Gause brought him in June, 1941, Rommel made his initial hostility unpleasantly clear. As one of his new staff officers vividly remembered:

> I shall never forget his reserved and frigid manner when he received us at Gambut. We were all very much officers of the General Staff, and yet we were all obviously new to African conditions. As a fighting soldier, Rommel looked at us with a sceptical eye; moreover he had never been on the General Staff himself and was clearly uneasy that we might attempt to surpervise and even supersede him. In actual fact there was never any question of our challenging Rommel's right to command; we had come to Africa to serve him and he soon realized that he could not command a large army without our help.[1]

For a large army it was to be. Rommel, now promoted full General, was to be entrusted with all Axis forces in Cyrenaica with the exception of XX Italian Armoured Corps (General Gastone Gambara with 'Ariete' and 'Trieste' Divisions) which was to remain under direct Italian command unless specifically transferred to that of Rommel. The latter was now enlarged to create *Panzergruppe* (Armoured Group) *Afrika*: a bi-national equivalent of the four groupings of panzer and motorized divisions carving their way eastwards across Russia. *Panzergruppe Afrika* was to consist of two corps. One was all-Italian: General Enea Navarrini's XXI Italian Corps, with 'Trento', 'Bologna', 'Brescia' and 'Pavia' Divisions. Rommel's second corps was his original command: *Afrika Korps*, now to be entrusted to a deputy commander. This was *Generalleutnant* Ludwig Crüwell, following in Rommel's footsteps by moving up from the successful command of a panzer division (in Yugoslavia) to that of a panzer corps.

The cutting edge of the *Afrika Korps* remained its original two panzer divisions: 15th Panzer and 5th Light, the latter now scheduled to receive a second panzer battalion and be up-graded to panzer divisional status, redesignated as 21st Panzer Division. The crying need for a division of

56

German motorized infantry to accompany the panzer divisions was to be met by using German units already in Africa to form three motorized infantry regiments: the 'Afrika Special Purpose Division',* afterwards redesignated as 90th Light (Afrika) Division. During its career, the new division was to gain a fine fighting reputation, recruited though it was from some of the most unorthodox human material in the entire Wehrmacht. This was typified by 90th Light's 361st Regiment, raised from German ex-members of the French Foreign Legion (hitherto barred from service in the German Army for having repudiated their country). Though no more German divisions were to be sent to Africa for nearly a year, the balance of the enlarged Afrika Korps was at least partially maintained by assigning the Italian 'Savona' Division to it.

Gause's staff became Haupquartier Panzergruppe Afrika on 31 July, 1941, and the Panzergruppe itself came officially into being on 15 August. This re-cast the Axis forces in Libya as follows:

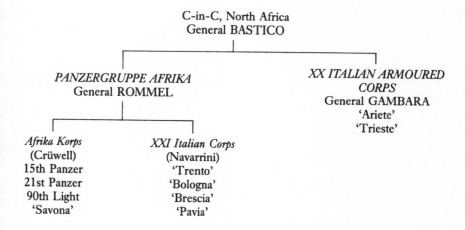

C-in-C, North Africa
General BASTICO

PANZERGRUPPE AFRIKA
General ROMMEL

XX ITALIAN ARMOURED CORPS
General GAMBARA
'Ariete'
'Trieste'

Afrika Korps
(Crüwell)
15th Panzer
21st Panzer
90th Light
'Savona'

XXI Italian Corps
(Navarrini)
'Trento'
'Bologna'
'Brescia'
'Pavia'

In the months of regrouping and build-up which followed BATTLEAXE, Rommel's basic strategy was to employ Navarrini's XXI Italian Corps to maintain the siege of Tobruk. The task allotted to Afrika Korps was to safeguard the Frontier until the time came for the decisive assault on Tobruk, to be launched, this time, from the south-east – the vulnerable Belhamed/Sidi Rezegh sector. To this end, Rommel positioned his Afrika Korps between the Tobruk siege perimeter and the Frontier, with his two panzer divisions always available for mobile defence in concentrated strength and the infantry entrusted with static defence.

* To avoid confusion with Afrika Korps the Afrika Division is here referred to throughout as 90th Light Division, by which title it will always be remembered.

57

The formation of 90th Light Division was a godsend, enabling Rommel to keep German garrisons in the most important Frontier strongpoints without drawing on the manpower of the panzer divisions, as he had been hitherto been forced to do. After the experience of BATTLEAXE, Rommel had no intention of leaving the defence of the Sollum/Halfaya/Sidi Omar sector entirely to the Italian 'Savona' Division. In detailing his German infantry for static defence, Rommel's standing order echoed Wellington's deployment of British infantry along the Allied line at Waterloo: 'A few German companies only are to be focused at certain points of the front in order to act as "corset stays" to the rest of the line.' This arrangement therefore split 90th Light Division between its main deployment on the eastern Tobruk perimeter (where it held the coastal sector) and its outposts along the Frontier.

Most army commanders delegate the minutiae of sector defence to the corps commander responsible, but that was not Rommel's way. At no stage did he leave the siting and deepening of the Frontier defences to Crüwell but supervised it himself, with constant surprise visits to the front-line positions. Between June and November, 1941, he visited gun positions, infantry foxholes, radio listening-posts and AA batteries, fact-finding and seeing for himself – and, no less important, being seen. The net result was to convince his men that they had an army commander prepared to see personally how they were getting on, appreciative of good work and merciless on the slack, leaving no weak links in the chain. Schmidt has a vivid description of the 'Rommel technique' in practice:

Punctually at 7 am we leave on one of our customary front-line visits . . . We drive past Capuzzo and through a gap in the wire entanglement on the frontier and rapidly head out into the Desert far beyond our front-line positions. On the horizon in no-man's-land we often spot enemy patrol cars. They cannot guess how fat a prize is moving within eye-shot of their binoculars.

Rommel studies our own positions from vantage points on the enemy's side. He examines them through his field-glasses with the painstaking care of a scientist using a microscope. He snorts: he has seen something that displeases him. We leap into the car after him. He stands up as we head straight for the strong-point he has surveyed.

The sentry on duty stares at Rommel wide-eyed. 'Why don't you salute?' the General barks. The soldier jumps to attention, petrified, speechless.

'Where is the outpost commander?' Rommel demands angrily.

'He is asleep, *Herr* . . . er . . . *Major!*' the sentry stutters. He is a recruit, new to the front, and has not seen Rommel before. The insignia of rank are confusing. He thinks anybody so authoritative must be of field rank; he takes a gamble on 'Major'.

'*Ja. Herr Soldat*,' snaps Rommel. 'It seems as if everybody is asleep here. Please wake this – gentleman.'

The sentry need not move. The flushed face of a young officer appears at the entrance of a dug-out nearby. When he sees the General he comes smartly to attention, salutes and reports: 'Outpost Franke – nothing special to report.'

'How do you know, *Herr Leutnant*?' Rommel raps out at him. 'You have been sleeping – and beautifully, too.'

The lieutenant has nothing to say. There is a grim pause. Rommel says, '*Herr Leutnant*, your post is not being run in accordance with my instructions. Your shelter is too prominent. The post is not camouflaged. Your men are running about – while you sleep! I shall return tomorrow and satisfy myself that my requirements are satisfied in every particular. Good morning, *Herr Leutnant*.'

He signs to the driver to start. The young officer stands rooted to the spot. Rommel has gone before he can ejaculate the customary '*Jawohl, Herr General*'. If he ever thought he would find the North African Desert romantic, he has received a rude shock now.

Our cars have been recognized before we reach the next outpost, which is named 'Cowa'. The strongpoint is alert. The lieutenant in command is on the *qui vive*. Rommel's manner changes completely. But nevertheless he delivers a little homily.

'A well-selected position, and good dispositions,' he comments. 'This is of the utmost importance. We cannot take chances. The problem of our supply lines over the Mediterranean make it difficult for us to provide equipment and rations for more troops than we already have in Africa. For this reason we must take the fullest advantage of natural features and whatever else we have at our disposal. One good strongpoint must serve as well as two indifferently planned and manned.'

'*Jawohl, Herr General*'.

'How are you off for ammunition and supplies?'

'We have plenty of ammunition, *Herr General*, and food for three days.'

'For three days, my friend? You require provisions for three weeks. But . . . never mind, we will see to that.' With a short 'Thank you!' Rommel is on his way again.

At every outpost the General leaves his car. Although nearly twice my age, he shows no sign of fatigue; my legs are sore and heavy as lead, for it is heavy going in the sand. I make endless notes and write down every request, every order, every observation. When we get back it is my duty to bring everything relevant to the notice of the Chief of Staff or the Chief Staff Officer.[2]

It was small wonder that Rommel strove in this way to get the utmost out of his human and material resources. Though no logistician, he could not escape from the supply nightmare into which his own successes had plunged him. When the *Panzergruppe* was formed, it had about 2600 tons of road transport capacity. Expressed in terms of 3-ton trucks, this came to 870 vehicles – each of which consumed three-quarters of a ton of fuel in the 14-day round trip between Tripoli and Tobruk. Of every 1000 tons of fuel landed at Tripoli, therefore, 652.5 tons was devoured by the transport fleet merely in getting to the front and back. Then there was the increasing worry over how many supplies *would* arrive every month. Between June and October, 1941, British aircraft, submarines and surface warships sank forty Axis merchant ships bound for Libya, with a total tonnage of 178,577 – an average of eight merchant ships (35,715 tons) lost every month. In addition there were the ships damaged or prevented from sailing by the British bombing and mining of Italian ports, losses which Italy's limping mercantile construction could never begin to make good. But, though the *Panzergruppe* could not move an inch without fuel, it could not live by fuel alone. Of the cargoes which did reach Libya, the average monthly ratio of general military cargo (troops, guns, ammunition, transport and stores) to fuel was 3.42:1. And only in one month, June, did all fuel shipments reach Libya intact. In July, August, September and October, 1941, the average loss-rate of fuel in transit to Libya was 21.75 per cent.

The net result was that in July, 1941, Rommel's forces were receiving 200 tons of food and fuel per day, when they needed at least 370 tons just to maintain themselves where they were. With these hard facts weighing upon him, Rommel was very much on his own, with little or no help (let alone comfort) from OKW and OKH. OKW's solution was to wash its hands of the whole transport problem, opining that it was an all-Italian responsibility. The 'Staff solution' of the OKH experts was to play with figures, starting with rejecting the figure of 11,000 tons of road transport required for the capture of Tobruk as 'unacceptable'. The figure of 5400 tons was conjured out of the air as 'jam tomorrow', transport which would be released from the Eastern Front after the Soviet collapse. This figure, added to the 2600 tons already in Libya, would amass 8000 tons of transport for the sustenance of future operations in North Africa. A further 1732 tons could be found by economies – relying more on fixed defences and advancing only by cautious stages. (This latter strategy was precisely what Graziani had tried to execute in September–December, 1940, but there is no evidence that OKH ever made a serious assessment of the Italian débâcle. To the German High Command there could be, of course, no serious comparison between the experiences of Italian and German troops.)

For the moment, however, the transport economies preached by OKH made sense and coincided with the *Panzergruppe*'s needs. Reliance on static defences and cautious manoeuvring made no sense at all for every other panzer army in the *Wehrmacht*. For *Panzergruppe Afrika*, obliged to secure its back while it took Tobruk, a reinforced static defence line along the Frontier was not only ideal but essential. Hence Rommel's tirelessness in personally overseeing the state of the Frontier defences, while making sure that every man knew what he was there for. According to Schmidt, it was also Rommel who came up with the best solution to the exasperating transport obstacle created by the Tobruk perimeter. The Australian defences denied a 22-mile stretch of the Via Balbia to the Axis supply convoys, forcing them to make a costly 35-mile detour to the south. This detour across the Desert punished trucks and exhausted drivers, and it was to cut down wastage of both that Rommel proposed the building of a bypass road across the Desert. This task proved ideally suited to the Italians of XXI Corps, whose construction battalions fell to with a will. Using local stone and sand, they completed an invaluable metalled road in three months (August–October, 1941).

Building the bypass road was a most useful exercise in shaking down the new *Panzergruppe*, giving its German and Italian elements a mutual interest and mutual respect. As the work proceeded Rommel made repeated visits to the Italian construction battalions, with excellent effect; Italian troops engaged on such duty were not used to seeing much of their own generals, let alone German ones. Rommel's praise for the Italians' efforts was unfeigned; he was not a man who handed out easy compliments, and what he saw gave him a new respect for what the Italian soldier could achieve when properly motivated. The Italians rounded off the job by erecting an imposing concrete monument at the Gazala end, complete with bas-reliefs of the Duce and Fascist emblems. The bypass road was promptly christened *Achsenstrasse* – 'Axis Road' – and it remained a permanent feature of the Desert War, used by both sides, for the rest of the conflict.

Building up the fixed defences and completing the *Achsenstrasse* were, however, little more than emergency ploys to offset the *Panzergruppe*'s inherent supply crisis. Between June and November Rommel received virtually no panzer reinforcements at all, though about 100 of the weak

Italian medium M-13 tanks were delivered to the doubtful benefit of 'Ariete'. For its most important combat element – the tank strength of *Afrika Korps* – the *Panzergruppe* was left to its own resources. Former battlefields were therefore scoured for damaged and abandoned tanks of all types, British as well as German, which could be repaired and re-armed for future service with *Afrika Korps*. Excellent work in the German field-repair workshops raised the combined strength of 15th and 21st Panzer Divisions from 180 to 250 between August and October, 1941.

Over these three months the *Panzergruppe*'s work was not restricted to strengthening its Frontier strongpoints, building the *Achsenstrasse* and repairing tanks. It was a time of intense training, under Rommel's personal supervision, for the attack on Tobruk which Rommel was determined to make at the end of November. This was the first time Rommel had had occasion to make specific plans for an attack on a 'set-piece' objective since he had prepared 7th Panzer Division for its crossing of the Meuse back in May, 1940. The work he put into this training gives the lie to accusations that Rommel was merely a tactical opportunist, a brilliant improviser. So indeed he was, but his preparation for the attack on Tobruk shows that his talents had genuine depth. It involved exhaustive rehearsals by all arms, with every platoon made familiar with its objectives by means of aerial photographs and sand-table models. Nothing could have been in greater contrast to Rommel's first and admittedly slapdash attempts to take Tobruk. The November operation was to see 'the attack as it should be delivered'.

For *Afrika Korps*, to be entrusted with the main weight of the attack and its rapid conclusion, the training was directed towards ever closer collaboration between tanks and artillery, with anti-tank guns well to the fore. This was the result of Rommel's dissatisfaction with the failure of 5th Light Division to finish off 7th Armoured Brigade during the final phase of BATTLEAXE. He hammered home the principle that *Afrika Korps* must be ready to react to every opportunity and crisis of battle, attacking or counter-attacking in maximum concentrated strength in whatever direction might be instantly required. This was a pitch of battle training which the British would take over a year to attain, overcoming the preference for roving probes by brigade groups in inadequate strength. Rommel's honing of *Afrika Korps*' tactical skills between August and November was to have lasting effect and win spectacular successes in the months ahead.

Yet there was a price to be paid for all this concentrated effort. The very intensity of Rommel's preparations for the Tobruk attack ended by giving him a bad case of strategic 'tunnel vision' – the inability to take the enemy's intentions and capabilities into account. (Napoleon had called this obsession 'making pictures' and claimed, presumably from personal experience, that it was the worst error into which any commander could fall.) Between August and November, 1941, Rommel displayed an increasing reluctance to consider the likelihood of the British attacking the *Panzergruppe* before the *Panzergruppe* could attack Tobruk. This would probably not have been the case if British security on the eve of the BATTLEAXE attack had not been so bad; certainly that experience, added to what Rommel *wanted* to believe as a result of his obsession with Tobruk, gave him a definite mental block. His Italian colleagues, mindful of the traumatic experience of COMPASS, were not so sanguine. Italian Intelligence could not help seeing the British mishandling of BATTLEAXE in a very different light, as the exception rather than the rule; but they failed to convince Rommel.By the time that the countdown to the *Panzergruppe*'s attack on Tobruk approached its final week in mid-November, 1941, Rommel's reluctance to consider a pre-emptive attack by the British had become a myopic refusal. Secretly massing across the Frontier Wire, the new Desert Army created by General Auchinleck was about to emulate 'Wavell's Thirty Thousand' and achieve complete surprise in its first attack.

The creation of Eighth Army

Auchinleck had taken over the Middle East Command from Wavell on 5 July – eighteen days after the failure of BATTLEAXE, thirteen days after the German invasion of Russia. Even if Auchinleck had not inherited two unfinished campaigns (in Syria and Ethiopia), he would have needed a modicum of time to familiarize himself with his new command and assess the reasons for the recent defeat on the Libyan Frontier. Yet Churchill wasted no time in urging the new C-in-C to attack Rommel at the earliest possible moment. Indeed, Churchill's first communication arrived four days before Auchinleck's formal take-over in Cairo, with his kit scarcely unpacked after his journey from India. 'You should,' wrote Churchill on 1 July, 'have regard especially to the situation at Tobruk and the process of enemy reinforcement in Libya and temporary German preoccupation in their invasion of Russia.' To leave Auchinleck in no possible misapprehension, Churchill added: 'The urgency of these issues will naturally impress itself upon you.'

Churchill never forgave Auchinleck for stubbornly refusing to launch a Desert offensive until four and half months later. Part of this resentment was certainly due to Churchill's feeling that he had been sold a pup. The Prime Minister had misinterpreted the speed with which

Auchinleck, from India, had despatched resources for the suppression of Iraq while Wavell (as Churchill chose to see it) merely made difficulties. Finding that Auchinleck was no less stubborn than Wavell was a bitter personal blow to Churchill, though this was scarcely Auchinleck's fault. But, in all justice, Churchill, as the man at the top of the British Empire's war effort, was under even greater pressure than that he exerted on his subordinates. The pressure on Churchill was fourfold, and only a quarter of it was due to Churchill's obsession with beating Rommel and feeling of personal defeat by Rommel in BATTLEAXE. Of course Churchill wanted an early clear-cut victory over Rommel to present to the British people after gruelling months of unbroken defeat abroad and air raids at home. But none of the British Service Chiefs in Whitehall believed that the Soviet Union would survive the German invasion. They were unanimous in advising Churchill that the *Wehrmacht's* commitment to its new Eastern Front presented Britain with a unique opportunity in the Mediterranean. This impression was naturally strengthened by the ULTRA decrypts from intercepted German signals, revealing Rommel's parlous supply situation.

The third source of pressure on Churchill came direct from Britain's new ally; non-stop Soviet demands for Britain to launch a 'Second Front' in the West – maybe in Norway, preferably in France, ideally in both. With Britain's mercantile and naval shipping already stretched to the limit by the Battle of the Atlantic and the need to supply the Middle East theatre, there was no chance of assembling such an amphibious invasion and no reserves of trained troops to man it anyway. Stalin and his advisers remained deaf to these realities; and, though Churchill gave as good as he got in rebutting Stalin's hectoring and charges of British cowardice, there could be no denying that the Russians had a point. The only answer Churchill had for Stalin was that an embryonic 'Second Front' already existed in the Mediterranean, whither German resources had already been drawn thanks to British prowess. Stalin, however, thought and argued in divisions. Given the enormous scale of operations in Russia, he refused to accept that the North African theatre, Britain's only active front, was anything more than a derisory sideshow. Viewed from Moscow, it seemed that Britain's commitment to the defeat of Germany was no more serious than it had been during the following exchange during the abortive Anglo-Soviet negotiations in the summer of 1939:

'How many divisions,' Stalin had asked, 'will France send against Germany on mobilization?' The answer was 'About a hundred.' He then asked, 'How many will England send?' The answer was 'Two and two more later.' 'Ah, two, and two more later,' Stalin had repeated. 'Do you know,' he asked, 'how many divisions we shall have to put on the Russian front if we go to war with Germany?' There was a pause. 'More than three hundred.'[3]

Stalin's scepticism over active British commitment in July, 1941, twenty-three months into the war, is easy enough to understand. Expressed in terms of divisions at the front, it came down to 'three, and two later': 7th Armoured Division and 4th Indian Division, plus 9th Australian Division in Tobruk, with the New Zealand Division recuperating from Crete and the 1st South African Division yet to muster in Egypt. These faced seven Italian and two German divisions of which three were armoured – small beer indeed to a Soviet Army already cracking and splitting under the impact of 120 German divisions, eighteen of which were armoured. This disparity of scale outweighed Churchill's counter-arguments that the British Imperial forces in Egypt were holding down three times their number of Axis divisions, which would otherwise be available for despatch to the Eastern Front (though Mussolini was anxious for Italy to share in Hitler's 'Crusade Against Bolshevism', he only had three spare Italian divisions to send to Russia; these saw their first action on the Eastern Front in August, 1941). It was therefore all the more infuriating for Churchill to find Auchinleck adding weight to Stalin's reproaches by refusing to rush into premature battle with Rommel.

Churchill's fourth source of anxiety was the need to impress upon the still-neutral United States that supplies of war materials to Britain would not be wasted, or put to better use at home. Since the outbreak of the European war, President Roosevelt had stretched American neutrality as it had never been stretched before, starting with the 'Cash and Carry' law permitting France and Britain to pay cash for American war materials and ship them home. After the fall of France and the early depletion of Britain's last dollar reserves, Roosevelt had contrived the principle of Lend-Lease to continue supplies of war materials to Britain. (To sell the idea to the American people, Roosevelt used the parable of the good neighbour lending – not selling – a garden hose to help put out a mutually dangerous fire.) Immediate benefits under Lend-Lease were foodstuffs and steel, followed by fighter aircraft and medium bombers. But there were great hopes that the latest American tank designs would close the gap between Brtish and German tank design, and here the problem was that the US Army needed tanks even more than the British. Churchill's fear was that, unless American tanks shipped overseas took part in an early British victory, the US Army chiefs would insist on

Roosevelt re-equipping the US Army with its own tanks before sending any more abroad.

Had they done so, it would have been hard to blame them. When the Lend–Lease Act became law on 11 March, 1941, the US Army was only just beginning to rearm against the probability of involvement in the war. So far as tank production was concerned, the fire had not even been lit under what Lord Grey had once called the 'gigantic boiler' of American war industry. In the whole of the United States, only sixteen tanks were manufactured during the month of March, 1941. By a singular mercy, however, American peacetime neglect of armoured development was about to reap a unique benefit to the advantage of the whole Allied war effort, for it meant that wartime tank production in the United States began virtually from scratch. American production lines were not obliged, like those in the United Kingdom, to keep turning out tanks of known obsolescence because of the frantic precedence of quantity over quality. And by April, 1941, the first of a trio of American tanks destined, over the next four years, to serve in every theatre of the war, was poised to enter mass production.

This was the Stuart M-3, designated 'light' in American parlance but at 13½ tons comparable to the flimsy British cruiser tanks of 1940–1. Its name (in honour of 'Jeb' Stuart, the famed Confederate cavalry leader of the American Civil War) was not the best of omens. The Stuart was indeed designed more as a mechanized cavalry mount than as a modern battle tank, in which speed mattered less than endurance, protection and hitting-power. The tall and angular profile of the Stuart, hard to conceal even on the most undulating battlefield, betrayed the inevitable lack of combat experience; its main armament was the 37mm gun, on a par with the short-ranged British 2-pounder; the high-octane fuel on which the Stuart ran created a separate logistic headache and was coupled to a short endurance. Yet the Stuart's overriding advantages were its speed and agility at speed, added to a refreshing freedom from the usual gamut of breakdowns suffered by British tanks. These advantages were exactly what British tank men had been praying for ever since they had first encountered the superior range of German tank and anti-tank artillery.

To earmark no less than 300 Stuarts for Lend-Lease export to the Middle East, at a time when American units had yet to be equipped with the type, was a lavish gesture of faith in British prospects of victory. To Churchill it was a gesture which not only deserved but demanded early justification in battle (if similar largesse was to be expected in the future) under Auchinleck's command. By the end of July forty-one American ships carrying Lend–Lease cargoes had already delivered the first eighty-four Stuarts to Egypt via the Red Sea, along with 164 fighter aircraft, twenty-four 3-inch AA guns, nearly 10,000 trucks, and generous stocks of road-making and engineering plant and tools. Churchill's interpretation of these deliveries was that they corresponded to that of the TIGER convoy in May, and that Auchinleck had no excuse for refusing to put these resources to immediate use.

Auchinleck, however, adamantly refused to comply with Churchill's demands and remained adamant when summoned to London on 29 July. He insisted that the Egyptian base must be rendered completely secure before there could be any thought of Western Desert offensive. By 'completely secure', Auchinleck meant not only the pacification of Syria and Iraq but the final conclusion of the Ethiopian campaign and the adequate defence of Cyprus for good measure. He rejected the Whitehall assessment that a Desert offensive was considered essential by mid-September at the latest. Though it was true that Middle East Command had already been restored to a tank strength of 500, this was nowhere near enough for a decisive assault on Rommel's *Panzergruppe*. Given the proven wastage rate of previous Desert campaigns, Auchinleck pressed the case for a margin of at least 50 per cent superiority in tank strength. Nor, he pointed out, was a mere 'head count' of tanks any sound indication of readiness for battle. BATTLEAXE had proved that the British in North Africa were not merely confronted by superior tanks, they were up against superior organization and tactics. Auchinleck therefore refused to contemplate battle without enough of a safety margin in tank strength. Before he tackled the *Afrika Korps* on its own ground, he wanted two and preferably three armoured divisions, fully equipped and trained. This, he argued, was the only guarantee of the victory which Auchinleck desired to win no less than Churchill and the Chiefs of Staff.

If Auchinleck's case was unanswerable, so was the retort of the Chiefs of Staff that there was absolutely no chance of concentrating three armoured divisions in the Middle East in the foreseeable future. It would, however, be possible to send out 22nd Armoured Brigade from 1st Armoured Division in the United Kingdom, accepting that time would be needed to convert this unit from anti-invasion expertise in England to Desert battle-worthiness. The arrival of 22nd Armoured Brigade (estimated at first for mid-September) would give Auchinleck three armoured brigades (7th, 4th, and 22nd). These, heavily reinforced with new tanks, guns and transport, should suffice to beat Rommel's three armoured divisions, under-strength and starved of reinforcements as these were correctly estimated to be. The Desert Air Force was also to be strongly reinforced, giving Auchinleck air superiority for the coming offensive, for which he was expected to be ready by the end of October.

Having won the first trick and avoided being prodded into a premature offensive as Wavell had been in June, Auchinleck returned to Egypt at the beginning of August in the knowledge that the old order in the Middle East was dead. The concept of a British 'Army of the Nile', required to dissipate its forces north and north-east into Syria and Iraq, overseas to Greece and Crete, west into Libya and south into Ethiopia and Somaliland, had been ground to extinction by the course of events since June, 1940. It was now time to reorganize the Middle East Command on a proper basis. The final operations in Ethiopia were to be entrusted to an entirely separate East Africa Command based on the Sudan, while Palestine and Transjordan became the base area for a new army, the Ninth, entrusted with the security of Syria and Iraq. This would leave Egypt as the base area for the new Eighth Army to be assembled for the conquest of Axis Libya.

Auchinleck's command re-shuffle sent Lieutenant-General Beresford-Peirse to the Sudan to take over the new East Africa Command, while General Sir Maitland Wilson was appointed to Ninth Army. To command Eighth Army, Auchinleck chose the victor of Ethiopia, General Sir Alan Cunningham. Western Desert Force was again designated XIII Corps. Its command passed from Beresford-Peirse to Lieutenant-General Godwin-Austen who, after his fine performance at Tug Argan during the withdrawal from British Somaliland, had gone on to command 12th African Division under Cunningham. But by far the most important element in Auchinleck's forward planning for Eighth Army's first offensive was the formation of a specialized armoured corps, which gradually took shape as XXX Corps. From the outset XXX Corps was assigned one overriding task: to engage and destroy the *Afrika Korps*. Wherever the *Afrika Korps* went, XXX Corps would go, constantly harrying Rommel's armour, denying it freedom of movement and keeping the panzers off the infantry as XIII Corps advanced into Cyrenaica. In creating XXX Corps, the built-in discrepancy between British infantry and cruiser tanks would be accepted – and exploited. The faster cruisers would be concentrated in XXX Corps; the infantry tanks would provide close armoured support for the infantry divisions of XIII Corps.

Never content with the record of his own successes in command of Eighth Army, won with double the resources that any of his predecessors had ever enjoyed, Field-Marshal Montgomery was later to claim that the formation of a specialized armoured corps for Eighth Army was his idea, and his alone. This typically misleading passage from Montgomery's *Memoirs*, referring to his thinking in August, 1942, is a near-perfect 'ghosting' of Auchinleck's conclusions thirteen months earlier. It could well have been penned by Auchinleck himself, in the memoirs which – determined to let the record speak for itself, as Montgomery rarely did – Auchinleck never deigned to write:

> I came to the conclusion that the Eighth Army must have its own Panzer Army – a corps strong in armour, well equipped, and well trained. It must never hold static fronts; it would be the spearhead of our offensives. Because of the lack of such a corps we had never done any lasting good. The formation of this corps of three or four divisions must be a priority task.[4]

The novelty of the thinking behind the formation of XXX Corps, and the importance attached to its role, was reflected by its first choice of commander. This was Lieutenant-General V.V. Pope, former Director of Armoured Fighting Vehicles at the War Office; but he never lived to complete the task of preparing XXX Corps for battle. On 5 October Pope and two of his brigadiers (Russell and Unwin) were killed in one of the recurrent air crashes cynically regarded by aspiring British officers as 'good for promotion'. Pope's replacement was Major-General Willoughby Norrie, hitherto commanding 1st Armoured Division.

As the cutting edge of Eighth Army, Norrie's XXX Corps fell woefully short of the two-division minimum considered essential by Auchinleck. It amounted to one and a half armoured divisions, or three armoured brigades. The full division was 7th Armoured, commanded by Desert veteran 'Strafer' Gott (now a major-general), with 7th and 22nd Armoured Brigades. The half-division was the expanded 4th Armoured Brigade Group under Brigadier Alec Gatehouse, DSO MC, 'who could best be described', as one of his troop commanders admiringly put it, 'as a tank officer as distinct from a cavalry officer, and who was probably the best handler of armour in the Desert at the time.'[5]

Though Auchinleck was denied the use of full-strength armoured divisions in the formation of XXX Corps, he was determined that its component armoured brigades should have the strength to operate on independent axes, as Rommel's panzer divisions had done in BATTLEAXE. The deepest initial penetration, on the far left flank, would be made by the veteran 7th Armoured Brigade; 4th Armoured Brigade would operate on the centre and right of XXX Corps' front, keeping touch with the left flank of XIII Corps. The protection of XXX Corps' line of communication was entrusted to 22nd Armoured Brigade, and the securing of gains made by the armour was entrusted to the two infantry brigades of 1st South African Division (Major-General G.L. Brink).

With the cruiser tanks creamed off to meet the fluid, long-distance role envisaged for XXX Corps, the slow Valentine and Matilda 'I' tanks were concentrated into two new army tank brigades. One of these, the 1st Army Tank Brigade, was to advance with Freyberg's New Zealand Division and Messervy's 4th Indian Division, as the cutting edge of XIII Corps. After the losses of BREVITY and BATTLEAXE, there were to be no more costly head-on attacks on Rommel's positions along the Sollum/Halfaya/Capuzzo sector. These were to be engulfed by XIII Corps in a bypassing advance through the Frontier Wire south of Sidi Omar, north to Sidi Azeiz, then west to Gambut and Tobruk. This time the Tobruk garrison would be waiting to enter the fray at the earliest possible moment and turn their besiegers into besieged. To this end the 32nd Army Tank Brigade was built up within the Tobruk perimeter. Its role was to spearhead the breakout attack by the Tobruk garrison which, in conjunction with the westward approach of XIII Corps from Gambut, was intended to catch Rommel's infantry divisions between hammer and anvil.

This was the audacious concept which had lain dormant ever since Wavell had given the order, back in April, that Tobruk was to be held until relieved. But the troops who had made it all possible – Morshead's 9th Australian Division, the 'Rats of Tobruk' – would be denied their share in the great offensive. For this the men of 9th Australian Division had their own politicians to thank, and the growing pulse of Dominion self-assertion in the British Empire's bloodstream.

The Australians leave Tobruk, August–October, 1941

From mid-July, 1941, political restlessness in Australia saw the administration of Robert G. Menzies give place to that of Arthur Fadden, and finally the Labour Government headed by John Curtin destined to carry Australia through the rest of the war. Though Australia's commitment to the British war effort was never in doubt, this loyalty did not exclude criticism of the Mother Country's use of Dominion forces, and by the summer of 1941 this had become a major political issue in Australia. All opposition cliques and parties objected loudly to the constant piecemeal deployment of Australian divisions in the Middle East, while the bulk of the British Army remained in the United Kingdom. These objections pointed to the isolation of 9th Australian Division in Tobruk, dwelled on the apparent danger of its destruction, and culminated in a sustained demand for the Division's early relief. The withdrawal of 9th Australian Division from Tobruk was formally requested as the preliminary to the unification of the Australian divisions in a single command, on the lines of the Australian and New Zealand Army Corps (ANZAC) of the First World War.

In Britain, Churchill's instincts as a politician had always winced at the gift such criticisms presented to Axis propaganda, and had done ever since the outbreak of the war, when the German Propaganda Ministry had assured the French Army that 'The English will fight to the very last Frenchman'. As he expressed the problem,

> I was sensitive to the hostile propaganda which asserted that it was the British policy to fight with any other troops but our own and thus avoid the shedding of United Kingdom blood. British casualties in the Middle East, including Greece and Crete, had in fact been greater than those of all our other forces put together, but the nomenclature which was customary gave false impression of the facts. The Indian divisions, of which one-third of the infantry and the whole of the artillery were British, were not described as British-Indian divisions. The armoured divisions, which had borne the brunt of the fighting, were entirely British, but this did not appear in their names. The fact that 'British' troops were rarely mentioned in any reports of the fighting gave colour to the enemy's taunts, and provoked unfavourable comment not only in the United States but in Australia.[6]

Another count in Churchill's score of grievances against Middle East Command had been Wavell's apparent inability to recognize the importance of this problem, and welcome the despatch of more 'British' divisions from the United Kingdom. Given the time it took for new arrivals to acclimatize themselves and work up to full combat efficiency, and the multiplicity of urgent combat tasks demanding 'ready-use' forces attuned to the theatre, Wavell preferred drafts and replacement equipment for the units already under his command. After Wavell's departure Churchill was incensed to find Auchinleck equally reluctant to place 'British' divisions fully in the limelight. Instead of immediately employing the newly arrived 50th (British) Division in the Western Desert, Auchinleck sent it off to build defences in Cyprus instead. And, when the time came to make the first token withdrawal of Australian troops from Tobruk, Auchinleck's choice of replacements only seemed to make matters worse on the propaganda front: not British, Indian, or Dominion troops, but Poles.

These were the men of Lieutenant-General Stefan Kopanski's Polish Carpathian Brigade, who had crossed into Rumania in the dying stages of the 1939 Polish campaign, determined to carry on their country's struggle. After a difficult journey via Rumania and Turkey, the Poles joined General Weygand's French command in Syria, but after the fall of France they decamped to the British in Palestine (causing great nostalgia to the cavalry diehards in Cairo by arriving with two squadrons of horsed cavalry). Kopanski's Poles readily adjusted to the conditions of the Western Desert and asked nothing better than the chance of fighting Germans. By the time of BATTLEAXE in June, 1941, the Carpathian Brigade was serving as the garrison force at Mersa Matruh where, according to Sir David Hunt, its presence was of great benefit in the interrogation of German prisoners of war:

> Most Germans had either a bad conscience about their own treatment of the Poles or else were convinced that the Poles had been in the habit of treating the Germans in Poland with great brutality; in either case they disliked the idea of being in Polish custody. And a hint that in return for a co-operative attitude they would be handed over to British troops to be looked after used to work wonders in loosening their tongues. As a matter of fact they were all going to be handed over to British troops anyway as soon as they left Matruh and furthermore we were obliged to get them away as quickly as possible in order to save on food supplies.[7]

In the event, Auchinleck's choice of Tobruk as the next assignment for the Carpathian Brigade proved inspired. The aggressive spirit of the Poles was perfectly suited to maintaining the reputation established by Morshead's Australians in Tobruk, where they replaced 18th Australian Infantry Brigade in mid-August, 1941. The Poles wasted no time in putting the fear of God into the 'Brescia' Division on the western sector of the perimeter. They also worked heroically at deepening and strengthening the defences, gradually converting surface scrapes just capable of concealing a prone infantryman into deep walkways where it was possible to walk upright without exposure to the besiegers' fire.

The evacuation of 18th Australian Infantry Brigade only intensified the demands of the Australian government to speed up the relief of the whole division. The task not only threatened to distract from Eighth Army's build-up in Egypt but was also intensely dangerous, with the ships involved being exposed to Axis air attack all the way in and out of Tobruk. Relief runs could therefore only be made at night – and, for maximum safety, during the 'dark nights' of each month's New Moon period. It would therefore be impossible to bring out the last elements of 9th Australian Division before the last week of October. Auchinleck formally requested that the relief should be postponed until the build-up in the Western Desert was complete, but the politicians had their way.

There was nothing for it but to proceed with the relief operation and hope that the pessimistic fears of excessive Australian losses (so far not realized on land) would not be realized on sea.

The division chosen by Auchinleck to take over Tobruk from 9th Australian *was* a 'British' division, the 6th, but it was not a division which had been shipped out intact from the United Kingdom. It was in fact a well-acclimatized Middle East unit, having been formed on the nucleus of 16th Infantry Brigade when the Greek expedition had first been mooted in autumn, 1940. The envisaged role for 6th Division was an attack on the Italian-held Dodecanese Islands, always one of Churchill's favourite schemes. Wavell had earmarked 6th Division for preliminary service in Crete, and its 14th Brigade was sent there in November, 1940; but the Division was still lacking its artillery and supporting arms when Rommel's first attack came at the end of March, 1941. The German arrival on the Egyptian Frontier nevertheless left Wavell with no option but to send 6th Division forward to Mersa Matruh, to block any further German move into Egypt.

Though 6th Division played no part in either BREVITY or BATTLEAXE, all three of its brigades nevertheless distinguished themselves in action between May and July, 1941. The 14th Brigade stoutly defended Heraklion on the north coast of Crete until its evacuation on the night of 28/29 May, losing 800 men to German air attack on the voyage back to Egypt. The 16th and 23rd Brigades were 'blooded' in the Syrian campaign against the Vichy French, performing well on the Damascus sector. It was, therefore, a battle-proved force, if yet to go into action as a complete division, which Auchinleck selected to join the Poles in Tobruk. Reformed as 70th (British) Division, it was commanded by Major-General R.M. Scobie. In his new command, Scobie wore a 'second hat' as commander of the entire Tobruk garrison force in succession to the redoubtable Morshead. The relief proceeded between 19 and 27 September when 16th Infantry Brigade Group was shipped into Tobruk with the Headquarters of 32nd Army Tank Brigade, and 24th Australian Infantry Brigade Group was brought out. It was resumed in the October 'moonless' period – 12–25 October – but with mounting losses to Axis air and submarine attack.

These losses led Admiral Cunningham, whose Mediterranean Fleet was now dwindling to alarming proportions, to insist that no further relief runs were to be made to Tobruk. The last battalion and a half of 9th Australian Division therefore remained in Tobruk under Scobie's command. On all counts the Royal Navy's contribution to the long siege had been magnificent. From April to October, 1941, 47,280 men (including wounded and prisoners) had been shipped out of Tobruk, and 34,113 had been carried in, together with 33,946 tons of stores. The cost – bearing in mind the Mediterranean Fleet's savage losses during the evacuation of Greece and Crete in the same period – had been thirty-four warships and merchant ships sunk while running the Tobruk gauntlet and another thirty-three damaged. By the end of October, however, Australian political demands had been (temporarily) met with the evacuation of 9th Australian Division. In its place stood Scobie's 70th Division and Kopanski's Poles, looking to the day when they could convert Tobruk into a sally-port against Rommel's *Panzergruppe*.

Churchill never forgave Auchinleck for the long lull on the North African front which followed BATTLEAXE: 'I nevertheless record my conviction that General Auchinleck's four and a half months' delay in engaging the enemy in the Desert was alike a mistake and misfortune.'[8] He would have preferred to see Auchinleck launch a persistent series of spoiling attacks across the Frontier to force Rommel into an early crisis of inadequate supplies and dwindling resources. As if to purge his memory of how shattered he had been by the failure of BATTLEAXE, to which he had attached such inflated hopes, Churchill now insisted that BATTLEAXE had been vindicated because it left the Germans 'utterly unable to advance'. Seized by an attack of 'tunnel vision' comparable with Rommel's obsession with the capture of Tobruk, Churchill refused to accept that repeat performances of BATTLEAXE after the June failure should only have depreciated Auchinleck's reserves far quicker than Rommel's.

Auchinleck, however, never wavered from his determination to atone for the delay on which he had insisted by delivering the goods in full. His objective, as agreed with Churchill and the Chiefs of Staff at the end of July, went far beyond that of BATTLEAXE: the relief of Tobruk. His sights were set on Tripoli, following the trail blazed by Wavell and O'Connor. To this end Auchinleck invited General Cunningham to consider two alternatives: a deliberate engagement with the *Panzergruppe* in the killing-ground between Tobruk and the Frontier, or a long-distance advance across the Desert to reach the Via Balbia south of Benghazi, cutting the *Panzergruppe*'s vital land supply-line and bringing about a second Beda Fomm. Cunningham's reaction was that a major effort across the Desert towards Benghazi was easily the worst option. The distance to be covered created insuperable problems of supply and vehicle wastage, during which advance the bulk of the Axis armour would be left intact. The further west Eighth Army advanced without pushing the Axis air squadrons off their airfields, the heavier the Axis air attacks were bound to grow, further reducing Eighth Army's capacity,

74

with the decisive battle still to be fought. Cunningham therefore opted for an early and decisive showdown with the *Panzergruppe* while Eighth Army's resources were greatest and its supply lines shortest.

'CRUSADER', the final plan for the long-awaited offensive, was therefore a pragmatic mixture of past experience and new ideas. The past experience (both of COMPASS and BATTLEAXE) served as a reminder of the prizes to be gained by the fluid use of armour on the inland Desert flank. It also showed the losses to be expected in any deliberate butt at the German Frontier defences. The new ideas therefore included an unprecedentedly deep outflanking advance into Cyrenaica by both XIII and XXX Corps, bypassing the entire defended Frontier sector between Sidi Omar and Sollum. Once through the Wire, XIII Corps would wheel north to begin the measured isolation of the Axis Frontier defences, which would end with the latter isolated from *Afrika Korps* and XIII Corps astride the road to Tobruk. No further dramatic advance was envisaged for XIII Corps until the armour of XXX Corps, striking north-west from the Wire straight for Tobruk, had brought the *Afrika Korps* to battle and defeated it.

Once the decisive armoured battle had been fought and won by XXX Corps, it would be time for XIII Corps to resume its westward advance and join XXX Corps in attacking the Axis divisions investing Tobruk from the east and south-east, while simultaneously 70th Division launched its breakout attack from within the perimeter. Success in these operations, and an energetic pursuit of the survivors, should result in the total destruction of Rommel's forces. The road to Benghazi, El Agheila and ultimately Tripoli would then be open to Eighth Army.

Though rejected by Cunningham as the main axis for Eighth Army's advance, the southern Desert flank – the straight road to the Benghazi/El Agheila sector – was not neglected. While the *Panzergruppe* and XXX Corps came to grips in the north, 'Oasis Force' – 29th Indian Infantry Brigade Group, with the 6th South African Armoured Car Regiment – would advance from Jarabub to Jalo Oasis. Its other objective was to seize and secure a new Desert landing ground known as 'Landing Ground 125', 100 miles north-west of Jarabub. From this new base the Royal Air Force would begin attacks on Rommel's supply line south of Benghazi, forcing him to look over his shoulder while the decisive armoured battle moved to its conclusion. The general task assigned to Oasis Force was to simulate a major British offensive in the south, and to reinforce this impression dummy camps, fuel and stores dumps, and tank parks would be ostentatiously created south of Jarabub.

Such were the outline and the objectives of CRUSADER, Eighth Army's first offensive. Regardless of the relief of the Tobruk garrison imposed by Australian pressure, its original D-Day was set for the first week in November, but the all-important preliminary work of troop training and supply-dumping remorselessly imposed their own imperatives, forcing the impatient Churchill to accept yet more delays.

The build-up: Eighth Army, October–November, 1941

CRUSADER was the ultimate proof, if proof had still been needed, of the German-coined truisms that the Desert was 'the tactician's paradise and the quartermaster's hell' and that 'supply is the basis of the battle'. It was comparatively easy to assess the Axis resources and work out a tactical plan for their destruction, but there were no easy answers to the logistic problems on whose solution all depended.

The success of CRUSADER would depend on Eighth Army's ability to make a rapid and unimpeded advance 130 miles to the Frontier from its nearest supply railhead. Once past the Frontier it would have to advance another 50 miles at least (more likely 80 miles) to the area of the anticipated main battle. This was to be fought by the highly mobile armoured columns of XXX Corps, whose demands for fuel and ammunition were bound to be voracious. To add to the conundrum the CRUSADER plan deliberately ruled out any attempt to allow the early establishment of direct supply by land, along the coastal road, whose sector from Halfaya through Sollum to Bardia was to be bypassed by Eighth Army's initial advance. This left the Western Desert railway as the main supply artery, and the extension of the railhead to the west became of the utmost importance. Wavell had begun this task back in May, before BATTLEAXE; but a railway, unlike the *Panzergruppe*'s *Achsenstrasse* round Tobruk, cannot be built from local materials. From June to September, 1941, the New Zealand 10th Railway Construction Company, labouring manfully under constant shortages of materials and plant, only managed to push the railhead 20 miles west of Mersa Matruh. Vital deliveries of Lend–Lease engineering materials, plus the reinforcement by a second New Zealand Construction Company (the 13th) raised the rate of track construction to two miles a day in October. But despite the heroic work of the New Zealanders, the railhead site marked down as essential for the launching of CRUSADER – Misheifa, 80 miles west of Matruh and 60 miles east of the Frontier Wire – was not reached until 15 November. The completion of the railhead extension was rounded off with construction of a dummy railhead to minimize the effect of Axis air attacks.

The extended railway, however, could not carry all Eighth Army's needs. Though the Army would be unable to advance or fight without fuel and amunition, it would be equally helpless without that bulky essential of Desert survival – water. Entrusting bulk water supply to wheeled transport was out of the question: there was neither the transport nor the fuel to spare. The only answer was the building of a new water pipeline up to the railhead, but this task, too, was seriously delayed. On 11 October a long-range German air raid on Fuka, 40 miles east of Matruh, destroyed the pumping stations and reservoirs storing all accumulated water stocks awaiting transfer west of Matruh. The need for repairs and replenishment meant that it was 13 November before the flow of piped water reached Misheifa. The extended pipeline and railway gave Eighth Army a rail supply link and piped water 270 miles from Alexandria, but these facilities were never intended to sustain Eighth Army throughout CRUSADER. So far as supplies were concerned, the plan envisaged the relief of Tobruk by the end of the first week, enabling the port to receive shipments of supplies direct to the battle front. Within another week – fourteen days after the launching of the offensive – it was expected that the water problem would have been solved by reaching the abundant water of the Jebel Akhdar. But if the battle went badly, the men of Eighth Army, whose initial water ration was only ¾ of a gallon (3.4 litres) per day, would inevitably face an escalating crisis of supply.

To sustain the westward advance Eighth Army was to use an expanded version of the mobile Field Supply Depots (FSDs) which had performed well during the advance of 'Wavell's Thirty Thousand' from Sidi Barrani to El Agheila. The initial deployment of Eighth Army would be supplied from three Forward Bases: one at Sidi Barrani, for the XIII Corps troops intended to mask the Axis Frontier positions from the east; one at Thalata 8 miles south-west of the railhead, for the rest of XIII Corps and the whole of XXX Corps; and one at Jarabub for Oasis Force alone. From these Forward Bases supplies would be fed westward, keeping pace with the advance of the front, to a lengthening chain of Field Maintenance Centres (FMCs). Each of these would consist of a Field Supply Depot, Field Ammunition Depot, Water Issue Section, plus separate dumps for Engineer, Ordnance and Medical stores. These FMCs, once established, would take up 6 square miles of desert *each*. It was therefore small wonder that the strictest attention was paid to layout, dispersion and, above all, camouflage. If, in the cut and thrust of the armoured battle, enemy armoured forces should happen to surprise and destroy the FMCs, immediate retreat would be XXX Corps' only hope of survival. No armour could be spared for the defence of the FMCs, though 22nd Guards Brigade was entrusted with their defence. Their best security lay in the ability of the Desert Air Force to retain control of the air, preventing Axis air reconnaissance from detecting the FMC sites.

The Desert Air Force

The provision of a specialized armoured corps for Eighth Army was matched by the build-up of a tactical air force under General Cunningham's opposite number in the RAF, Air Vice-Marshal A. Coningham. The role of the Desert Air Force was to assure Eighth Army of control in the air, not just during the initial advance and armoured battle, but for as long as CRUSADER lasted. The Desert Air Force was therefore to advance with the Army, to which fell the responsibility for constructing and protecting forward airfields. Under the direction of Air Marshal Tedder, the RAF theatre C-in-C, RAF squadron training since the retreat from Cyrenaica in April had concentrated on improvements in field maintenance and repair, with the maximizing of local resources. Like Wavell with the ground forces, Tedder was less interested in asking for more squadrons than in the number which could actually be kept, fully armed, fully manned, fully equipped, at maximum readiness.

Squadron training for CRUSADER therefore devoted much time and thought to the ability to move at such short notice, leap-frogging forward to new bases, with as much of the squadron as possible remaining operational while the move was achieved on the ground. Here the RAF's problem was the universal one – lack of sufficient transport vehicles as the lion's share went to the Army. It was to dog the Desert Air Force throughout CRUSADER, imposing a never-ending demand for ingenuity and flexibility. Advance planning to cope with the problem in the field split each squadron's maintenance staff into three: a base party, to stay with the squadron workshops at the base airfield; a rear party, to cope with day-to-day maintenance at operational fields; and an advanced party, whose main task was acting as the all-important refuelling team when moving forward to new airfields.

Every other RAF station in the Middle East was milked to create the Desert Air Force, expanding it from the original No.204 Group, as Eighth Army had been built up from the original Western Desert Force and XIII Corps. Coningham's main force consisted of three tactical reconnaissance squadrons, eight medium bomber squadrons, and sixteen fighter squadrons (single-engined and twin-engined). The heavy bombing role was filled by the Wellingtons of No.205 Group, and the Desert Air Force also had the periodic use of a Fleet Air Arm squadron of bombers, plus several long-range reconnaissance and transport aircraft. Squadron strengths were raised from sixteen aircraft to eighteen, with seven more held in immediate reserve, yielding a 'front-line' strength of 486 aircraft and an immediate reserve of 112. Lend-Lease supplies of American aircraft greatly eased demands on British aircraft production and ferrying schedules; two of the most useful and ubiquitous American types were the Curtiss P-40 Tomahawk fighter and the Douglas A-20 Boston medium bomber. Between mid-October and mid-November 232 more aircraft were delivered to the replacement pools created to feed the front-line squadrons. The main problem of the Desert Air Force was not the supply of aircraft or even fuel. It was men – corresponding supplies of fully trained pilots and crews.

As the aircraft continued to swell the replacement pools of the Desert Air Force, the new tanks were arriving in the expanded vehicle parks of XXX Corps. Of these by far the most exciting were the 163 Stuarts (excluding reserve machines) which went to Gatehouse's men of 4th Armoured Brigade:

The really intriguing things about the M-3 were its engine and the tracks. Drivers gasped in astonishment when the back covers were lifted off . . . it was simply an aeroplane engine stuck in a tank, with radial cylinders and a fan that looked like a propeller. Fuel was to present a new problem to the supply services, as the engine ran efficiently only on high octane aviation spirit. But this was not our problem, and the consensus of opinion was that anything that was likely to assist in a fast take-off was probably a good thing.

After the engines had received their share of comment, we gave our undivided attention to the tracks. There had never been anything like them in the British Army. Each track link was mounted in solid rubber blocks on which the vehicle moved. After one look we wondered why the hell British tank designers had never thought of it.

As soon as I could, I got my crew into one of the Stuarts and headed out of Heliopolis for the first patch of open, sandy desert – not always as easy to find as you might think. We tested her for speed first, and found that on good going we could get up to 40 mph. It was a comforting thought, in the circumstances, to know that the German Marks III and IV could manage only 20 or so.

Then I told my driver, Whaley, to make a few fast turns, and waited with some foreboding for the inevitable bang-clatter and swerving halt that meant a broken track. Nothing happened. It was wonderful. That tank handled like a well-trained cow-pony.

'Let's see just what it will take,' I said down the intercom. 'Try and shed one of these tracks.'

Whaley put her through a variety of turns and manoeuvres that made the sandy floor of the Desert look like an ice-rink after a hockey match, spurting up great fountains of sand and dust behind the tracks.

'That'll do,' I shouted to the driver at last. 'We're beginning to wear out the Desert.'[8]

As with every other American weapon adopted for British service, the Stuart was re-christened on its arrival in Egypt. This time, however, the new name was not prescribed by the War Office. It was bestowed by the troops, delighted by the sweet handling qualities of their new mount: in Eighth Army service the advent of CRUSADER converted the Stuart into the 'Honey'.

But not everything in the build-up for CRUSADER went according to plan. Apart from the worries over the time taken to extend the railhead and water pipeline to Misheifa, the dumping schedule in the Forward Bases was repeatedly interrupted by the transport shortage. Then there were the late arrivals. The third claw of XXX Corps, 22nd Armoured Brigade, only arrived in Egypt on 4 October, nearly three weeks late. The time required for Desert refits and training left Auchinleck with no option but to postpone CRUSADER until 11 November, but even this deadline had to be revised again to 15 November. This, however, failed to meet the needs of General Brink's 1st South African Division, without which the tanks of XXX Corps would have to advance unsupported. It was the old problem, the transport shortage, particularly serious for a division intended to operate as part of an armoured corps. General Brink was forced to apply for three final days to bring his division up to full operational capacity, putting back D-Day for CRUSADER to 18 November.

A typical example of the myriad last-minute hitches besetting Eighth Army was the panic over the Honey tracks. The 80-mile approach march of 4th Armoured Brigade from Bir el Kenayis to Halleqat, south of Sidi Barrani, wrought havoc on the pristine rubber blocks of the tank tracks, prompting an SOS from Brigadier Gatehouse to Auchinleck. Gatehouse was ordered to fly to Cairo with a specimen, upon which Auchinleck ordered the tracks to be stripped from every reserve Honey in the rear echelons and rushed west to 4th Armoured Brigade by rail. Transporters were then to be used to carry the Brigade to its penultimate jumping-off points. This completely unforeseen problem was sorted out in three days (10–13 November) – good training, it had to be admitted, for the many similar crises which the progress of the coming battle was bound to create.

Between the 13th and the 17th, as XXX Corps stole westwards to the Frontier by carefully staging night marches, the tank men had one last item of training to perfect:

> Here, too, we learnt for the first time the art of night leaguering, though it was a familiar enough blackboard diagram. It was a simple and effective manoeuvre for getting all tanks in a compact square, with the thin-skinned vehicles inside, ready to fan out at first light into an offensive formation. We practised it and practised it until we could do it blindfold – which was more or less the way we had to do it in the pitch dark of the Desert night after disengagement from battle at last light.[9]

The final approach night march of XXX Corps was timed to bring the leading regiments, accompanied by engineers to break the Wire, up to the Frontier by midnight on D −1: 17 November. The move into Cyrenaica would begin at first light on the 18th. As luck would have it low cloud and bad weather, producing a storm of astonishing violence after midnight on the 17th/18th, helped conceal XXX Corps in the final stage of its stealthy approach; but this most welcome help from the elements detracted nothing from the excellent security achieved by Eighth Army over the preceding week. Strict radio silence had been ordered and duly preserved, yet another painful lesson from BATTLEAXE. The tanks of XXX Corps had been disguised with temporary frameworks and hessian screens to present the dumpy, rectangular silhouettes of trucks. These 'Sunshields' were to be kept in position for as long as possible during the advance into Cyrenaica, so that any Axis reconnaissance aircraft which managed to escape the Desert Air Force and spot the oncoming columns would, it was hoped, report them as motorized and not armoured troops. Radio silence was to be preserved until the first order of CRUSADER – 'Drop Sunshields' – was given. Also during the approach, great attention had been paid to camouflage, dispersion, and driving discipline to prevent straggling. All these precautions paid off in full.

The Panzergruppe *on the eve of* CRUSADER, *October–November, 1941*

Auchinleck, Cunningham and the Eighth Army Staff planners had always known that no matter how tautly security might be preserved on the eve of CRUSADER, there would nevertheless be certain obvious indications of a coming British offensive which the *Panzergruppe*'s Intelligence sections could hardly misinterpret. The most unmistakable of these was the marked acceleration of the Desert railway's westward extension during October. By 17 November, however, it was becoming evident at Eighth Army Headquarters that, however Rommel might be planning to counter a new British offensive, this did not include any dramatic change in his dispositions around Tobruk. There was no sign of any significant movements of Axis armour south or south-east, in the direction of XXX Corps' planned lines of advance. All the signs were that both divisions of his *Afrika Korps* were still positioned up in the coastal sector, east of Tobruk. There could be little doubt that the panzer divisions would move fast enough as soon as XXX Corps' approach was detected. For the moment, however, Eighth Army had won the first trick. Nothing Rommel could do would prevent the planned lodgement of XXX Corps deep in the rear of the Axis garrisons holding the Frontier.

There were of course, sinister overtones to the *Panzergruppe*'s apparent lack of defensive precautions; XXX Corps would have to be on its guard to prevent a sudden counter-attack from slicing across its lines of communication. It was for this very reason that 4th Armoured Brigade had been assigned a 'bridging' role, preventing any dangerous gap from opening between XXX Corps and the left flank of XIII Corps. At the same time 7th Armoured Division, the spearhead of XXX Corps' advance, would not be exposed to the risk of being cut off by advancing too far; there was to be a deliberate halt at Gabr Saleh to await developments. Whatever Rommel did, it was expected that XXX Corps must certainly be in some kind of contact with the *Afrika Korps* by nightfall on the 18th at the latest. The fact remained that in CRUSADER, conceived as an offensive and preceded by a well-planned advance deep into Axis territory, the actual fighting was to begin with a deliberate abandonment of the initiative to Rommel.

Auchinleck was, in short, deliberately flouting one of the most sacred of all military precepts, the necessity of 'maintaining the initiative' in order to 'achieve the objective'. But it was a carefully calculated risk. Auchinleck accepted that setting traps for the enemy is always dangerous: there is always the risk that he will not only take the bait but smash the trap at the same time. It was for this very reason that Auchinleck had resisted the temptation to let Rommel start his attack on Tobruk before unleashing CRUSADER. Auchinleck feared, and his view was shared by General Scobie, that there was every chance of the *Panzergruppe* storming Tobruk before Eighth Army could come to the rescue. Exposing XXX Corps in an ostentatious 'wave of the matador's cape' would simultaneously force Rommel to shelve the attack on Tobruk, while enabling Eighth Army to begin a battle of quantity versus quality – superior British numbers and reserves versus the known superiority of German fire-power. But in all the British weighing of the odds on the eve of CRUSADER one possibility had never been seriously considered. This was the incredible fact that Rommel had succeeded in convincing himself that a full-blooded British offensive, launched before he had attacked and taken Tobruk, was out of the question.

Perhaps the best evidence for the magnitude of Rommel's self-delusion is the yawning gap in his own writings: the German *Krieg Ohne Hass* ('War Without Hate') of 1950, and Liddell Hart's edition of *The Rommel Papers* of 1953. Both reveal that the fighting of November–December, 1941, and Rommel's preparation for it, did not constitute an experience on which he had any inclination to dwell. But there is a relative wealth of evidence from senior officers of the *Panzergruppe*, Italian as well as German. All have stories of Rommel's often explosive refusal to accept warnings of a new British offensive. But the root of the trouble seems to lie in a premature armoured raid across the Frontier, not only ordered by Rommel but personally directed by him, which ended by giving the German commander an entirely false impression of Auchinleck's intentions.

This raid was code-named 'MIDSUMMER NIGHT'S DREAM' and it went in on 14 September. In part it was intended as an end-of-training 'exercise with live ammunition' for 21st Panzer Division, but the aim was to investigate and destroy reported supply dumps apparently made in preparation for a repetition of BATTLEAXE. As we have seen, if Churchill had had his way such dumps would actually have existed at this time, and such an attack (or more than one) would actually have been made by the British. Though reconnaissance soon established that no such dumps existed in the reported area, 15 miles south-east of Sidi Omar, Rommel ordered the raid to proceed. This was stark folly. Panzers were Rommel's most precious asset, yet here he was recklessly exposing them in broad daylight, first to the fire of 7th Support Group's 25-pounders, then to repeated air attacks by Desert Air Force bombers. The first of these came close to killing Rommel, who was not inside his armoured 'Mammoth'; a bomb splinter ripped off his left boot-heel and his driver was badly wounded. He ordered a withdrawal to the Axis lines, only to be left stranded for hours in no-man's-land when one of the 'Mammoth's' tyres collapsed. The wheel-change took hours, thanks to inadequate tools, while the wireless-operator listened-in to the ominous progress

83

of the British pursuit. In the end Rommel's party made it back to the Frontier Wire just as day was breaking.

Rommel's whole performance during the MIDSUMMER NIGHT'S DREAM spree was emphatically not that of the cool mind which had won BATTLEAXE. Schmidt's account of the adventure is revealing (and heartfelt – he had to do the lion's share of the work in changing the wheel). The impression he gives is of Rommel joyfully gulping a dose of front-line action as an antidote to weeks of inspection trips and gruelling hard work in training. 'Rommel and von Ravenstein were as gleeful as a pair of boyish rascals over their little plot. "I'm coming with you!" Rommel announced. . . . He was in an unusually jovial mood and shouted out with an even more unusual boisterousness: "We're off to Egypt!"' And this feeling of happy irresponsibility is given a serious twist when Schmidt quotes Rommel as brushing aside Ravenstein's glum warning 'that a number of panzers had moved into position during the [previous] day and might have been spotted by British aircraft'.[10]

The sole gain was the capture of a couple of soldiers in a truck, together with documents which appeared to include codes. No doubt clutching at straws, Ravenstein assured Rommel that 'the capture of these documents alone is enough to have justified the expedition'. But the captured papers contained no hint of any imminent British offensive, let alone the fact that Rommel had unwittingly traversed the terrain west of the future Misheifa railhead where, in two months, Eighth Army's first FMCs would be established as XIII Corps concentrated for CRUSADER. Rommel therefore chose to interpret MIDSUMMER NIGHT'S DREAM as personal confirmation that the British were far from ready for any attack which would justify postponement of the *Panzergruppe's* attack on Tobruk.

After MIDSUMMER NIGHT'S DREAM Rommel therefore intensified his preparations for the Tobruk attack, closing his eyes and ears to the growing evidence of unwelcome British preparations in the Western Desert. The quickening work on the Desert railway was duly detected by *Luftwaffe* reconnaissance; but Ravenstein was present when Rommel threw the photographs on the ground, refusing even to look at them. His orders for the attack, scheduled for 15–20 November (later confirmed for 23 November) were issued on 26 October. The Italian Intelligence officers of Rommel's nominal theatre commander, General Bastico, were convinced that a British attack was brewing; Rommel told his German staff officers to radiate confidence and play down the possibility of a British advance in discussions with Italian colleagues. This is confirmed by Mellenthin: 'I deliberately minimized the possibilities of a British offensive whenever I spoke to our allies.'[11] But this official stance

5. (*left*) Major-General Bernard Freyberg, VC, Commander of the New Zealand Division.

6. (*below left*) Major-General Alan Cunningham

7. (*below right*) Major-General Alfred Godwin-Austen

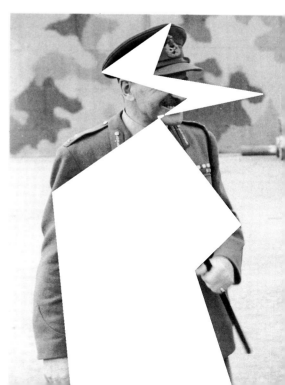

8. Major-General Willoughby Norrie

9. Major-General Neil Ritchie

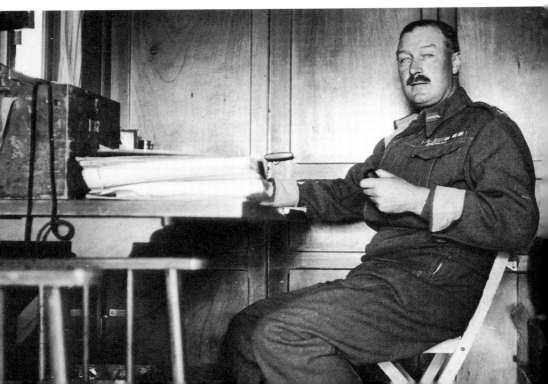

was in total contrast to the private conviction of the German Intelligence section concentrating on the British order of battle, where there was general agreement that an offensive was brewing. With this inside information, junior officers on the *Panzergruppe* staff, like Schmidt, laid private bets that the British would attack before the end of the year at the latest.

By the second week in November the Italian High Command was doing all it could to bring about a postponement of the Tobruk attack. Its case was strengthened by continuing supply losses. After a deceptively good month in September, the *Panzergruppe*'s supply crisis peaked again in October with 62 per cent losses (49,365 tons) of the total supplies shipped from Italy. Not only was there no let-up in November, but on the 9th the Malta-based British 'Force K' scored the first total liquidation of an Axis convoy to Libya. In a radar-guided night attack the 'Duisburg' Convoy of six merchant ships and a tanker was sent to the bottom in ten minutes, closely followed by one of the escorting Italian destroyers. This disaster intensified Supremo Comando protests to OKW, already uneasy over Intelligence of the coming offensive provided by *Abwehr*, OKW's own Intelligence branch.

Pressure from OKW for a postponement of the Tobruk attack took Rommel to Rome in mid-November. 15 November was his birthday, and he took Ravenstein with him; the wives of the two generals had travelled south to Rome for a brief reunion with their husbands. Ravenstein was again present during the stormy scene in Rintelen's office, when Rommel insisted on telephoning General Alfred Jodl (OKW's operations chief). He brushed aside Jodl's fears about the British offensive by insisting that 21st Panzer Division had been positioned to beat off any spoiling attack which the British might attempt. And when Jodl asked him to guarantee that there was no danger, Rommel shouted down the line, 'I will give you my personal guarantee!'[12]

With this exchange Rommel obtained OKW's grudging permission (approval was hardly the word) to attack Tobruk. But if he lacked the confidence of the Italian and German High Commands, Rommel had the approval of at least one Italian: Mussolini. Not that the Duce was ever shy of claiming all the credit for himself, as Ciano records:

Mussolini tells me that he has persuaded Rommel to hasten the attack at Tobruk and that it is to begin some time this month. I recall that Gambara [commanding XX Armoured Corps] says he is distinctly opposed to this because he fears that when we attack Tobruk this will be followed by a British attack on our flank at Sollum which he feels we cannot resist.[13]

(This piece of cheek by Mussolini matched that of the film, *On From Benghazi*, which the Italians proudly showed Rommel during his stay in Rome. This purported to show his triumphant advance of April but no German troops were shown, only heroic Italians. 'Very instructive' was Rommel's deadpan comment.)

So it was that Rommel got his way: the *Panzergruppe* would assault Tobruk on 23 November. He set off on the return trip to Libya via Athens to give the final orders to his forces. It was, by any standards, a most paradoxical balance of power. With a line-up of only one and a half armoured divisions, two infantry tank brigades, three divisions of motorized infantry and a solitary infantry division in reserve (2nd South African Division, commanded by Major-General I. P. de Villiers), Eighth Army was advancing to tackle no less than ten Axis divisions, of which three were armoured. In fire-power the *Panzergruppe* held most of the important cards. Of Rommel's total of 390 German and Italian tanks, 174 – the 139 Pzkw.IIIs and 35 Pzkw. IVs – could out-gun every tank in Eighth Army's array of 477 cruisers and 261 'I' tanks. A second factor to pit against Eighth Army's impressive numerical advantage in tanks – there were over 250 tanks of all types in reserve, while the *Panzergruppe* had virtually none – was the superb German anti-tank artillery. The gunners of Eighth Army had no weapon to match the tank-killing range of the new German 50mm anti-tank gun, of which *Afrika Korps* had ninety-six. As for the dreaded '88s', Rommel now had twenty-three 88mm guns dug in on the Frontier, and another twelve on wheeled mountings accompanying the *panzerjägers* ('tank-hunting' anti-tank gunners) of the *Afrika Korps*. A final German advantage in the tank balance was the technique of recovering tanks from the battlefield for field repairs. The *Afrika Korps* had this down to a fine art by 18 November, while the British were still learning the knack. For many reasons, therefore, the destruction of Rommel's armour was bound to present a much harder task than the mere numerical balance of tanks suggested at first sight.

The air balance was different. The British started CRUSADER with a total of 550 aircraft of all types serviceable out of a total of 650-odd machines, with another sixty-six serviceable aircraft on Malta able to strike at Axis sea communications. The combined *Luftwaffe* and *Regia Aeronautica* strength was 342 out of 536. How many of the 750 German aircraft based on Sicily, Greece, Crete and other bases might be fed into the battle remained to be seen; but the Desert Air Force went into battle with undoubted command of the air, and no dramatic reverses ever threatened to reverse this. Evidence from every level of command, from the troops 'at the sharp end' to the generals in their mobile HQs, agrees that CRUSADER was a total novelty: the first battle of the war in which a

British army fought under skies which were not, and never were to be, swarming with enemy aircraft. But the threat of sneak attacks, especially by low-level strafing fighters, was always present. Though every man in Eighth Army, high and low, had been trained to dig himself a slit trench on halting, the stony and rocky terrain of the CRUSADER battlefield repeatedly made this impossible. The only recourse was constant vigilance and maximum use of the terrain, piling up makeshift stone shelters where it was impossible to dig.

Prelude to battle: the 'Keyes Raid' on Rommel's HQ

Rommel's stop-over in Athens on his way back to Libya meant that he was hundreds of miles away when British Commandos made a daring attempt on his life. The raid, led by Lieutenant-Colonel Geoffrey Keyes, has passed into Commando legend: twenty-four men, landed by submarine 250 miles behind the Axis lines, their mission to capture or kill Rommel, paralyse the Axis command centre and sever Axis communications with the rear on the eve of the British attack. It was a brilliant concept, and the first British attack of its kind; the odds against success were immense, the value of the stakes infinite. Perhaps it is true that the 'Keyes Raid' was naturally suited to that facet of the British mentality which loves to dwell on gallant failures. The courage and sacrifice of the raid have never been in doubt; Keyes died in the futile attack on Rommel's supposed HQ at Beda Littoria in the Jebel, winning a posthumous Victoria Cross, and only two men escaped to tell the tale. But in truth the Keyes Raid was not a good omen for CRUSADER. The British Intelligence behind the Raid was shockingly bad – not in itself, but in its lack of coordination. The basic reason for the failure of the Keyes Raid was the assumption that Rommel, like Auchinleck and Cunningham, commanded from the rear. It was true that Beda Littoria had been the original *Panzergruppe* headquarters, but Rommel had quickly abandoned it precisely because it *was* too far to the rear; he had moved his own head-quarters east to Gazala, then even further east to Gambut. The Intelligence for the Keyes Raid was based on locally-gathered 'cloak-and-dagger' information, and not on a cold analysis of Rommel's actual movements:

> It was a bad characteristic of the various private armies to try to collect their own intelligence. They were particularly fond of asking odd questions of the [Eighth Army] Intelligence Branch without revealing the purpose for which the information was wanted. . . . If Intelligence had been properly taken into the confidence of the persons organizing the raid they could have been told that Rommel would not be at his HQ that day.[14]

The armies on the brink, 17 November, 1941

The facts about the ill-starred Keyes Raid did not come out in full until the only two Commandos to escape death or capture, Colonel Laycock and Sergeant Terry, met the advancing spearheads of Eighth Army at Cyrene in late December, after forty-one days on the run. Even so, the mood of Eighth Army was buoyant on the night of 17/18 November, 1941, and nowhere more so than among the tank men of XXX Corps, those who, from painful experience, had best reason to know the advantages still enjoyed by their antagonists: the *panzertruppen*. There was an overriding feeling that this time 'They', the politicians at home and the Top Brass in Cairo, had got it right; that this time Rommel was going to be caught napping and forced to fight the way the British wanted, under RAF-commanded skies.

This eve-of-battle exhilaration certainly held true of 4th Armoured Brigade, whose role in the coming battle was the least defined of all. The XIII Corps generals, Freyberg most emphatically, were far from content with the sluggish and meagre helping of armoured protection offered by their accompanying infantry tank brigade. They wanted stand-off cruiser tank support as well, to prevent *Afrika Korps* from breaking through to close with the infantry of XIII Corps. Cunningham had acceded to Godwin-Austen's demand that 4th Armoured Brigade should operate in close touch with XIII Corps. Clearly this would have a highly weakening effect if a full-blooded tank battle broke out on XXX Corps' front while 4th Armoured Brigade was supporting XIII Corps. Norrie's counter-demand that XXX Corps must remain concentrated for its coming trial of strength clashed with Godwin-Austen's insistence that XIII Corps must not be left without the cruiser tank support of 4th Armoured Brigade. This effectively left 4th Armoured Brigade in the unenviable position of 'pig in the middle', to be hauled to and fro between XXX Corps and XIII Corps as the crises of the battle dictated. And yet, as Crisp records, there was no depression at the prospect in 4th Armoured Brigade:

> It seemed that the role of 4th Armoured Brigade was to do most of the destroying in the centre, while the other two covered our flanks and joined in whenever possible. It seemed a pretty good idea to me, and when I showed the troops my map and where we were going, deep into enemy territory, their eyes popped and their lips whistled. It was all they could do to stop themselves cheering. We were all a bit like schoolboys on the last night of term.[15]

Behind the Axis lines nightfall on the 17th found the *Panzergruppe*'s staff still awaiting the return of Rommel from Greece to supervise the final preparations for the Tobruk attack, now only five days away. On the previous day the units of Major-General Sümmermann's 90th Light Division on the Tobruk perimeter had been briefed on their role in the attack, and the artillery of 15th Panzer Division had begun to move into position to support it.

Hopes that the attack would, after all, proceed unmolested by the British were mingled with anxiety. It was forty-eight hours since the *Panzergruppe*'s Wireless Intercept Service had first reported that 1st South African Division was now apparently heading west from the Mersa Matruh area (as indeed it was – moving into position behind the armoured columns of XXX Corps). The last intercepts, on the 16th, had confirmed this impression, but since then the British had been keeping an impenetrable radio silence. Ravenstein, for one, was uneasy. With Crüwell's approval, he decided to take out a little insurance, by sending a *panzerjäger* company to give some anti-tank teeth to 21st Panzer Division's reconnaissance screen. This was patrolling the yawning gap on the *Panzergruppe*'s southern flank, between the armoured concentrations of 'Ariete' at Bir el Gubi and 21st Panzer south-east of Gambut.

With the air waves now silent, there was no other way of discovering what the British were up to. Air reconnaissance was out of the question: from 16 November wretchedly deteriorating weather, with violent storms and torrential rain developing from the west, had converted every airfield in Cyrenaica into a quagmire. Nothing like these conditions had ever been seen since the German arrival in Africa. 'Bridges were carried away, roads became rivers, and all our airfields were under water. For days it was impossible for any aircraft to take off, and our air reconnaissance was reduced to nothing.'[16] There was consolation in the hope that British airfields must be similarly affected, but they were not. Most of the Desert Air Force's advance bases on the eve of CRUSADER lay just outside the foul-weather zone, which advanced east to drench the advancing masses concealed east of the Wire by the pitch-dark night of the 17th/18th, but petered out roughly midway between Sollum and Sidi Barrani. Rarely have the elements so favoured a British army on the eve of battle, since the cloudbursts of 17–18 June, 1815 made it impossible for Napoleon to get his artillery into position on the morning of Waterloo. By first light on 18 November, with the British signal wavelengths still as silent as the grave and all Axis airfields flooded out, the *Panzergruppe* was deaf and blind to Eighth Army's approach.

CHAPTER 3

THE BATTLE

Day 1: 18 November

Eighth Army: XXX Corps

For Eighth Army it had been a miserable night, with the troops forced to bivouac in a ceaseless downpour of rain laced with sleet. The dull explosions up ahead as the engineers blew gaps in the Wire were soon drowned out by thunder. The men of XXX Corps had an easier time of it. They were able to use groundsheets and bivouac tents to reinforce the hessian 'sunshields' disguising their tanks, creating tolerably rainproof shelters. At last, with the first streaks of grey in the sodden eastern sky, the sprawling columns began to stir. Had any aircraft been overhead it would have seen Eighth Army pricked out with thousands of tiny flames, as the troops lit petrol-soaked scoops of sand ('Benghazi cookers') for the day's first life-giving 'brew' of tea.

First through the Wire were the armoured-car squadrons of 7th Armoured Division – the 11th Hussars and the King's Dragoon Guards. Their time-honoured role was to spread out in a wide screen ahead of the advancing spearhead of XXX Corps. As the first air patrols of the Desert Air Force roared past overhead with not an Axis aircraft to be seen, the feelings of confidence dampened by the night's downpour swiftly revived. 'We knew that we could hit nothing and nothing could hit us without the air being full of the crackling message from the recce men in front.'[1] Until that vital first contact, however, strict radio silence was maintained, with Eighth Army staff accepting the inevitable disadvantage of not knowing precisely where every unit was. Behind the armoured cars came the cruisers of 7th Armoured Brigade, nosing up to the XXX Corps gap in the Wire south of Fort Maddalena with innumerable stops and starts. It was impossible not to think of Bank Holiday traffic jams back home, with the difference that here there was no shortage of traffic marshals and (military) police.

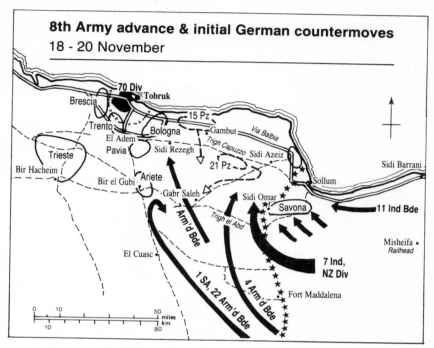

At 0700, an hour after 7th Armoured Brigade, the Honey crews of 4th Armoured Brigade received the word to move, but they were not fed through the now well-worn gap until 1000. After topping up with fuel from dumps assembled west of the Wire, the first advance of the campaign began in a sense of distinct anti-climax; the psychological boost of crossing the Wire was short-lived. As Crisp put it, the sand and scrub of Cyrenaica was exactly the same as that of Egypt.

The empty terrain into which XXX Corps was now heading was bounded to the north by the low escarpments sloping down to the Via Balbia between Tobruk and Bardia; to the south it was distinguished only by the ancient Desert trackways or *trighs* worn by centuries of Arab commerce. Two of these were destined to become household names to both armies in the weeks ahead. The first was the Trigh Capuzzo, which ran east from the Tobruk perimeter at El Adem to the Frontier at

Capuzzo. Its east-central section, Sidi Rezegh/Sidi Azeiz, was occupied at the outset of CRUSADER by Ravenstein's 21st Panzer Division. Some 25 miles to the south, running roughly to the Trigh Capuzzo, was the Trigh el Abd. It came down from the west through Bir el Gubi, 20 miles south of El Adem, to reach the Frontier at Sheferzen (the designated crossing-place of XIII Corps). A third trackway, running south-west from Sidi Azeiz to Gabr Saleh, connected the Trigh Capuzzo and Trigh el Abd; a fourth, the Tobruk–Jarabub track, crossed the Trigh Capuzzo at El Adem and the Trigh el Abd at Bir el Gubi. Within the rough quadrilateral thus formed, though repeatedly flooding over its confines, the long-awaited armoured clash between XXX Corps and the *Afrika Korps* was to take place over the next three weeks.

After the traffic jams and congestions of the Frontier crossing down at Maddalena, the three armoured brigades of XXX Corps fanned out in a rapid advance. The left-flank prong, Brigadier J. Scott-Cockburn's 22nd Armoured Brigade, carried the outermost sweep of XXX Corps' northward wheel into Libya. Its line of advance ran roughly 10 miles east of the Tobruk–Jarabub track and was aimed at Bir el Gubi. The three regiments of 22nd Armoured Brigade were the 3rd and 4th County of London Yeomanry and the 2nd Royal Gloucestershire Hussars, all making their combat début in the North African theatre. The Brigade totalled 158 Crusader tanks straight out from the United Kingdom. Because of their late arrival in Egypt, these tanks had been hastily converted for Desert operations but their crews had not been granted the time for more than the most rudimentary Desert training. Perhaps fortunately, this inexperience made 22nd Armoured Brigade the only one of the three not to reach its initial objective on 18 November. True to their bad mechanical form, the Crusaders of 22nd Armoured Brigade were reduced by 11 per cent on their first approach run of 65 miles, with eighteen tanks breaking down. As a result, 22nd Armoured Brigade went into its defensive leaguer for the night of the 18th/19th some 20 miles south of where the 'Ariete' Armoured Division was holding the Bir el Gubi crossroads.

The centre prong of XXX Corps was Brigadier G. O. M. Davy's 7th Armoured Brigade: 7th Hussars, 2nd Royal Tank Regiment, and 6th Royal Tank Regiment. As 7th Armoured Brigade was entrusted with the deepest initial penetration of the CRUSADER advance it enjoyed considerably more fire-power than the 22nd Armoured Brigade on the left: 4th Regiment, Royal Horse Artillery (RHA), minus the lone C Battery serving with 22nd Armoured Brigade. The armoured units of 7th Armoured Brigade all had plenty of Desert experience, but unlike the two flanking armoured brigades the composition of 7th Armoured

Brigade was motley. Out of the total of 168 tanks, no less than ninety-six were outmoded A-13s (71) and even older A-10s (25), for which transporters were required in the advance from the Frontier. Not surprisingly, this threadbare collection suffered even more breakdowns during its 85-mile advance on the 18th than the new Crusaders of 22nd Armoured Brigade. By the time 7th Armoured Brigade leaguered for the night, 10 miles north of the Trigh el Abd, forty-nine tanks had fallen out with mechanical defects and the Brigade was reduced to 119 'runners'. This represented a 'wear and tear' percentage loss of 29 per cent, fully justifying Auchinleck's insistence on sizeable tank reserves.

It had been a very different story with the Honeys of 4th Armoured Brigade under Brigadier Alec Gatehouse. The refuelling arrangements to counter the Honeys' high fuel consumption worked smoothly and they completed their 65-mile advance with little or no trouble, proving that the previous week's panic over their rubber-faced tracks had been a false alarm. (The speed at which the 'factory-fresh' rubber blocks wore down had unduly alarmed their new British operators, who now found that after due running-in there was no further deterioriation.) The disguising 'sunshields' were jettisoned on receipt of the order 'Drop Sunshields' at 1530, whereupon

the wireless aerials were released, and floating from the top of them were the twin yellow pennants which each British tank carried for identification. In moments of quick decision it was assumed that tanks or armoured cars without pennants were hostile. Very often the masts were lowered to assist concealment, and undoubtedly a number of Eighth Army v. Eighth Army encounters took place as a result.[2]

But there were no such encounters for the tank crews of 4th Armoured Brigade on the 18th. At 1630 its three regiments – 8th Hussars, 3rd Royal Tank Regiment and 5th Royal Tank Regiment – arrived at the day's objective of 'Point 185' on the Trigh el Abd, midway between Bir el Gubi and Sidi Omar. In its advance from the Frontier, 4th Armoured Brigade had not seen a single Axis aircraft or patrolling vehicle.

As the tanks of XXX Corps went into defensive leaguer for the night of 18/19 November, the main sensation of Cunningham, Norrie, and Gott was one of bafflement. Rommel was reacting, or, more accurately, failing to react at all, in wholly unexpected fashion. His inactivity had permitted XXX Corps to establish itself along an arc extending 50 miles west into Cyrenaica, with 7th Armoured Brigade barely 30 miles from the Tobruk perimeter itself. The 1st and 5th Brigades of Brink's 1st

South African Division were already well up the Jarabub–Tobruk track, advancing behind 22nd Armoured Brigade to consolidate the western extremity of this deep bridgehead pegged out in Axis territory. The only sight of Rommel's armour on the 18th had, as expected, been his armoured cars on the northern horizon. Desultory fire-fights in the afternoon between the 11th Hussars and the 3rd Reconnaissance Unit, all well north of the Trigh el Abd, had in every case found the German armoured cars to be completely unsupported by panzers. The Germans engaged had wasted little time in withdrawing north where the bulk of the *Panzergruppe* apparently still lay inert.

The question now to be decided was what to do next. Should XXX Corps stick to the original plan, sit tight and wait for Rommel to do something? There was much to be said for this; all brigades of XXX Corps were in close touch still, well enough placed to support each other in a general action. On the other hand, Cunningham was painfully aware of CRUSADER's built-in supply problem, and the need to achieve the relief of Tobruk as quickly as possible. A *coup de main* by 7th Armoured Brigade, storming on to the north-west past Sidi Rezegh, could well result in XXX Corps joining hands with 70th Division before the all-important panzer divisions could do anything to stop it. Cunningham's decision for XXX Corps' operations on the 19th was to tidy up on the left, push on a little further in the centre and consolidate on the right. The 22nd Armoured Brigade was to carry on to Bir el Gubi and see if 'Ariete' was there in strength; 7th Armoured Brigade was to advance to Sidi Rezegh, 10 miles from the Tobruk perimeter; 4th Armoured Brigade and Brigadier Campbell's Support Group were to stay where they were, covering the Desert flank of XIII Corps as it continued its outflanking of the Axis Frontier garrisons.

Eighth Army: XIII Corps

The task for Godwin-Austen's XIII Corps on 18 November was altogether more straightforward than that of XXX Corps, carried out in the foreknowledge that there was little or no possibility of an armoured counter-attack out of the blue. Freyberg's New Zealanders and Messervy's 4th Indian Division had moved into position for CRUSADER side by side, with 4th Indian on the coastward flank; now the New Zealanders eased into the lead, leaving 4th Indian Division to wrap itself like a watertight pad round the Egyptian front of the Axis Frontier positions. Brigadier A. Anderson's 11th Indian Infantry Brigade moved forward to secure the Sollum-Halfaya road and contain the Halfaya garrison; this time there were to be no costly attacks on the Pass itself.

94

The 7th Indian Infantry Brigade (Brigadier H. R. Briggs) moved on to straddle the Frontier south of the two Axis strongpoints at Sidi Omar (Libyan Omar and Sidi Omar Nuovo). To discourage any aggressive German move from Halfaya, the cruisers *Euraylus* and *Naiad* had treated the Halfaya garrison to a bombardment on the previous night.

The net effect was to establish a powerful blocking force at each end of the Axis Frontier defence. Patrolling the plateau above Halfaya Pass, armoured cars of the Central India Horse kept watch on the 15-mile sector held by the 'Savona' Division between Sidi Omar and Halfaya. The 'I' tanks of Brigadier H. R. B. Watkins' 1st Army Tank Brigade leaguered for the night in close support of 7th Indian Infantry Brigade south of Sidi Omar. Meanwhile, 10 miles further south, the New Zealand Division had crossed the Wire south of Sheferzen to halt for the night 5 miles west of the Frontier.

These modest opening moves by XIII Corps laid the groundwork for the coming advance north to the Via Balbia, which would complete the isolation of the Axis Frontier forces. Once this had been achieved, XIII Corps could regroup for its westward advance towards Tobruk. But if there was nothing spectacular about the advance of XIII Corps, there was plenty of tension. This cautious deployment amounted to a house-that-Jack-built, ultimately propped up by the XXX Corps armour out to the west, the New Zealand Division shielding 7th Indian Infantry Brigade, and 4th Armoured Brigade in turn shielding the New Zealanders. In the days to come, the magnetic eastward pull exercised by XIII Corps was gravely to impede 4th Armoured Brigade.

The Panzergruppe

Rommel did not get back to *Panzergruppe* headquarters at Gambut until the afternoon of 18 November, to find that the day had begun with the Wireless Intercept Service still reporting complete British radio silence. With every Axis airfield awash with mud after the recent cloudbursts, no reconnaisance sorties could be flown to confirm what the British were doing. Though the rains had converted the Desert softlands to a quagmire and filled the *wadis* (normally dry watercourses), adding to the problems of wheeled vehicles, the *Panzergruppe* had no choice but to rely on Ravenstein's armoured car patrols south of the Trigh el Abd.

While awaiting Rommel's return, his staff officers were officially taking the line that the British could be no better off, and that no news was good news. They were also keeping up the confident front ordained by Rommel for the benefit of the Italians. Calling on his Italian opposite number, Lieutenant-Colonel Mario Revetria, Mellenthin began with the cheerful greeting: 'Well, everything seems quiet today.'[3] This was at noon – six hours after the leading tanks of XXX Corps had begun their advance from the Frontier.

The picture began to change in the afternoon with the first alarm-calls from 3rd Reconnaissance Unit 30 miles away to the south: large numbers of British armoured cars, heading north towards the Trigh el Abd. Having returned from Rome with his mind seething with details for the attack on Tobruk, Rommel reacted testily. Armoured cars were armoured cars, not armoured divisions of tanks. The British were doing what he had done with MIDSUMMER NIGHT'S DREAM in September, and carrying out a reconnaissance in force; Ravenstein would see them off if they came too close. By nightfall on the 18th the Tobruk attack plans were still the dominant item of business at *Panzergruppe* headquarters.

Good tank man that he was, Crüwell was not so sure. He did not like the wide dispersion of the Axis armour: 'Ariete' away to the south-west at Bir el Gubi; 15th Panzer Division 40 miles north-east of 'Ariete' on the coast, with its artillery already siphoned off for the Tobruk attack; 21st Panzer 20 miles south-east of 15th Panzer, down on the Trigh Capuzzo. Crüwell told Rommel that he fully shared Ravenstein's uneasiness at the British activity in the south and had approved Ravenstein's request to send a panzer battle group south to Gabr Saleh in the morning. But Rommel reacted angrily when Crüwell added that he had briefed Neumann-Silkow to be ready to take 15th Panzer south-east to join Ravenstein if need be. Telling Crüwell that 'We must not lose our nerves',[4] Rommel not only countermanded the order to 15th Panzer but forbade any advance of Ravenstein's armour to Gabr Saleh. The reason Rommel gave Crüwell – 'for fear of discouraging the enemy too soon' – sounds lame even with the benefit of hindsight. Given the dispersion of the *Panzergruppe*'s armour, if there were British tanks south of Gabr Saleh, then the sooner they were discouraged the better. But Rommel's real reason was that he did not want 21st Panzer diverting its armoured strength southward on the eve of the Tobruk attack. As a sop to Crüwell, however, Rommel did instruct General Gambara that 'Ariete' must maintain 'increased vigilance' east and south of Bir el Gubi, along the axis of the Trigh el Abd. This request was to have unexpected results on the following day.

Here again was proof of how badly the Tobruk virus was affecting Rommel's clarity of decision. Back in June he would never have dreamed of leaving *Afrika Korps*' most vulnerable sector in Italian hands. Venturing into speculation (there is no documentary proof), Rommel may also have been 'playing politics'. He had passed the ball to Gambara with the innermost knowledge that even if the Italians made a hash of things, *Afrika Korps* could still save the day – and the case for bringing Gambara's corps under Rommel's direct command would be answerable. If Rommel was scheming on these lines, his hopes were to be dashed by 'Ariete's' performance next day.

Crüwell did not, however, cancel his alerting order to 15th Panzer Division; nor did he order Ravenstein to recall the panzer regiment which Ravenstein had sent to reinforce 3rd Reconnaissance Unit on the afternoon of the 18th.

Day 2: 19 November

Eighth Army: XXX Corps

For XXX Corps 19 November was the day when the last illusions of a surprise victory were sharply dispelled. The only real success of the day was scored, in the absence of armoured opposition, by 7th Armoured Brigade in its advance on Sidi Rezegh. By 1400 Davy's leading armoured cars had reached the low escarpment south of Sidi Rezegh airfield, waiting for the tanks to come up. The German infantry regiment posted east of Sidi Rezegh to defend the airfield was unsupported even by armoured cars and had very few anti-tank guns. It was therefore completely unable to prevent the tanks of 7th Armoured Brigade from roaring straight on to the airfield while aircraft were still taking off, capturing nineteen Italian aircraft. By nightfall 7th Armoured Brigade, now barely 15 miles from the Tobruk perimeter, was established on the Sidi Rezegh escarpment with Brigadier 'Jock' Campbell's Support Group heading north to join the armour.

By this time, however, 25 miles to the south, 22nd Armoured Brigade was painfully counting the cost of a bruising, unmitigated defeat at Bir el Gubi. The existence of a strong Italian force at Bir el Gubi was confirmed by the armoured cars of the 11th Hussars in the morning, while Gott was paying a visit to 22nd Armoured Brigade. This was perhaps unfortunate, for Gott's thinking was naturally coloured by the spectacular Italian collapse in the previous December and January. In any event, Gott ordered Brigadier Scott-Cockburn to attack at once – without proper reconnaissance, with only one 25-pounder battery and one company of motorized infantry in support – and paid for it heavily in tanks and casualties. Gambara's Italians had done an excellent job of digging themselves in at Bir el Gubi and their position was no obstacle to set before green yeomanry regiments sailing into their first battle. Though the attack was pressed with the high courage of sheer inexperience and many sectors of Italian infantry trenches were overrun, 22nd Armoured Brigade lacked enough infantry to consolidate such gains. By nightfall Scott-Cockburn's Crusaders had been beaten back from Bir el Gubi, having lost twenty-five tanks knocked out in the attack and another forty-five immobilized by battle damage and breakdowns. The first forty-eight hours of CRUSADER had reduced the fighting strength of 22nd Armoured Brigade by 50 per cent.

The defeat of 22nd Armoured Brigade was a resounding success for 'Ariete', one of the many good performances by the Italian Army to be either ignored or glossed over in British accounts of the Desert War. The Italians had fought with tenacity and no little coolness, overrun infantry being quick to resume their fire positions on realizing that the British cruisers lacked the backing of infantry. As if reluctant to admit the fact, the British Official History is circumspect about the reasons for the failure at Bir el Gubi:

> It has been suggested by some who were present that the Ariete Division was met in unexpected strength at Bir el Gubi. Its composition was accurately known, however, and a document issued by 7th Armoured Division on 15 November shows that the Ariete Division was thought to have moved forward to the Bir el Gubi area.[5]

If that was the case, why was the attack ordered? The only answer is that 'Ariete' had been left out of nearly every British calculation of the odds before CRUSADER as a negligible threat; its location south of Tobruk had been a good reason to assign the inexperienced 22nd Armoured Brigade to the inland flank. In other words, 'Ariete' had been unwisely written off by the British as something of a pushover, hardly more formidable than an Italian infantry division and a fit opponent on which 22nd Armoured Brigade could cut its teeth. In fairness to Gott, British Intelligence had not noted the fact that 'Ariete' was the only Axis armoured division to have been brought fully up to strength in the weeks before CRUSADER. But the results were bad enough. Instead of advancing past Bir el Gubi on the 19th to close up within 10 miles of 7th Armoured Brigade, 22nd Armoured Brigade had been checked south of Bir el Gubi, in a severely weakened state, and over 20 miles from the other tank brigades of XXX Corps.

Gatehouse's operations with 4th Armoured Brigade were a micro-cosm of XXX Corps' overall activities that day: an increasing fragmenta-tion of effort in different directions, with nothing concrete to show for it. Shortly after first light the day's combat began with armoured-car clashes between the King's Dragoon Guards and the German 3rd Reconnaissance Unit, and a squadron of 3rd Royal Tank Regiment was sent off in support. The other two squadrons first headed east to intercept a (non-existent) Axis column heading south, then north-east to ambush a column of Axis transport heading east along the Trigh Capuzzo. This column, when surprised by the charging Honeys, scattered wildly to the north-east with the Honeys in pursuit. It was an exhilarating but untrammelled chase, with all the fox-hunting excess zeal of the British cavalry tradition at its worst. Though it saw the Honeys of 3rd Royal Tank Regiment score their first kills against the armoured cars and light Pzkw.IIs of 3rd Reconnaissance Unit, it also scattered the Regiment all over the Desert; the foremost Honeys, one of them Crisp's, advanced so far that they came within sight of Bardia. The pursuers far outran their supplies and the price was empty fuel tanks on the way back to Brigade at the end of the day. Gatehouse was therefore left without his screening armoured cars and one of his tank regiments when, at long last, Rommel's panzers counter-attacked in force.

Eighth Army: XIII Corps and Desert Air Force

19 November saw XIII Corps improving on the initial deployment of the previous day. HMS *Euryalus* and *Naiad* had returned in the night to keep up the pressure on the Halfaya garrison with another bombardment of 5.25-inch shells; but no offensive moves were planned against the eastern end of the Axis Frontier barrier. Godwin-Austen was nevertheless briefed to do whatever he could to reduce the sharp Axis salient, around which most of Eighth Army's overland supplies would have to flow. The only way to achieve early results would be to take Libyan Omar and Sidi Omar Nuovo. With this end in view Brigadier Briggs pushed the inland flank of his 7th Indian Infantry Brigade north to invest Libyan Omar from the west as well as the south. Keeping pace further inland, Freyberg's New Zealanders advanced another 5 miles to reach the Trigh el Abd 10 miles west of the Frontier.

For the second day the Desert Air Force operated largely unmolested, with the Axis squadrons still nearly all immobilized on their boggy airfields. Long-range Beaufighters attacked the main Stuka base at Tmimi, 60 miles west of Tobruk, while the Wellington bombers again concentrated on grounded aircraft at Gazala, Tmimi, and Derna and Martuba in the eastern Jebel. The results of the long-range foray by 3rd Royal Tank Regiment were detected, with sightings of many Axis tanks and vehicles between Gambut and Capuzzo. From their movements it was deduced that the main trend of Axis movements was westward, away from the Frontier instead of towards it as had been expected.

The Panzergruppe

In the continued absence of 'instant' Intelligence by air reconnaissance, the *Panzergruppe*'s reactions were necessarily subject to a time-lag of at least six hours. On 19 November the morning clashes between 3rd Reconnaissance Unit and the tank-supported King's Dragoon Guards sent Crüwell back to *Panzergruppe* headquarters at noon. Crüwell insisted that with British tanks now reported north of the Trigh el Abd, it was obvious that the *Panzergruppe* was no longer confronted with a mere reconnaissance in force. This was a major operation on a much more ambitious scale than the BATTLEAXE offensive back in June, and an early counterblow by *Afrika Korps* was essential.

Pressed by Ravenstein and Crüwell, Rommel gave way. He not only agreed to Ravenstein's plan for an armoured foray south towards Gabr Saleh, but authorized the move of 15th Panzer Division to a new assembly area south of Gambut. The Battle Group from 21st Panzer, to be commanded by the aggressive Lieutenant-Colonel Stephan of 5th Panzer Regiment, was assembled without delay: 85 Pzkw. IIIs, 35 Pzkw.IIs, four 88 mm guns and twelve 105mm guns. About an hour after its departure at 1430, when Rommel drove south to see for himself, the Stephan Group came suddenly upon Gatehouse's attenuated 4th Armoured Brigade about 5 miles north-east of Gabr Saleh. The result was the first serious tank-versus-tank encounter of CRUSADER, lasting until both sides disengaged and went into leaguer for the night.

Gatehouse, deprived of his reconnaissance screen by the helter-skelter foray of 3rd Royal Tank Regiment north of the Trigh Capuzzo, was caught with the 8th Hussars and 5th Royal Tank Regiment 10 miles apart. The German blow fell on the 8th Hussars first, with 5th Royal Tanks piling into the fray from the east with the last of the daylight, and the resultant confusion was witnessed by war correspondent Alan Moorehead:

Dark rainclouds were pressed solidly onto the eastern horizon. Against this backcloth a line of grey shell-bursts flared up, and soon there were so many of them that a series of twenty or more were hanging together on the skyline. As the battle joined more closely these bursts grew together and made a continuous curtain of dust and smoke and blown sand. This was the battle of the guns reaching its climax – German guns on our tanks, our guns on the Germans; the range perhaps five thousand yards. Then came the tanks.

What a moment it was. These light Honeys with their two-pounder 37mm gun, their ugly box-shaped turrets, their little waving pennants, had never seen the battle before. They had come straight from the steel mills of America to the desert, and now for the first time we were going to see if they were good or bad or just more tanks.

Gatehouse, with his heavy head, his big hooked nose, and his deep-set eyes, sat on his tank watching the battle, estimating the strength of the enemy, the position of the sun, the slope of the ground. Then he lifted up his radio mouthpiece and gave his order. At his command the Honeys did something that tanks don't do in the desert any more. They charged. It was novel, reckless, unexpected, impetuous and terrific. They charged straight into the curtain of dust and fire that hid the German tanks and guns. They charged at speeds of nearly forty miles an hour and some of them came right out the other side of the German lines. Then they turned and charged straight back again.[6]

What Moorehead saw was the Honeys using their only advantage over the panzers – speed – to get within range of their 2-pounder guns before they were knocked out themselves. Many failed to make it; the evening's fighting cost the 8th Hussars twenty tanks knocked out and 5th Royal Tank Regiment three, though twelve of these were retrieved and repaired for action within forty-eight hours. The Honey crews reckoned that they had done well enough, claiming nineteen panzers destroyed for sure and maybe as many as twenty-six knocked out. But they were reckoning without the excellent German tank-recovery crews, and forgetting the inevitable tendency (as with fighter pilots after an air 'dog-fight') to count cripples as kills. *Afrika Korps'* tally for the encounter came to only three panzers destroyed and four disabled.

For Cunningham and Norrie the situation on the night of 19/20 November was little clearer than it had been at daybreak. The day's operations by XXX Corps seemed to add up to one definite setback on the left flank (22nd Armoured Brigade's repulse at Bir el Gubi), and – according to the first, over-optimistic figures from the crews of 4th Armoured Brigade – one drawn tank battle on the right. The only clear-cut gain of the day had been 7th Armoured Brigade's advance to Sidi Rezegh in the centre. But a major question mark still hung over the whereabouts of XXX Corps' real objective: the main concentration of *Afrika Korps*. The tank battle of the late afternoon had not imperilled the steady advance of XIII Corps, where all was going according to plan, but it had clearly not involved the bulk of the German armour. Before he returned to his rear Army Headquarters to confer with his staff, Cunningham therefore ordered 1st South African Division to close up to Bir el Gubi and take over the investment of 'Ariete' from 22nd Armoured Brigade. In the centre, reinforcing success, Campbell's 7th Support Group was to press on and join Davy's 7th Armoured Brigade at Sidi Rezegh. On the right, Gatehouse was to stay where he was in the Gabr Saleh area, offering the continued guarantee of armoured support to the left flank of XIII Corps.

Similar uncertainty prevailed at *Panzergruppe* headquarters, where the only solid achievement of the 19th seemed to be a fine job of work by Gambara's Italians down at Bir el Gubi. The arrival of British armour at Sidi Rezegh, so close to the Tobruk perimeter, was a new worry; if quickly reinforced it could constitute a real threat to the maintenance of the siege. Sümmermann was therefore ordered to re-deploy 90th Light further to the south, acting now as a hard core in the middle of the 'Bologna' Division, and sending a blocking force down to Sidi Rezegh. But the greatest concern was that aroused by the activities of the British armoured force north-east of Gabr Saleh. The fast-moving new British tanks had cause considerable trouble to Stephan's tank and *panzerjäger* gunners, and his Battle Group had certainly not inflicted any crushing defeat on the British armour. Still more confusion was caused by vague reports from the far south of British forces moving west from Jarabub, Brigadier Reid's Oasis Force excellently fulfilling its role as a diversion in its second day's advance.

Nor, as Crüwell interpreted the day's events, was the force encountered by Stephan Group the only British tank concentration north-east of Gabr Saleh; there was that deep-ranging British advance across the Trigh Capuzzo to be considered. If there was a third British tank force, able to operate between *Afrika Korps'* main assembly area and the Frontier, then the sooner it was destroyed the better. To this end, for 20 November Crüwell ordered his two panzer divisions to launch their first joint foray eastward towards Sidi Omar. *Afrika Korps* was therefore set in motion to seek out and destroy a non-existent enemy – one wild-goose-chase (that of 3rd Royal Tank Regiment) begetting another. As the rival armoured corps continued to grope for each other the 'fog of war' was thickening fast.

Day 3: 20 November

Eighth Army: XXX Corps

Events on the morning of 20 November encouraged an illusion of victory, all the more cruel because it was brief-lived. The day began with a flare-up of action on 4th Armoured Brigade's front, as Gatehouse sought to renew the previous evening's battle with Stephan. It was an inconclusive fight, with each side repeatedly going for the opposition's flank; it was also one-sided, because Stephan was trying to break away to the north-east and join the rest of *Afrika Korps* in its eastward advance to the Frontier. All this manoeuvring quickly drained the fuel tanks of the Honeys and prevented Gatehouse from giving chase, but he naturally interpreted the disappearance of the German armour as a heartening victory for 4th Armoured Brigade.

Up at Sidi Rezegh, dawn on the 20th saw Davy's 7th Armoured Brigade come under its first counter-attacks from Sümmermann's 90th Light Division. This attempt by infantry to dislodge tanks was by no means as hopeless as it sounds, for three reasons. First, Sidi Rezegh airfield was overlooked from all sides by low ridges, with plenty of 'dead ground' on the reverse slopes to conceal the approaching attackers. Second, the defending armour was deprived of its supreme advantage, mobility. Third, the tanks were on their own, Campbell's Support Group not having yet arrived. If 90th Light had had its full complement of artillery it might have been a different story; 7th Armoured Brigade would also have been hard-pressed if Sümmermann's two regiments (361st and 155th) had been granted the time to launch a simultaneous, converging attack. As things were, 7th Armoured Brigade beat off the westward attack of 361st Regiment, launched at dawn from the direction of Point 175, then faced about to drive back a second attack by 155th Regiment from the west, at 0800.

At 0940 Gott arrived at Sidi Rezegh shortly in advance of the leading elements of Campbell's Support Group. Davy's account of the two German defeats convinced him that the ideal moment was at hand for the relief of Tobruk to be launched. As Campbell's Support Group began to take over Sidi Rezegh airfield from 7th Armoured Brigade, Gott informed Norrie that there was every chance of a successful link-up between 7th Armoured Division and 70th Division on the following day.

Norrie relayed this enticing information to Cunningham, who was now back at Eighth Army Headquarters at Maddalena. There Cunningham had been given the air reconnaissance appreciation of the previous evening, suggesting a general westward movement of Axis forces. This appreciation was, of course, always tentative at best, and it was now hopelessly out of date, as the main Axis movement on the morning of the 20th was *eastward*. But, vague though it was, it conjured up in Cunningham's mind the glorious image of *Afrika Korps*, surprised by Eighth Army's advance and initial successes, recoiling westward – to be trapped by the opening of the corridor into Tobruk and the link-up of

70th Division and XXX Corps. He saw the bulk of the Axis divisions – 'Bologna' and 90th Light, 15th and 21st Panzer, 'Savona' and the Halfaya garrison – penned within an arc of British-held territory stretching from the coast at Tobruk to the coast east of Sollum. Even if Rommel managed to break out, he would have little option but a retreat to the west. And if he failed to break out he would suffer what every British general had dreamed of inflicting on the German Army for the past 18 months: Dunkirk without the evacuation facilities. Unable to resist the prospect, Cunningham endorsed Gott's proposal: 70th Division was to begin its breakout from Tobruk at dawn on the 21st.

In this way, Cunningham made the decision which was to balance Eighth Army's chances of victory in CRUSADER on a knife-edge. It was a decision made for all the wrong reasons: imprecise and out-dated Intelligence, ignorance of the enemy's true position, deference to an over-optimistic subordinate unable to see the whole picture. Indeed, Cunningham's own view of the whole picture (or what he conceived it to be) was as wrong as that of every other general, in both armies. And no matter how fairly it can be justified, it was a decision which brought down the keystone of the original CRUSADER plan: that the destruction of Rommel's armour must precede all subsequent operations. Offering Rommel the initiative after the initial advance had not helped bring forward that destruction: a cardinal military principle had thus been sacrificed in vain. But in determining that from now on Eighth Army would snatch and hold the initiative, Cunningham violated a far more sacrosanct principle: the need to stick to a sound plan once made. Three curt words spelled out that principle, in what had become a time-tested British military proverb: 'Order – counter-order – disorder'. In prematurely approving the Tobruk breakout before the destruction of *Afrika Korps*, Cunningham was issuing one of the most important counter-orders of the Second World War. And he was never to find an answer to the disorder into which it cast his Army's prospects.

At least it can be said in Cunningham's favour that he did not make this momentous decision lightly. It took him nearly six hours, from about 1000 to 1600, when the fateful order was issued. But this was only because Eighth Army Intelligence came up with intercepted German signals suggesting that both panzer divisions were preparing for a joint attack on 4th Armoured Brigade. Here was an even more pressing reason for postponing the opening of the Tobruk corridor until the armoured battle had been fought and, hopefully, won according to the original plan. But Cunningham issued his counter-order before the armoured battle had even been joined, an extraordinary display of confidence in the outcome. Apart from the pressing need for Eighth Army to secure Tobruk as a base for supplies, and the wondrous prospects of an 'African Dunkirk' outlined above, over-confidence certainly seems to have been as much to blame as anything. Here Cunningham, Eighth Army's first commander, had done his job rather too well in preparing his new command for battle. The Army in general, and XXX Corps in particular, had gone into CRUSADER 'with its tail well up', a little too much so for its own good. A little less reliance on morale and mere superiority in numbers, and a little more weighing of the actual tactical odds, was wanting at all command levels down to brigadier on 20 November 1941.

Norrie was a case in point. After throwing his weight behind Gott's enthusiastic urging, Norrie issued a combination of orders which asked far too much of the weakest link in XXX Corps: Brink's 1st South African Division. He ordered 22nd Armoured Brigade to disengage from Bir el Gubi and head east down the Trigh el Abd to reinforce Gatehouse at Gabr Saleh; Brigadier D. H. Pienaar's 1st South African Infantry Brigade was to take over the 'masking' of 'Ariete' from 22nd Armoured; Brigadier B. F. Armstrong's 5th South African Infantry Brigade was to advance 20 miles to reinforce 7th Armoured Division at Sidi Rezegh for the break-in to Tobruk. These orders, if fulfilled to the letter, would virtually have completed the fragmentation of XXX Corps with the armour split between Sidi Rezegh and Gabr Saleh, and 1st South African split between Bir el Gubi and Sidi Rezegh. This was averted for the painful reason that Brink did not consider Armstrong's brigade capable of safely reaching Sidi Rezegh in a night march and asked for the transfer to be postponed until first light on the 21st.

Fuel crisis for Afrika Korps

Certainly as late as noon on 20 November Rommel was still reluctant to admit that he had a major British offensive on his hands. He continued to hope that Crüwell would quickly smash the British armour north of the Trigh el Abd and return 15th Panzer Division for the planned attack on Tobruk. A major mystery, on which no light has been cast by any former officers of the *Panzergruppe*, is the time it took Rommel to appreciate the threat posed by 7th Armoured Division at Sidi Rezegh. Given the delusions common to both sides during CRUSADER, Rommel may have decided that Sümmermann's morning attacks, though unsuccessful, had rendered 7th Armoured Division incapable of further advance. This would explain Rommel's hope that *Afrika Korps* would quickly sweep the British armour south of the Trigh el Abd (after which 7th Armoured Division's position would become highly critical), but it was a hope which rapidly waned on the afternoon of the 20th.

Crüwell's drive east to Sidi Azeiz, intent on trapping the British armoured force which had thrust across the Trigh Capuzzo on the previous day, accomplished nothing but the dislocation of *Afrika Korps* due to fuel shortages. Finding nothing as far east as Sidi Azeiz, Crüwell ordered a sweep to the south-west, back to towards Gabr Saleh; but 21st Panzer Division was soon stranded for want of fuel and ammunition, leaving 15th Panzer to go on alone. Radio security went to the winds as the operators of 21st Panzer besought *Panzergruppe* Headquarters for more fuel. The true nature of the German supply crisis does not seem to have been appreciated by Eighth Army's signal interceptors, but they did detect the continuing advance of 15th Panzer Division. This was the attack which 4th Armoured Brigade was briefed to expect in the afternoon.

Eighth Army: XIII Corps and Desert Air Force

On 20 November XIII Corps was looking ahead to the attack on Sidi Omar Nuovo by 7th Indian Infantry Brigade, and to the advance north towards Sidi Azeiz by the New Zealand Division. The 'I' tanks of 4th Royal Tank Regiment were pushed north, taking up a forward position 6 miles north-west of Sidi Omar Nuovo. Encouraged by the apparent ease, success and range of 4th Armoured Brigade's operations since the advance had begun, Freyberg was not disconcerted by the news of the incoming German attack. He also offered to move north-west in support of Gatehouse, whose decline of the offer seems to have been based more on over-confidence than on fears that the New Zealanders might be surprised while still on the move.

The Desert Air Force continued to attack the Stuka base at Tmimi, though now beginning to encounter fighter opposition as the Axis airfields dried out. In the afternoon air reconnaissance noted 15th Panzer Division's advance to the south-west; these sightings, added to sightings of traffic down the *Achsenstrasse* speeding Sümmermann's redeployment of 90th Light to the north of Sidi Rezegh added to Eighth Army's impression of a westerly trend to Axis movements. But the chronic inability to act swiftly on such reports failed to save 4th Armoured Brigade from being surprised when 15th Panzer Division actually attacked and a medium-bomber strike arrived too late to catch the German columns on the move in the open Desert.

15th Panzer Division attacks 4th Armoured Brigade

It was less than an hour before sunset when 15th Panzer's blow fell on 4th Armoured Brigade. This gained complete surprise because

Neumann-Silkow circled wide to the west in order to attack out of the setting sun – at this time still a novel tactic to XXX Corps, though soon to become accepted as commonplace and even predictable. The tank strength of 15th Panzer would seem to be less than the thirty-eight Pzkw. IIs, seventy-six Pzkw. IIIs, and twenty-one Pzkw.IVs listed in the British Official History. Schmidt's last staff job for Rommel, before requesting a transfer to a combat unit, was to draw up a report on 15th Panzer which noted that the Division was nearly 50 per cent under its 'paper' manpower strength.[7] Further light on the matter is offered by Crisp, who noted that by the time of the German attack

most of us were developing a sort of wolf-wolf complex, but we were startled into reality by a frantic call for help from B Squadron, who screamed that they were being attacked by over 100 tanks. The desert air was suddenly full of high explosive and the terrifying swish of armour-piercing shells. Coming in from the west very fast, with the sun behind them shining straight into our gunners' eyes, were scores of the dark, ominous shapes of German panzers. Going even faster a few hundred yards ahead of them were B Squadron's Honeys, together with half a dozen soft-skinned vehicles.

They came hurtling back through A Squadron, whose commander started yelling into his microphone: 'Halt! Halt! the lot of you. Turn round and fight, you yellow bastards. I'll shoot the next tank I see moving back.'

... Movement was the obvious answer, but movement in a direction which could only be described as running away. I could see the panzers clearly now, coming down a broad depression in line abreast, 40 to 60 of them, easy enough to exaggerate into a hundred and more. On my left was a low ridge, the southern edge of the depression, and I made for this flat out with my troop conforming, in the hope of getting on the flank of the advancing juggernauts and getting out of the direct line of fire.

Once over the ridge I turned back along the crest to see what was happening and whether it would be possible to do any damage. The enemy onslaught was losing some of its impetus, owing to lack of opposition, and with darkness falling fast the Germans could not have claimed a great deal of success – although it must have given them a good deal of self-satisfaction.[8]

The battle petered out in the gathering dusk, which enabled Honey commanders like Crisp to rally and press close-range attacks on the panzers. Neumann-Silkow therefore disengaged as darkness fell, going into leaguer about 5 miles to the north. Through the night the sentries in the blacked-out British leaguers at Gabr Saleh watched their German counterparts across the Desert sending up their usual non-stop firework display of white and green flares to prevent surprise. 'It was a convenient arrangement,' reflected Crisp, 'and it was just as well that at least one side knew where the other was during the hours of darkness.'[9]

The lateness of 15th Panzer Division's attack on the 20th, plus the agility and speed of the Honeys in evading it, saved 4th Armoured Brigade from losing more than twenty-six tanks destroyed and damaged. The effect of these losses was virtually cancelled by the belated arrival of 22nd Armoured Brigade from Bir el Gubi. Once again, British claims of German casualties were sadly exaggerated; of the thirty panzers claimed as knocked out German records refer to none. The third day of CRUSADER therefore closed with 22nd and 4th Armoured Brigades united at Gabr Saleh, 4th Armoured having survived its third brush with *Afrika Korps*. As Mellenthin later noted, albeit with hindsight and all the information so sadly lacking that day, the *Panzergruppe* had unknowingly let slip the chance of a shattering early victory over XXX Corps:

> There is no doubt that we missed a great opportunity on 20 November. Cunningham had been obliging enough to scatter the 7th Armoured Division all over the desert, and we had failed to exploit his generosity. If *Afrika Korps* had concentrated at Gabr Saleh on the morning of the 20th, it could have wiped out the 4th Armoured Brigade; on the other hand, if it had moved towards Sidi Rezegh it could have inflicted a crushing defeat on the British forces there. In that case we would have won the CRUSADER battle very easily, for the whole Eighth Army had been dispersed in a gigantic arc stretching from Sollum to Bir el Gubi. These operations show the need for caution and the careful weighing of all Intelligence reports, before committing one's main armoured force in a great mobile battle.[9]

At 2100 that evening thousands of men in both armies gathered to hear the one Intelligence source which any radio operator could tap: the BBC 9 o'clock News. Out into the Desert air the measured voice announced that 'the Eighth Army, with about 75,000 men excellently armed and equipped, has started a general offensive in the Western Desert with the aim of destroying the German–Italian forces in Africa'. Much has been made of this broadcast as one of the earliest feckless breaches of security in modern warfare by the broadcasting media. It is still widely believed that Rommel had the BBC to thank for the information that the *Panzergruppe* was facing a major offensive.[9] But it is unlikely that the broadcast did more at *Panzergruppe* Headquarters than confirm the decision to which Rommel had already come: that Eighth Army had stolen a three-day march on him and was poised for the relief of Tobruk. When Crüwell arrived at Gambut for his evening conference with Rommel, it was to be given a top-priority objective for the morrow. Crüwell was to rush *Afrika Korps* north-west to Sidi Rezegh, in full strength and at top speed, there 'to attack and destroy the enemy force which has advanced on Tobruk'. On 21 November, D+4 of CRUSADER, the battle would break loose in full and chaotic earnest.

Day 4 – 21 November

The night of 20/21 November was a troubled one for Rommel, as *Panzergruppe* wireless intercepts confirmed intensified activity within the Tobruk perimeter. He had now accepted the incredible truth that 7th Armoured Division, with South African reinforcements on the way, was poised to break through to 70th Division at the precise point of his own long-cherished attack on Tobruk. Rommel hounded Crüwell to get *Afrika Korps* moving on Sidi Rezegh at the earliest possible moment, at 0400 warning Crüwell that 'the situation in this whole theatre is very critical'. Though nothing could be done to re-create the wasted opportunity of the previous day, Crüwell's superb response on the morning of 21 November nevertheless succeeded in frustrating the first British attempt to relieve Tobruk.

Eighth Army: 70th Division and XXX Corps

Inside Tobruk Scobie's 70th Division had been working on its breakout drill for the past month. Through the night of 20/21 November the south-east corner of the Tobruk perimeter was a scene of intense activity, reminiscent more than anything else of the eve of a 'big push' on the Western Front in the First World War. The Tobruk breakout was in fact the first British 'set-piece' attempt to pierce a belt of fixed defences in similar depth; the Italian defences encountered at Sidi Barrani, Bardia and Tobruk, during the first Desert offensive, had been easy meat by comparison. On 21 November, 1941, 11 miles separated 70th Division's start-line from 7th Armoured Division at Sidi Rezegh. To facilitate rapid penetration in the greatest possible depth, as much preparatory work as possible was tackled under cover of darkness; wire and inner minefields gapped and marked, and the anti-tank ditch bridged at four places. Spare bridges had been provided for each crossing-point to enable swift replacement, and an interesting feature was the deployment of armoured-car teams, trained in mine clearance, to push ahead and gap the outer minefields. Before the invention of mine-clearing flail tanks, this was the best that could be done. But despite all these preparations, in what can only be described as typical fashion for CRUSADER, the long-awaited pincer-movement to raise the siege of Tobruk was not executed as planned. The simultaneous converging attacks by 70th and 7th Armoured Divisions did not take place.

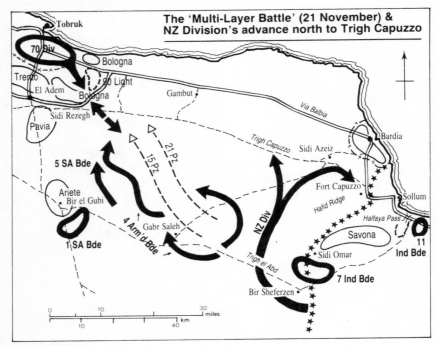

One reason for this was the unexpectedly tough resistance encountered by both attacking forces. The original breakout plan had envisaged a clean punch through the centre of the Italian 'Bologna' Division. But since the morning of the 19th the besiegers had fielded a last-minute substitute, with the unexpected southward deployment of 90th Light Division. This was a factor which had scarcely been considered. In the plan to 'open the corridor' through to Tobruk, the only serious German opposition had been seen as coming from *outside* the siege perimeter: the attempts by the remains of an already-defeated *Afrika Korps* to stop XXX Corps from breaking in. The likelihood of unexpectedly tough opposition to the breakout considerably changed the odds, but too late for anything to be done about it.

110

By the morning of 21 November Rommel had been forced to spread 90th Light Division, his only source of German infantry, to its maximum effective limits. First, the take-over from 'Bologna' on the Tobruk siege perimeter had given 90th Light a front-line sector two miles broad, backed by over four miles of defensive positions. The right flank of this position commanded the Via Balbia, only two miles from the coast. Fourteen miles to the south-east, holding Point 175 and effectively blocking the Trigh Capuzzo, was 361st Regiment. Six miles west of Point 175, commanding the escarpment north-west of Sidi Rezegh airfield and blocking 7th Armoured Division's path to Tobruk, was 155th Regiment. No other division on the CRUSADER battlefield occupied a more extraordinary position that that of 90th Light: three main concentrations at the angles of a distorted triangle some 50 square miles in area. And two of those concentrations would have to be crushed before XXX Corps and 70th Division could join hands.

The assault from the north by 70th Division, which opened at daybreak on 21 November, was accompanied by diversionary attacks on the southern and western sectors by Kopanski's Poles and the 23rd Infantry Brigade. The main attacking force on the south-east sector – 2nd Black Watch and 1st, 4th, and 7th Royal Tank Regiments – found the going tough right from the start. The attack happened to fall on the divisional 'join' in the Axis front between 'Bologna' and 90th Light Division, normally a natural weak spot in a defensive front, but not in this case. The initial attack opened a 2-mile breach in the Axis front and, though broadening attacks found more success in the Italian sector than in the German, the Italians again fought unexpectedly well. That morning, indeed, 70th Division took more German prisoners than Italian: 550 Germans and 527 Italians.

The painful advance south-east towards 7th Armoured Division was impeded in particular by four Axis strongpoints, code-named 'Lion', 'Tiger', 'Jack' and 'Jill'. The toughest nut to crack was 'Tiger', which cost the Black Watch 75 per cent casualties before it fell. The minefields, and intense artillery fire repeatedly called down by the defenders, also sent the tank casualties rocketing to sixty out of the original 109. By noon on the 21st, after four hours of heavy fighting, 70th Division had hammered a lozenge-shaped salient 4 miles deep into the Axis front. Despite its losses, 70th Division was fit to struggle on towards El Duda, still 4 miles away, but Scobie now had no choice but to order what he hoped would prove a temporary halt. He knew that the expected break-in by 7th Armoured Division had not materialized and, pre-empted by the dramatic intervention of *Afrika Korps*, 7th Armoured Division was fighting for its life.

Daybreak had found 7th Armoured Division poised to launch the break-in attack north-west towards El Duda. This was to be carried by 1st King's Royal Rifle Corps, 6th Royal Tank Regiment and a company of 2nd Rifle Brigade. Artillery support was provided by 3rd and 4th Regiments, Royal Horse Artillery, with the 7th Hussars and 2nd Royal Tank Regiment in reserve. The first objective was to push the German 155th Regiment off the ridge north-west of Sidi Rezegh airfield. The attack would then develop across the Trigh Capuzzo towards *Achsenstrasse* at El Duda 5 miles away, the expected link-up point with 70th Division. But at 0800, only half an hour before the attack was due to go in, 7th Armoured received the electrifying news that both divisions of *Afrika Korps* were closing fast from the south-east.

Davy's courageous decision was that even in this supreme crisis he could not leave 70th Division's attack wholly unsupported. Campbell therefore took over the attack to the north while Davy turned with the 7th Hussars and 2nd Royal Tank Regiment to face the oncoming panzers. Thus sliced in half by *Afrika Korps'* unexpected approach, 7th Armoured Division's break-in to Tobruk was reduced to little more than a token gesture made at great cost. The KRRC and Rifles stormed their way onto the ridge, gaining part of their first objective. This partially opened the door to permit 6th Royal Tank Regiment to get across the Trigh Capuzzo, only to be battered to a halt by artillery fire from the ridge at Belhamed and left with only twenty-eight operational tanks. Even as Campbell's gallant attack went in to the north-west, the leading German tanks were sighted by Davy's two regiments 5 miles south-east of Sidi Rezegh airfield.

0830, 21 November: the 'multi-layer' battle

The unbelievable situation prevailing at 0830 on Friday 21 November, 1941, has no equal anywhere in modern warfare. Indeed, in all military history there is only one approximate equivalent, and for that one has to go back to the first century BC.[10] It was so chaotic that it could not endure; within a few hours a saner pattern began to re-emerge. But, when 'frozen' for examination in detail, nothing better illustrates the unique fluidity of the CRUSADER fighting, in which the battle repeatedly passed beyond control of the rival generals. It is hard indeed to better the verdict of the British Official History: that the situation, 'if suggested as the setting of a training exercise, must have been rejected for the reason that in real life these things simply could not happen'.[11] The favourite metaphor is that of a Neapolitan layer-cake and, though the impression this gives is much too tidy, a better one is hard to find. From north-west

112

to south-east, over the 50 miles between Tobruk and Gabr Saleh, the tangled sequence of interlocked units was as follows:

a   British 70th Division trying to batter its way out of Tobruk, still pressing its attack on

b   'Bologna' and 90th Light, the latter division simultaneously fighting off

c   the northern half of 7th Armoured Division, whose southern half was reversed to face

d   Crüwell with both panzer divisions of *Afrika Korps*, advancing from Gabr Saleh while swatting off attempts to attack its flanks by

e   Scott-Cockburn and Gatehouse with 22nd and 4th Armoured Brigades, who had got moving too late to prevent Crüwell's advance with a pre-empting attack.

The chaos of the situation may be judged by the wholly mistaken impression at XXX Corps Headquarters that *Afrika Korps*, battered by 4th Armoured Brigade in the previous day's fighting, was not advancing but *retreating*. Nothing else seemed to explain the indecent haste with which *Afrika Korps* took off to the north-west at first light (0720) without so much as a preliminary spoiling attack. This could only mean that the German tank losses on the 20th, so far from having been exaggerated, had been much higher than originally estimated. Davy's 7th Armoured Brigade, so far from being in danger at Sidi Rezegh, would therefore have a fine chance to step up the attrition rate as it nudged *Afrika Korps* along its westward retreat. It was in this hopelessly wrong interpretation of the battle that Cunningham took the decision destined to win the battle. With *Afrika Korps* heading off to the west, Godwin-Austen could now begin the northward advance of XIII Corps.

As the situation on the ground became increasingly chaotic, so the onus of command tended to shift downwards on the British side. The decisions which mattered on 21 November were taken at divisional and brigade level, not corps or army. It was Gott, not Norrie, who ordered Gatehouse and Scott-Cockburn to try and pin down *Afrika Korps* at Gabr Saleh; Gott who ordered the green 5th South African Brigade, moving up to Sidi Rezegh, to halt and keep out of the developing maelstrom. Moving down a further rung, it was Davy, not Gott, who ordered Campbell to attack towards El Duda while he faced about to fend off *Afrika Korps*. But on the German side there was, if anything, a tendency for command to shift upwards. On the first two days of CRUSADER it was Ravenstein's uneasiness over 21st Panzer's southern flank which dictated the first tentative German counter-moves. By 20 November the leadership had shifted up to Crüwell, who by the following morning was wielding the German armour with a concentrated decisiveness never attained by his British opposite number, Norrie.

The upshot of Crüwell's advance on Sidi Rezegh early on the 21st was the destruction of 7th Armoured Brigade as a fighting force. The main shock fell on the 7th Hussars which by the afternoon had virtually ceased to exist, reduced to a total strength of twelve tanks, most of them hit or damaged. The brave efforts of 2nd Royal Tank Regiment to attack the left flank of 15th Panzer Division during this slaughter were beaten back by the *panzerjägers*, whose 50mm guns did great execution. While Neumann-Silkow fell upon 7th Armoured Brigade, Ravenstein took 21st Panzer further to the north and hooked savagely into the right rear of Campbell's Support Group. Ravenstein's leading tanks attacked the support company of the 2nd Rifles, which gallantly engaged them with 2-pounder *portées* – 2-pounder crews mounted, unarmoured and exposed, on the backs of trucks – and 25-pounders firing over open sights. In this brutal action 2nd Lieutenant G. Ward Gunn, who died while directing the fire of his dwindling 2-pounder crews to the last, won a posthumous Victoria Cross. This was only one of the four Victoria Crosses awarded during the desperate fighting for Sidi Rezegh between 21 and 23 November.

And yet, despite the flaying of 7th Armoured Brigade, 21 November ended in yet another disappointment for Crüwell. Thanks largely to the inspiring leadership of 'Jock' Campbell, racing from crisis-point to crisis-point in an open car and winning one of the most popular Victoria Cross awards of the campaign, 7th Support Group just managed to hold on at Sidi Rezegh. For *Afrika Korps* had its troubles too, and its frustration on the 21st perfectly illustrates the extraordinary difficulty of manoeuvring and fighting armoured formations in the Desert. In the Battle of France, with abundant fuel and good roads, Rommel had driven 7th Panzer Division on a record-breaking 150 miles in a single day. But on 21 November, 1941, Crüwell's 30-mile advance across the Desert from Gabr Saleh to Sidi Rezegh left *Afrika Korps* gasping for resources and unable to clinch its victory. By the afternoon both panzer divisions were suffering from fuel and ammunition shortages after the manoeuvring and fighting of the past two days, while 22nd Armoured Brigade's attacks dogged the German flank and rear. Refuelling problems prevented 4th Armoured Brigade from giving any effective relief to 7th Armoured Division on the 21st.

As night fell *Afrika Korps* withdrew to leaguer north and east of Sidi Rezegh. Crüwell intended to give 7th Armoured Division the *coup de grâce* on the following day, knowing that he had dealt the 7th Armoured Brigade a mortal blow. Out of the 141 tanks with which 7th Armoured Brigade had gone into battle on the morning of 21 November, only twenty-eight remained fit for battle at the end of the day, once the last stragglers had come in. Gott nevertheless proposed to resume the defence of Sidi Rezegh with the Support Group backed by 22nd Armoured Brigade (plus 7th Armoured Brigade's gallant remnants) with Gatehouse's 4th Armoured Brigade providing mobile cover from the south-east. Armstrong's 5th South African Brigade was to take the escarpment south of the airfield, and the aim was to resume the opening of the Tobruk corridor as soon as possible with 70th Division holding its new positions until this could be done.

Eighth Army: XIII Corps

While the breakout was suspended and the armoured battle raged around Sidi Rezegh, XIII Corps began its first major advance into the rear of the Axis Frontier positions. As mentioned above (p.113), this was based on the entirely false deduction that *Afrika Korps* was withdrawing westward. While 7th Indian Infantry Brigade squared up to attack Sidi Omar Nuovo, Freyberg's New Zealanders moved off to the westward, driving north towards Sidi Azeiz and encountering no opposition. Nightfall on 21 November found an entirely new situation rapidly developing in the eastern sector of the CRUSADER battlefield. Freyberg's leading brigade, 6th New Zealand, was preparing for a night march to reach the Trigh Capuzzo, 12 miles west of Sidi Azeiz. The 5th Brigade was in Sidi Azeiz itself and had also taken Capuzzo from the west, not only severing the telephone link between *Panzergruppe* Headquarters and the Frontier garrisons, but shutting off the water pipeline supplying the latter. Freyberg's 4th Brigade had meanwhile continued north to arrive on the escarpment overlooking Bardia.

Eighteen miles south of Sidi Azeiz 7th Indian Brigade had managed to take Sidi Omar Nuovo after an unexpectedly tough fight. This was one of the rare 'set-piece' attacks specifically envisaged in the CRUSADER plan and had been carefully prepared, not only with air reconnaissance photography but with a Desert Air Force bombing raid to supplement the opening bombardment. Earlier patrolling had located the minefield gap left by the defenders, but the terrain around the Omars was as flat as a billiard table, with no dead ground to assist the attack. Supported by Matildas of the 42nd and 44th Royal Tank Regiments, the infantry of the Royal Sussex was treated to a vigorous bombardment as they advanced. The siting of artillery and machine-gun positions was good, and the Italian infantry fought as toughly as their comrades had done at Bir el Gubi. Even after Sidi Omar Nuovo was declared secure at 1500, isolated pockets of resistance still had to be cleared. Resistance was even harder at Libyan Omar, where the attack was made by the 4/10 Punjabis, and by nightfall the northern sector of the perimeter was still holding out. Briggs decided to regroup for another attack, having already suffered 500 killed and wounded, with thirty-five 'I' tanks knocked out by mines and anti-tank fire. Despite these unexpectedly high losses at Sidi Omar, XIII Corps had nevertheless made an unqualified success of their first real day of action. By nightfall on the fourth day of CRUSADER XIII Corps had accomplished the isolation of the Axis 'Frontier triangle' – Halfaya/Sidi Omar/Bardia – and had taken the first step in its piecemeal reduction.

Panzergruppe *and Eighth Army: assessment and plans*

As a direct cause of the New Zealanders' advance, Rommel ordered a precautionary shift of his *Panzergruppe* Headquarters, from Gambut 35 miles west to El Adem. But this did not mean that Rommel had fully appreciated the new menace taking shape to the eastward. His full attention was still focused on Sidi Rezegh. There the morning's northward attack by Campbell's forces had prompted Rommel's first personal intervention in the CRUSADER fighting; he had taken command of 3rd Reconnaissance Unit and supervised its establishment with 88mm guns at Belhamed, halting the 6th Royal Tank Regiment. On the evening of the 21st Rommel placed 90th Light Division under Crüwell's direct command and told him to keep up the pressure on Sidi Rezegh: the British attempt to break through to Tobruk must be defeated at all costs.

Crüwell, however, was inclined to a gloomy view of the day's fighting. Though *Afrika Korps* had undoubtedly had the better of the engagement at Sidi Rezegh it had nevertheless failed to destroy XXX Corps, which had still been counter-attacking at last light. Crüwell's nightmare was a vision of his panzer divisions becoming sucked into a futile positional battle for Sidi Rezegh and being left stranded for want of fuel and ammunition, rapidly unable to move or fight. He tended to an over-generous estimate of British tank resources and was determined to keep a margin for manoeuvre for *Afrika Korps*, the instincts of a professional tank soldier for whom manoeuvrability was all. For this reason, while leaving 21st Panzer Division at Belhamed and 8th Panzer Regiment 6 miles south-east of Sidi Rezegh, Crüwell ordered Neumann-Silkow to withdraw 15th Panzer Division to the east and re-group south of Gambut. This would leave *Afrika Korps* with a mobile reserve, even though it allowed 7th Armoured Division to be joined by 22nd Armoured Brigade at Sidi Rezegh.

In the British camp the communications failure between the front-line

116

10. A Stuart M-3, known as the Honey (see p. 79) passing a knocked-out Panzer Mk III.

11. Infantry ('I') tanks, better known as Matildas, of the 4th Royal Tank Regiment.

12. A knocked-out Crusader (see p. 143)

13. Bren-gun carriers on the road to Derna (see p. 193)

units and Eighth Army Headquarters at Maddalena continued to deny Cunningham any accurate appreciation of what had happened at Sidi Rezegh that morning. He had 'made a picture' of a force of maybe sixty German tanks hemmed in by Norrie's three armoured brigades, while the Support Group dominated Sidi Rezegh; and he could not understand why it was taking Norrie so long to open the corridor to Tobruk. Pressurized by Cunningham to resume the northward drive into Tobruk without further delay, Norrie therefore proposed to bring up Armstrong's 5th South African Brigade and dominate the southern escarpment overlooking Sidi Rezegh. Once the last element of 90th Light had been swept from the slight but commanding ridges to south and north of the Sidi Rezegh airfield, the advance on Tobruk could be resumed from a secure start-line. With luck XXX Corps would have reached El Duda by the afternoon of the 22nd; until then Scobie was not to resume 70th Division's attack from the Tobruk breakout salient.

Such was the British plan for 22 November: sweep the Sidi Rezegh escarpments clear of 90th Light, then resume the opening of the Tobruk corridor. On the 22nd, however, 'the bear blew first', and his breath was to come with shattering force.

Day 5 – 22 November

By the fifth morning of CRUSADER both armies were settling into a discernible daily campaign routine. It began with the breaking of the defensive leaguers at first light, followed by a morning of outpost and rearguard clashes between the forces in contact with the enemy. By the time that each side had made its appreciation of the latest situation and seen to replenishment and refuelling (when possible without a necessary wait for supply transport), it would be afternoon before any decisive moves could be made. And these were likely to have, at most, only three or four hours of declining daylight before the rapid descent of the winter night. Norrie's plan for the 22nd was for XXX Corps to end the day in full command of the Sidi Rezegh area, with the intitiative on the El Duda/Tobruk axis back in its hands. But this encouraging programme was crushed between the jaws of a pincer movement by *Afrika Korps*, executed quite by chance as the result of independent decisions taken by Rommel and Crüwell.

Eighth Army: XXX Corps

The morning of 22 November began with Campbell's force at Sidi Rezegh awaiting the arrival of 22nd Armoured Brigade and Armstrong's

5th South African Brigade, with outpost actions to the south and east as 15th Panzer Division completed the withdrawal ordered by Crüwell the night before. The disappearance of the last panzers by noon encouraged a feeling of optimism at Gott's Headquarters, but the time it took delayed the northward approach of 5th South African Brigade. It also enabled the southernmost troops of 90th Light Division (155th Regiment) to strengthen their hold on Point 178, south-west of the airfield; and when 5th South African Brigade tentatively attacked Point 178 at 1500 it was beaten back. Thus only 22nd Armoured Brigade, after a morning of rearguard clashes with 15th Panzer Division, came up from the south at 1400 to reinforce Campbell and Davy on Sidi Rezegh airfield. Minutes later Gott's incompletely concentrated force was fighting for dear life against a converging attack by 21st Panzer Division.

The Panzergruppe: *21st Panzer Division's attack*

By noon on the 22nd Ravenstein had 21st Panzer concentrated north of Sidi Rezegh on the Belhamed ridge, poised to counter-attack the expected resumption of the British northward advance; but Rommel had no intention of leaving the initiative to the British. Arriving at Belhamed, Rommel ordered Ravenstein to send his infantry south to clear the King's Royal Rifle Corps off the escarpment north of the airfield while 5th Panzer Regiment swept on to the airfield from the west. Ravenstein's attack remains a classic example of how a well-handled small tank force can overcome a disorganized (and outgunned) larger one. His 5th Panzer Regiment numbered only fifty-seven tanks, against a total of 107 in 7th and 22nd Armoured Brigades, but the cohesion, force and overall surprise of the German attack carried all before it. In desperate fighting the British forces were gradually forced off the northern escarpment and the airfield, giving ground to the eastward.

Eighth Army: XXX Corps – no help from 4th Armoured Brigade

As the German guns heralded the attack of Ravenstein's infantry from the north, Gott called on his only source of armoured support: Gatehouse's 4th Armoured Brigade, lying about 5 miles slightly south of east from Sidi Rezegh. Gatehouse responded by heading 3rd Royal Tank Regiment west to investigate, being, exactly like Crüwell, unwilling to commit his tank force *en masse* to a battle of position rather than manoeuvre, in which his cruisers would be bound to suffer heavy loss by being pressed into service as surrogate infantry tanks. Out in the lead of 3rd Royal Tanks, outpacing the rest of the regiment, were three Honeys: the depleted troop commanded by Crisp. They arrived on the rise at the eastern extremity of the airfield, staring in disbelief at the chaos below. The airfield was littered with wrecked aircraft and the burning Crusaders of 7th Armoured Division. The western end of the airfield and the ridge to the north were clearly in German hands, but on the airfield it was impossible to distinguish between derelict and stationary tanks, let alone friend or foe. Crisp, with his three Honeys, was still vainly trying to assess the situation, while the 100-odd tanks of 4th Armoured Brigade were (as he thought) coming up behind him, when he was brusquely commandeered by 'Jock' Campbell in his open car:

'What unit are you with?'
'Third R.T.R., 4th Armoured Brigade.'
'Good. There's a Jerry tank attack coming in from the west. We need you. Follow me.'
I said desperately: 'Sir, if you wait ten minutes the whole brigade will be up.'
'If you're there in ten minutes you'll be in time. If you're there in fifteen you'll be too late,' said the long brigadier. 'Follow me.'
He sat down, said something to the fair-haired driver sitting capless beside him, and shot off down the escarpment. I told my driver to follow the car, and we bounced down. Over my shoulder I could see Tom's tank lurching down behind . . . we were down the slope and in amongst the infantry and gunners. They were our own all right; the grimy, weary men yelling and giving 'Thumbs-up' signs. We went through and beyond them in a cloud of dust. . . . 30 yards ahead of me raced the little car, the blond head of the driver gleamed like the plumed helm of Navarre. Beside the driver sat the brigadier holding aloft a blue and white flag that stood straight out in the gale of their going. No wonder the dispirited troops cheered. It must have been quite a sight . . .
Now we were amongst the still-burning, depressing-looking Crusaders, and left them behind to speed through a few knocked-out Jerry tanks – a much pleasanter sight. Then we were through these onto the clean desert floor. . . . At last, on the opposite edge of the airfield, where the scrub grew again in a straight line, the car halted and my driver pulled back on the brakes. The long brigadier stood up, looked back at me, then waved his arm widely to the westward. . . . My stomach turned over. 1200 yards ahead of me stretched the array of

dark brown shapes, 60 to 70 monsters in solid line abreast coming
steadily towards the landing ground . . . towards me.[12]

Such was the irresistible leadership of 'Jock' Campbell vc on 22
November. Crisp and his crew came out of their ordeal 'wondering how
the hell we four had managed to be still alive', having been forced to bale
out of their burning Honey. As he had raced down the slope in
Campbell's wake, and as he dodged the German fire on the airfield,
Crisp had continually radioed news of his plight back to 3rd Royal
Tanks. None of his signals were acknowledged because none got
through – testimony to the badness of British tank radio communications in CRUSADER, which helped turn every action into the chaos of a
free-for-all that melted British tank reserves like snow. Only last light
and the end of the day's operations saw the scattered regiments
reassemble; when Crisp and his crew returned to 3rd Royal Tanks on
foot, it was to find that their regiment was momentarily unable to muster
more than four tanks. In fact Gatehouse had counter-attacked 21st
Panzer with 5th Royal Tanks, with several accidental encounters
between its Honeys and the Crusaders of 22nd Armoured Brigade.
Ravenstein's attack was already beginning to run out of steam for the
usual reason – fuel and ammunition – and was moreover confused by the
tangle of wrecks which had helped save Crisp and his crew on the
airfield. But the day ended with Sidi Rezegh once more in German
hands, while to the east of the airfield 15th Panzer Division completed
the scattering of 4th Armoured Brigade.

The Panzergruppe: *15th Panzer Division's attack*

About an hour after Rommel had descended on Ravenstein's Headquarters to order 21st Panzer's attack on the Sidi Rezegh airfield,
Crüwell had come to a wholly independent decision of his own. He
ordered Neumann-Silkow to turn 15th Panzer back to the west and
attack the flank of the British concentration at Sidi Rezegh, thus
unwittingly converting *Afrika Korps'* operations that afternoon into a
pincer attack on the armour of XXX Corps. After completing a
ponderous wheel to the south and replenishing, 15th Panzer was finally
ready to move off at 1530. Its 'march to the sound of the guns' took 15th
Panzer right through the Headquarters area of the 4th Armoured
Brigade as night was falling, scattering the 8th Hussars to the four winds
with the claimed capture of fifty tanks and 267 prisoners. It was to take
another 24 hours before 4th Armoured Brigade reassembled as a

fighting force; but those 24 hours were crucial. Whereas *Afrika Korps* ended 22 November with 173 battle-worthy tanks, XXX Corps was approaching its lowest ebb. The number of runners in 7th Armoured Brigade had dropped from twenty-eight to ten; in 22nd Armoured from seventy-nine to thirty-four. With 4th Armoured Brigade scattered by 15th Panzer Division, *Afrika Korps* had not only recovered Sidi Rezegh but gained a decisive superiority in tank numbers. Until XXX Corps had retrieved its stragglers and repaired its cripples, *Afrika Korps* could roam the battlefield at will.

Eighth Army: XIII Corps

On 22 November the only redeeming feature of Eighth Army's prospects was the continuing success of XIII Corps and its westward spearhead, the 6th Brigade of Freyberg's New Zealand Division. Though the battered armour of XXX Corps had received no help from its own 1st South African Division, help was at last on the way from the New Zealanders in the east. The upheavals of the armoured battle were beginning to cast the infantry brigades in an entirely new light. If it was still true that unsupported infantry could not fight tanks, infantry was still free of many restrictions limiting the freedom of movement of the armoured formations. Not only was an infantry unit free of an absolute dependence on fuel supply, but it did not have to go into leaguer when night fell: the infantry was trained to march and fight by night. This gave a steadiness to XIII Corps' advance which was about to reap dividends. 22 November was the first day of CRUSADER in which XIII Corps, so far from badgering XXX Corps for constant armoured protection, began to show that responsibility for the entire campaign did not rest solely on the shoulders of the tank men.

Despite his orders for a morning start the commander of 6th New Zealand Brigade, Brigadier H. E. Barrowclough, was unable to move off on the morning of the 22nd; the Valentine 'I' tanks of 8th Royal Tank Regiment were late in joining him. The 6th Brigade finally moved off at 1400 and was soon appraised of the latest crisis at Sidi Rezegh. In response Barrowclough's men turned in a fine 12-mile march in just over six hours, calling a halt at 2015 to eat and rest, and pressing on at 0100 on the 23rd. On the last stage of this night march, a navigational error landed 6th Brigade at Bir Chleta at first light, squarely among the command vehicles of *Afrika Korps*, whose encampment was beginning to stir after the night's leaguer. Yet another freak accident of Desert warfare left a general pondering his luck at having narrowly escaped capture with most of his Headquarters and staff. The New Zealanders had blundered into the Bir Chleta position only minutes after Crüwell had driven off to 15th Panzer Division.

Assessment, night 22 November

By midnight on the 22nd delusions about the true condition of XXX Corps continued to prevail at the upper command levels of Eighth Army. Cunningham was still obsessed with the delay in the breakthrough to 70th Division. He now saw this as being achieved by a collaboration of XXX Corps and the New Zealand Division, which was also to continue its attacks in the opposite direction against the Axis Frontier positions. Moreover, Cunningham believed that XXX Corps still had the ability to continue grinding down *Afrika Korps* while simultaneously providing armoured protection for the New Zealanders. Norrie's obsession was the need to concentrate 1st South African Division south of Sidi Rezegh, which meant hastening the relief of Pienaar's 1st South African Brigade at Bir el Gubi by 22nd Guards Brigade.

After the successes of *Afrika Korps* on the 22nd, Rommel was meanwhile preparing to take a personal grip on the battle in real earnest. The pincer movement achieved by *Afrika Korps* on the 22nd had been accidentally contrived; now he planned a repetition for the 23rd, deliberate this time, aimed at nothing less than the total annihilation of XXX Corps. He applied to Gambara to obtain the participation of 'Ariete': this was to be the first joint effort of the three Axis armoured divisions. *Afrika Korps* and 'Ariete' were to attack towards each other and smash everything between them. But once again the superb natural partnership between Rommel and Crüwell came into play. As he had done on the previous day, Crüwell changed the plan and infused it with much greater destructive potential. Crüwell's variant was for Ravenstein to remain in possession of Sidi Rezegh airfield, but release 5th Panzer Regiment to join 15th Panzer Division in the south-westerly drive towards 'Ariete'. Once the two forces had joined hands they were to sweep north, catching the British and South African forces between their hammer and Ravenstein's anvil.

Once XXX Corps had been destroyed, Rommel planned to sweep east and relieve what was becoming a major worry: the danger to his Frontier garrisons posed by XIII Corps. It was a good plan, ruthless and pragmatic, yet containing two weaknesses almost identical to those which had bedevilled Eighth Army's planning for the past three days. Rommel was beginning to estimate the overall British tank losses higher than they really were; he believed, too, that 4th Armoured Division had been liquidated on the 22nd, not merely temporarily dispersed. Both miscalculations were to cost the *Panzergruppe* dear in the long run. For the moment, however, the fortunes of *Afrika Korps* were about to reach their zenith.

Day 6 – 23 November

The Panzergruppe – Afrika Korps *triumphant*

For the German Army this Sunday, the last in November, was a day of special significance: *Totensonntag*, the 'Sunday of the Dead' – memorial day for the fallen of past wars. The relatively few *cognoscenti* in Eighth Army who understood the importance of *Totensonntag* to their enemy naturally hoped, at first light, that this leaden name would prove prophetic before the day was out. So indeed it proved, but not to the cost of Rommel's army. There were to be few sadder days in Eighth Army's entire history.

Totensonntag began for *Afrika Korps* with Crüwell moving off at 0730 with 15th Panzer Division, as yet unaware of the narrowness of his escape from capture by 6th New Zealand Brigade. Intent on snatching as big a time advantage as he could over the slower-moving British, Crüwell refused to wait for 5th Panzer Regiment to close up from 21st Panzer, but left orders for it to follow. Everything went wrong for XXX Corps from the start. On the previous day its armoured-car screens had failed disastrously to locate the approach of either Ravenstein or Neumann-Silkow; early on the 23rd 15th Panzer was spotted by the 4th South African Armoured Car Regiment as it set off for its rendezvous with 'Ariete', but the news was not believed. Still 'making pictures', XXX Corps decided that the South Africans had sighted 4th Armoured Brigade instead, though several days were to pass before 4th Armoured Brigade would be able to make a show of strength in any way resembling that of 15th Panzer Division that morning.

After this initial piece of good luck for Crüwell, a second followed at once when 15th Panzer ran straight across the transport of 7th Support Group and 5th South African Brigade. Ragged but furious opposition was improvised yet again by 'Jock' Campbell and Davy. The rear areas of 5th South African Brigade were wide open and Neumann-Silkow urged Crüwell to change the plan and seize such a golden opportunity, but Crüwell refused to be diverted from his planned junction with 'Ariete' and continued stolidly on course. By noon the last vehicles of 15th Panzer had disappeared to the south, leaving the South Africans to thank their lucky stars and resume the day's interrupted programme.

Mellenthin's opinion is that Crüwell's decision to stick to his original plan was a mistake. It missed the ideal opportunity to overrun what was left of 7th Armoured Division in a surprise attack, and gave the British the chance to cover 5th South African Brigade's front with artillery. But by 23 November Crüwell had had enough of premature attacks which stampeded the British into the empty Desert, there to re-form and return to battle. Panzer technician that he was, he was using his modern resources to pursue the classic ideal of Clausewitz: a *schlacht ohne morgen*, or 'battle without a morrow'. To be certain of catching the British with 21st Panzer at their backs and nowhere to run, it was well worth accepting loss of surprise, additional fuel consumption and the risk of higher tank losses. Nor was it true that the morning's running fight was wholly detrimental to Crüwell's prospects. As Mellenthin admits, it had the immediate and most desirable effect of preventing the planned concentration of 1st South African Division. Once Pienaar knew that a strong panzer column was on the loose in his area, 1st South African Brigade promptly froze in its tracks and stayed where it was for the rest of the day, leaving the 5th Brigade with only the remnants of 7th Armoured Division for protection.

The rendezvous with 'Ariete' took place shortly after noon, with 5th Panzer Regiment closing up soon afterwards, and Crüwell began the laborious task of realigning the combined Axis force: 'Ariete' on the left, 8th Panzer Regiment in the centre, 5th Panzer Regiment on the right. The Axis phalanx added up to the greatest tank concentration which had ever been achieved in Africa for a single attack. Apart from the ninety-odd indifferent M 13s of 'Ariete', the panzer concentration came to 162 tanks (eighty-seven down on *Afrika Korps*' original strength on 18 November). At 1500, closely supported by lorried infantry, Crüwell's tanks rolled into their attack.

Four miles to the north-east Armstrong and Campbell had done their best to exploit the respite given by 15th Panzer Division's inexplicable disappearance in the late morning. But the British commanders were faced with the task of contriving an all-round defence from wholly inadequate resources. Nothing could be spared for the northern flank, which came under heavy artillery fire from Ravenstein and Sümmermann shortly after noon. The last thirty-four tanks of 22nd Armoured Brigade were posted on the South Africans' western flank, and Campbell's Support Group on the east. Left to face Crüwell's assault on the southern flank was the 2nd Scots Guards' motor battalion from 4th Armoured Brigade, strengthened on Gott's advice by gunners from the Support Group. This gallant screen of defenders inflicted heavy losses on the oncoming masses of Axis armour and motorized infantry, but nothing could stop the onrush. The two panzer regiments smashed across Armstrong's infantry positions. The South Africans lost 224 killed and 379 wounded but nearly all of them, 2790 in all, were taken prisoner. Armstrong was also captured, though Campbell and Davy managed to fight their way out in the chaos. By nightfall on 23 November *Afrika Korps* had followed its previous victories over 7th and 4th Armoured Brigades with the total destruction of 5th South African Brigade as a fighting force.

But the cost had been heavy. 'Ariete', shying away from the heavy fire of Campbell's gunners, had emerged virtually unscathed from its first tank battle; but no less than seventy-two panzers had been knocked out in the attack, reducing the tank strength of *Afrika Korps* to ninety runners. *Totensonntag* had seen the greatest German tank loss for a single day, and only Crüwell's belief that he had scattered the last of the British armour made that loss tolerable. Conversely, the British did not yet know that Crüwell's tank losses had given XXX Corps a decisive tank superiority. With Gatehouse's squadrons still hopelessly dispersed, Crüwell's victory over 5th South African Brigade stood out in distorted enormity. At last light on *Totensonntag*, there was no way of realizing, in either army, that *Afrika Korps'* victory was a Pyrrhic one.

Rommel meanwhile had little idea of Crüwell's precise intentions, let alone whereabouts on 23 November. The day had begun well for the *Panzergruppe* commander, with the arrival of Mussolini's permission for Gambara's corps to come under Rommel's direct command. According to Mellenthin, Rommel had then set off from *Panzergruppe* headquarters with the intention of joining Crüwell; he planned to supervise the intended hammer-blow by *Afrika Korps* in person. But Rommel never reached *Afrika Korps* headquarters. Instead he became caught up in the continued spirited advance by Barrowclough's 6th New Zealand Brigade from Bir Chleta to Point 175, subjecting the German 361st Regiment to heavy attack. Taking heavy losses, over 400 casualties, the New Zealanders stormed the eastern defences of Point 175 before being halted, now only 6 miles east of Sidi Rezegh airfield. The night of 23/24 November saw Rommel and Crüwell still out of touch, with Crüwell finally heading for a rendezvous with Rommel on the *Achsenstrasse* at 0600 on the 24th.

Eighth Army – Cunningham loses heart

By nightfall on 22 November Cunningham's worries at Eighth Army headquarters were mounting fast. Though he still had no details from

125

Norrie about XXX Corps' actual losses over the past three days, it was already clear that the original CRUSADER plan had been put badly out of joint. It was *Afrika Korps* which held the initiative in the armoured battle, not XXX Corps, and the still-imprecise British tank losses seemed to be approaching crisis point. If the offensive were to be maintained, it must be drastically re-thought. By the morning of 23 November Cunningham was convinced that he must transfer the onus from XXX Corps to XIII Corps, with Godwin-Austen taking up the running and Norrie's survivors providing what armoured support could be afforded. It was a question of reinforcing the only concrete success achieved to date: the westward advance of Freyberg's New Zealanders from Sidi Azeiz.

On the morning of the 23rd Cunningham therefore drove to XIII Corps headquarters and ordered Godwin-Austen to take over responsibility for the relief of Tobruk, with the two South African brigades now passing from XXX Corps command to XIII Corps. Almost immediately, however, the impossibility of this revised plan became apparent with grim confirmation of the previous day's results. As Cunningham saw the situation, the tally amounted to the virtual destruction of 7th Armoured Brigade, the reduction of 22nd Armoured Brigade to thirty-odd runners, and near-total obscurity over the fate of 4th Armoured Brigade. This horrifying state of affairs seemed to leave *Afrika Korps* as a mortal threat to any continuation of the offensive. Though Godwin-Austen remained buoyant, pointing out that all was going well on XIII Corps' front and Norrie's surviving forces were still able to offer support from south of Sidi Rezegh, Cunningham remained unconvinced. He therefore asked for Auchinleck to fly up from Cairo, effectively to decide whether to continue the CRUSADER offensive or call it off.

Auchinleck reached Cunningham's Maddalena HQ just before nightfall on *Totensonntag*, to be greeted by the latest tale of woe from XXX Corps: the liquidation of 5th South African Brigade. Cunningham gave his opinion that the accumulating British tank losses had probably left *Afrika Korps* with superiority in cruiser types. (This, in itself, is an interesting comment on the British view of the opposition, because the British distinction between cruiser and infantry tanks did not exist in the panzer forces.) Such a superiority meant that the surviving British armour could no longer guarantee security to the infantry from German tank attack. According to all previous experience, Cunningham could only deduce that there was now every chance of the troops east and south of Sidi Rezegh being cut off. And if this were to happen Eighth Army would be left with no reserves to stave off a German thrust right across the Frontier to Egypt, and the fate of 5th South African Brigade could well presage the fate of Eighth Army as a whole. Having unfolded this glum hypothesis, Cunningham formally asked Auchinleck to make the decision: whether to carry on with the offensive and risk losing all, or order a retreat which would at least leave Eighth Army in being.

Auchinleck never denied that Cunningham could well be right about the risk, but he also sensed that Cunningham, overwrought with his own problems, had overlooked one vital point. This was the eternal military truism, never more true than in the Desert, that the enemy always has troubles of his own. Auchinleck knew that *Afrika Korps* had received no dramatic injection of fresh resources since the launching of CRUSADER, nothing to cancel Eighth Army's long-term advantages in a continued battle of attrition. Given those advantages, any local gain of tank superiority by *Afrika Korps* was bound to be short-lived. Auchinleck therefore had no hesitation in ordering Cunningham to proceed with the offensive.

It was a great decision by a great general; nor, as Auchinleck was to prove at Alamein in the following July, was it to be unique. For all that, it was another example of the right decision being made for the wrong reasons. Auchinleck could not know that so far Cunningham had been fighting Crüwell rather than Rommel; that the Germans did indeed have problems of their own, but that most of those problems were being caused by Rommel's fluky and disjointed conduct of the battle. Auchinleck was, in fact, 'making a picture' of his own: of Rommel the eternal opportunist, so far admittedly still in control of the situation, but not far off the verge of desperation as his armoured assets continued to wane. Auchinleck, in short, was only half-right. Rommel's worries were real enough, but by the night of 23/24 November he believed, wrongly, that XXX Corps had been written off. It was high time for *Afrika Korps*, exploiting the victory now in its grasp, to come to the aid of the embattled garrisons on the Frontier.

Turning-point of CRUSADER: *Rommel plans the 'Dash to the Wire'*

The result was what has been described as the most controversial act in the whole of Rommel's military career[13] – the 'Dash to the Wire'. This was Rommel's attempt to reverse the whole battle in one dramatic stroke, converting the British invasion of Libya into an Axis invasion of Egypt. Nothing better shows the total extremes of confidence to which the rival commanders had been driven by the end of the first week of CRUSADER – Cunningham over-pessimistic, believing that the time had come to play it safe and retreat; Rommel over-optimistic, believing that

127

total victory now lay within his grasp. Both assessments were based on wholly inadequate interpretations of the two armies' actual fighting capacities. In Rommel's case the decision was prompted by his having been close enough to the action on 23 November to get the impression of overwhelming success, yet not close enough to appreciate Crüwell's true losses. From what he had seen on *Totensonntag*, Rommel believed that Eighth Army was now tottering on a knife-edge and that its total defeat was only one hard push away. In such a state of mind it was not surprising that Rommel failed to see that all he had to do to be assured of genuine victory was to keep *Afrika Korps* at Sidi Rezegh and build on the solid success already won there.

There was, moreover, the undeniable evidence of earlier Desert battles, when energetic drives into the British rear areas had resulted in runaway German successes. Such well-timed moves had overrun Cyrenaica in April and hurled back the BATTLEAXE offensive in June. In judging that the moment had arrived for a similar coup, Rommel had weighed his opponent well so far as Cunningham was concerned. Not until far too late, however, did Rommel appreciate the resolution of Auchinleck, whose study of earlier German victories had resulted in a determination never to be stampeded by surprise German thrusts. The 'Dash to the Wire' was an attempt to repeat, on a far grander scale, the *Totensonntag* victory which had caught 5th South African Brigade between *Afrika Korps* to the south and the German guns to the north. After *Totensonntag* Rommel proposed to drive south-west with *Afrika Korps*, herding XIII Corps into instant retreat and eventual destruction with its back to the minefields of the Frontier. Not for a minute did he pause to consider where this would leave *Afrika Korps* if XIII Corps refused to be panicked and stayed where it was. Once again, Rommel's *fingerspitzengefühl* played him false. To quote Mellenthin's telling words, 'When he came back to El Adem that night 23 November he was in a state of excited exultation, and at once began to issue orders which changed the whole character of the CRUSADER battle.'[14]

That this 'excited exultation' took the form of a personal brainstorm is proved by the signal which Rommel sent to Berlin at about midnight on 23/24 November:

Intention for 24 November, a) To complete destruction of 7th Armoured Division. b) To advance with elements of forces towards Sidi Omar with a view to attacking enemy on Sollum front.

When he sent this signal Rommel had not consulted with either Crüwell, Ravenstein or Neumann-Silkow; indeed, he had no clear idea of their whereabouts, let alone of the drastic reduction of *Afrika Korps'* armoured strength on *Totensonntag*. His plan to use Sidi Omar as a 'corner post' onto which to slam Eighth Army overlooked the fact that Sidi Omar was now in Godwin-Austen's hands, Libyan Omar having also fallen to 7th Indian Infantry Brigade. The Sidi Omar minefields were therefore now working for the British, not against them. Much more serious was Rommel's impatient rejection of the warnings of his staff. Both Westphal and Mellenthin were concerned at the westward progress made by the New Zealand Division over the past two days. They noted, however, that the New Zealanders were coming up piecemeal, by independent brigades. Their advice, which Rommel rejected, was for *Afrika Korps* to be kept at Sidi Rezegh, poised to give the New Zealanders the same treatment as had been meted out to the South Africans. 'Indeed it is my conviction,' writes Mellenthin, 'that if we had kept the *Afrika Korps* in the Sidi Rezegh area, we would have won the CRUSADER battle. The Eighth Army had a fatal practice of committing its forces in succession, and we could have destroyed them one after the other.'[15]

Rommel seems to have been completely confident of plunging Eighth Army into headlong panic. This confidence prevented him from taking positive action to give substance to such panic. His plan for the 'Dash to the Wire' did not include the destruction of the vital British Field Maintenance Centres in *Afrika Korps'* path. This would have guaranteed the immobilization of the remaining British armour, left high and dry with empty tanks, within a matter of hours. Mellenthin claims that the position of the FMCs was known at *Panzergruppe* headquarters; but Young, when he interviewed Ravenstein and Crüwell's Chief of Staff, Bayerlein, after the war, had no doubt that 'the Germans did not know [the FMCs] were there'.[16] Ravenstein and Bayerlein both insisted to Young that 'if we had known about those dumps, we could have won the battle'.

This ignorance may be seen as interesting confirmation of the parallel confusion bedevilling both armies throughout CRUSADER, with vital information not being passed from army headquarters to the divisions 'at the sharp end'. But it must also be taken as yet another instance of Rommel's impatient tendency to neglect supply considerations, which so often brought him to grief. For the second time in the Desert War, Rommel's opportunism was to be wrecked by his opponent's resolution. In April Wavell had stopped the German advance by tying Rommel down in siege warfare at Tobruk. Now, in the last week of November, Auchinleck's determination was to leave Rommel empty-handed on the battlefield. Spectacular coup though it was, the 'Dash to the Wire' was fated to be remembered as a gamble which failed, devoid of the victory which had lain within the *Panzergruppe*'s grasp.

Day 7 – 24 November

'Dash to the Wire' – *the* Panzergruppe

Once he had 'made his picture' of Eighth Army's imagined condition and conceived the 'Dash to the Wire', Rommel was all impatience to direct his master-stroke in person. He left El Adem at first light on the 24th, taking his Chief of Staff, Gause, with him and leaving Westphal to hold the fort at *Panzergruppe* headquarters. This apparent insanity, which split the nerve-centre of his own headquarters, is explained by the fact that Rommel, heedless of the formidable distances to be covered, expected to be back within 24 hours, if not before. 'You have the chance of ending this campaign tonight!' he told Ravenstein, whose 21st Panzer Division was to lead the advance, with 15th Panzer following and 'Ariete' keeping pace on the southern flank. Crüwell finally caught up with Rommel on the *Achsenstrasse* at 0600 and was frankly staggered by Rommel's plan. If Crüwell had had his way, *Afrika Korps* would have stayed where it was on the 24th, resting, repairing and replenishing its tank strength. It was not to get the chance again for the rest of the CRUSADER battle.

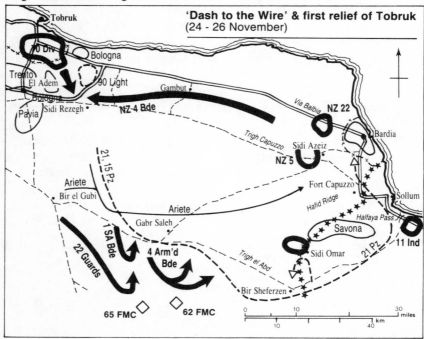

'Dash to the Wire' & first relief of Tobruk
(24 - 26 November)

From the outset Rommel's 'Dash to the Wire' bore little or no resemblance to the calculated, concentrated punch with which Crüwell had shattered 5th South African Brigade on *Totensonntag*. It began with the headlong advance of 21st Panzer Division shortly after 1030, with 15th Panzer and 'Ariete' belatedly following suit some two hours later. Out on its own, 21st Panzer roared south straight through the headquarters areas of 7th Armoured Division, 1st South African Brigade and XXX Corps at Bir el Gubi, encountering nothing but soft-skinned vehicles which scattered in panic – precisely the reaction for which Rommel had hoped. Rommel probably never knew how close he had come to capturing Cunningham himself, who had flown up that morning to confer with Norrie and Gott at Bir el Gubi. Amid the chaos, Cunningham was rushed back to his Blenheim aircraft which took off in the nick of time, narrowly missing a fleeing 3-ton truck. On the flight back to his headquarters, Cunningham was therefore left with the horrifying retinal image of XXX Corps scattered to the four winds.

If 21st Panzer had continued on its south-south-easterly course, giving the fleeing elements of XXX Corps no respite, Rommel's assurance to Ravenstein would almost certainly have come true. By 1130 there were no organized forces between 21st Panzer's spearheads and Eighth Army's two foremost Field Maintenance Centres. These were FMCs 62 and 65, less than 15 miles away and squarely in the path of 21st Panzer's onrush. But, as Hunt has put it, 'This battle is perhaps the best example of Rommel's ability to snatch defeat from the jaws of victory.'[17] On Mellenthin's evidence it is probably true to say that Rommel was heedless rather than ignorant of the nakedness of the FMCs. Cutting the logistic props from under Eighth Army played no part in his plans: he was obsessed with completing his advance to relieve the Frontier garrisons. For on reaching the Trigh el Abd 21st Panzer turned eastward along the desert track, heading for the Wire at Sheferzen and leaving the remnants of XXX Corps to continue their southward flight. The retreating British units included 22nd Guard's Brigade, dutifully resuming its original role of protecting XXX Corps' lines of communication. With 1st South African Brigade, the Guards eventually rallied to form a screen covering the two FMCs from the north. From then on, assuming that Norrie's forces were subjected to no further harassment, they would continue to draw vital sustenance from the FMCs.

By mid-afternoon on the 24th Rommel's dramatic intervention in the battle had prevented Eighth Army from regaining the initiative, but had also failed to destroy Eighth Army's forward source of supply. Rommel had injected a spectacular panic into the British rear areas, but he had not continued the destruction of Cunningham's forces. Worst of all, within 24 hours of Crüwell's three-division triumph on *Totensonntag*, Rommel had achieved the near-total dispersal of *Afrika Korps*. Rommel himself, with 21st Panzer Division, was approaching the Wire; Crüwell, with 15th Panzer, was labouring along the Trigh el Abd some 15 miles to the west; 'Ariete', having bumped into the rearguard of 1st South African Brigade, had never really got moving at all and was effectively stuck 10 miles south-east of Bir el Gubi. Nevertheless, blithely indifferent to what he had done to *Afrika Korps'* fighting strength by stringing it out over 40 miles of Desert, Rommel now sketched orders for a northward wheel to destroy 4th Indian Division with 15th Panzer attacking from the west and 21st Panzer from the east.

Crüwell again did his best to get Rommel to see sense. He pointed out that next to nothing was known of 4th Indian Division's true positions, whereas the dispersed *Afrika Korps* was again racked by supply problems. (Happily for Crüwell's peace of mind, he did not know how close *Afrika Korps* had come to solving all its supply problems by capturing the two British FMCs.) Nor did he believe that 'Ariete' would be able to give any effective assistance to 15th Panzer Division. But Rommel again overruled Crüwell and the two German commanders parted, each of them getting completely lost in the dark. By midnight on the 24th *Panzergruppe* headquarters at El Adem had no idea that a crucial attack was pending to the east while Rommel and Crüwell had disappeared, being forced to spend a miserably uncomfortable night out in the open, at the mercy of any passing patrol.

'Dash to the Wire' – Eighth Army: the great panic

24 November opened peacefully enough in the XXX Corps sector, a peace shattered in mid-morning by the lunging advance of 21st Panzer Division over XXX Corps headquarters and through the British transport areas. One very good reason why so many vivid accounts of the subsequent stampede back to the Frontier have been preserved is that they were written by war correspondents caught up in the rout. Perhaps the most famous is that of Moorehead, who had arrived at XXX Corps headquarters early that morning after witnessing the *Totensonntag* fighting of the previous day:

Another great swarm of vehicles rushed through the camp and now shells began to fall among them. It had been a bright early morning, but now the churned-up dust had blotted out the sun and visibility became reduced to two hundred yards or less. In this semi-darkness and confusion thousands of vehicles got hopelessly mixed so that men and vehicles of entirely different units travelled along together, and since many of the drivers had no orders they simply rushed ahead following anyone who would lead them. . . .

My party stuck to the Signals vehicle, but unknown to us the young officer inside had jammed his hand in the door and was semi-conscious. His driver simply went on as hard as he could in the direction away from the firing, which was south-east, and we followed blindly. Twice we stopped and, while men ran from one vehicle to another asking for orders and trying to find out what was amiss, more shells came over the horizon. We were being followed – and fast. So the hue and cry went on again. . . .

All day for nine hours we ran. It was the contagion of bewilderment and fear and ignorance. Rumour spread at every halt, no man had orders. Everyone had some theory and no one any plan beyond the frantic desire to reach his unit. We were just a few hangers-on of the battle, the ones who were most likely to panic because we had become separated from our officers and had no definite job to do. I came to understand something of the meaning of panic in this long nervous drive. It was the unknown we were running away from, the unknown in ourselves and in the enemy. We did not know who was pursuing us or how many or how long they would be able to keep up the pursuit and whether or not they would outstrip us in the end. In ourselves we did not know what to do. Had there been someone in authority to say "Stand here. Do this and that" – then half our fear would have vanished. So I began to realize, sitting there in the swaying car, how important the thousand dreary routine things in the army are. The drill, the saluting, the uniform, the very badges on your arm, all tend to identify you with a solid machine and build up a feeling of security and order. In the moment of danger the soldier turns to his mechanical habits and draws strength from them. . . .

These matters, I suppose, should have been obvious enough, but I personally only began to see them clearly during this ignominious retreat back into Egypt. I wanted badly to receive orders, and so, I think, did the others.

It was a crestfallen and humiliated little group of men that finally felt its way towards the frontier wire fence as dusk fell. We found a gap in the wire and as we plunged through it with a feeling of relief – even the fence between us and the unknown pursuer was something – a British major came up in a truck and began to organize us and knock some sense in us.[17]

In Eighth Army's 'great flap' of 24 November thousands of men shared the common experience of disorientation, fear, humiliation, and above all a horrifying sense that the whole military machine had inexplicably fallen apart. These sensations encouraged a conviction that Eighth Army's offensive had failed, or at the very least had suffered such a major reverse that large-scale withdrawals to re-group must ensue. But this was the logical reaction to a wholly illogical battle which had, in the space of a few hours, converted yesterday's battle zone into a rear area and yesterday's rear area into the new battle zone. Men closer to the real storm-centre of CRUSADER, the south-east approaches to Tobruk, saw the 'Dash to the Wire' very differently. 'To us,' wrote Crisp of 4th Armoured Brigade,

> it seemed as though Rommel had gone clean off his bloody head.
>
> We heard of the panic in the headquarters and supply areas, and were unpatriotically delighted at the thought of generals and staff officers fleeing for Alexandria or wetting themselves in slit trenches. It was the universal, if unmerited, reaction of the front-line troops to the thought of any form of disaster befalling the immunity of the rear areas. In this case we reckoned that the top command was making a complete mess of things anyway, and we could do just as well without them. We were also relieved to think that somebody else was getting the pasting and not us. . . .
>
> But back in the battle area – or what had been the battle area – the flap passed us by completely. We followed its course impersonally by the coloured arrows and rings on the map as though watching a blackboard exercise at OCTU. And never for one moment, either on the night when we got the first reports or at any time during the next few days when the crayoned arrows prodded deeper and deeper until they penetrated Egypt, did we have the slightest feeling of uneasiness about the situation in our rear. I do not think it an exaggeration to say that our twin emotions of relief that we were not involved, and gratitude for the respite it offered us, were the strongest things we felt about Rommel's raid. We just assumed that the German commander had made one hell of a blunder and in due course would get it in the neck.[18]

'Dash to the Wire' – Eighth Army: XXX Corps

Writing of the events of 24 November, Carver states that 'the rest of Eighth Army [ie those units not directly in the path of the German

134

advance to the Wire] was taking life remarkably serenely'.[19] Fair comment, perhaps, from an officer who had been swept up in the panic flight of XXX Corps and 7th Armoured Division headquarters that morning, but putting it rather mildly; the serenity or otherwise of 24 November depended very much on where you were.

The 24th was certainly a day of respite for XXX Corps, but by no means one of perfect peace. It saw the reconstitution of 4th Armoured Brigade as a fighting force, if only at half-strength for the moment, as tanks trickled in from all quarters on orders issued after a hard night's work by Gatehouse and his staff. This reassembly was still under way when Gatehouse had to launch his under-strength tank regiments against a large column of Axis transport heading south-east. The result was another helter-skelter encounter battle, with Gatehouse's Honeys enjoying the rare luxury of attacking without armoured opposition. The column was most satisfactorily scattered – revenge for the scenes of chaos at XXX Corps headquarters that morning – and, though the attack inevitably dispersed Gatehouse's tank strength again, the trade-off was of considerable importance, for the scattered transport had been moving up to join the armour of *Afrika Korps*, bringing not only badly-needed fuel and supplies but 88mm guns, and its failure to arrive in the Frontier zone delayed the arrival of 5th Panzer Regiment for the attack planned by Rommel for the morrow.

While 4th and 22nd Armoured Brigades hacked at *Afrika Korps*' supply line, the rest of XXX Corps was conforming to the American backwoods maxim: 'When they hand you a lemon, make lemonade'. Hustled south in the morning's flight, 22nd Guards Brigade and 1st South African Infantry Brigade redeployed in a protective screen north of the vital FMCs 65 and 62, 10 miles south of the Trigh el Abd. Campbell's 7th Support Group, drawing breath about 10 miles further east, faced about and prepared to harass Rommel's southern flank on the 25th.

'Dash to the Wire' – Eighth Army: XIII Corps

On Eighth Army's northern flank the 'Dash to the Wire' failed to prevent the continued westward advance of Freyberg's New Zealanders. The Frontier zone was left to 5th New Zealand Infantry Brigade, by now spread fairly thin on the ground between Sidi Azeiz, the western Bardia perimeter on the Via Balbia, and Capuzzo/Musaid/Sollum. This consolidated the gains made since Freyberg's northward push on 21 November, maintaining a breach in the original Axis Frontier barrier and keeping the Bardia garrison separated from the main body of the 'Savona' Division north-east of Sidi Omar.

Over 30 miles now separated 5th New Zealand Brigade's blocking force on the Via Balbia, west of Bardia, from the rest of Freyberg's division. In obedience to the changed CRUSADER plan, shifting the onus from XXX to XIII Corps, 4th New Zealand Infantry Brigade advanced west from Gambut to join the 6th Brigade, still holding its ground east of Sidi Rezegh. The New Zealanders were accompanied by Brigadier Watkins' 1st Army Tank Brigade, minus 42nd Royal Tank Regiment left back in the Frontier sector. Freyberg's armoured cover therefore consisted of eighty-six 'I' tanks (forty-nine Valentines with 8th Royal Tank Regiment and thirty-seven Matildas with 44th Royal Tank Regiment) with which to resume the northward drive and join up with 70th Division. This remained Godwin-Austen's overriding objective by nightfall on the 24th.

Eighth Army: Oasis Force and Desert Air Force

Reduced to its simplest terms, a diagram of the battle as it stood on the evening of 24 November would have shown the main forces of the two armies separated by about 50 miles and heading in opposite directions. *Afrika Korps* was stabbing eastward at the Frontier south of Sidi Omar; XIII Corps was stabbing westward at the Tobruk perimeter, which had been reduced to a wasp-waist by 70th Division's aborted breakout. But the leading unit of Eighth Army was now far off the map of the main battle area, nearly 250 miles away to the south-west. This was Brigadier Reid's Oasis Force, which had taken Aujila on the 22nd and followed its latest success by capturing Jalo on the 24th. Reid's men had excellently fulfilled their initial mission, taking out all the southern Desert airfields which the Axis air forces might otherwise have used. For the moment, however, Oasis Force had shot its bolt; its fuel consumption on the long detour via Landing Ground 125 had been far higher than expected and imposed severe limitations on subsequent patrol activity. At the same time Eighth Army's failure to relieve Tobruk and press on to the Jebel Akhdar according to schedule left Oasis Force dangerously isolated. After taking Jalo, therefore, Reid's men had no choice but to hang on where they were, living on half rations, until they could be relieved, nearly four weeks later. Though inevitably eclipsed by the high drama of events in the battle for Tobruk, the ordeal and successes of Oasis Force provide one of the finest achievements in the CRUSADER story.

Another notable achievement was that of the Desert Air Force, whose operations were inevitably dictated by the cut and thrust of the land battle. By nightfall on 23 November the short-range squadrons of the Desert Air Force had moved west to begin operations from the ground apparently secured by XXX Corps. The reconnaissance squadrons leap-frogged to new landing grounds at Sidi Azeiz and Gabr Saleh, while eight fighter squadrons began operations from the Maddalena region. All these new landing grounds, whose transplanted facilities were as incapable of instant flight as those of the sprawling FMCs, were imperilled by the 'Dash to the Wire'. With the Army no longer able to guarantee the security of his forward squadrons, Cunningham had no choice but to order their temporary withdrawal east of the Frontier. This withdrawal inevitably led to overcrowded airfields on the night of 24/25 November, but happily the opposition missed the chance of exploiting it. The temporary retreat of the Desert Air Force, pushed off its forward airfields by the 'Dash to the Wire', was largely cancelled out by the advance of the New Zealanders which pushed the forward Axis air squadrons off *their* forward airfields at Gambut. Finely executed as it was, the retreat of the Desert Air Force kept the considerable British advantage in air resources in being.

Though close integration between air and ground forces continued to elude the British, the troops remained deeply appreciative of the efforts of their airmen. 'It is significant,' writes Crisp, 'that up to this eighth day I have barely mentioned activity in the air. It was going on all the time, but in the tank units we were not involved beyond the sight of occasional packs of Stukas going over to dive-bomb our supply vehicles – though "dive-bombing" was a flattering description of the hurried passes which the Germans made in their anxiety to carry out their orders and get away again.'[20] It was a very different story 'on the other side of the hill'. 'Continuous heavy raids in the Sidi Omar area,' lamented the *Afrika Korps* War Diary for 25 November, the day after the Desert Air Force's hasty withdrawal, be it noted. 'Heavy losses among our troops. Where are the German fighters?'

Day 8 – 25 November

Afrika Korps *frustrated; unease at* Panzergruppe *Headquarters*

After dislocating *Afrika Korps* by the sheer pace of the 'Dash to the Wire' on 24 November, daybreak on the 25th saw Rommel complete the process by ordering piecemeal attacks on the scantiest of Intelligence.

Grudgingly accepting that 'Ariete' had been blocked out of play, Rommel ordered a simultaneous northward advance by both panzer divisions on either side of the Frontier, 15th Panzer against Sidi Omar, 21st Panzer via Halfaya against Sollum and Capuzzo. Rommel also ordered Neumann-Silkow to detach a force from 15th Panzer for a southward pounce on Jarabub, 120 miles to the south. Fortunately for 15th Panzer this move never got under way, being cancelled in favour of the northward drive; but the necessary orders and counter-orders were symptomatic of the operational malaise imposed by Rommel, over Crüwell's head, on *Afrika Korps*.

Not content with ordering *Afrika Korps* to advance north, south, and north-east, Rommel brusquely completed the work begun by 4th Armoured Brigade's attack on *Afrika Korps'* supply column on the previous afternoon. As the sorely-tried 5th Panzer Regiment came struggling up to the Frontier, Crüwell ordered it to rejoin 21st Panzer Division without delay; but Rommel immediately intervened again. He cancelled Crüwell's order and flung 5th Panzer Regiment into an attack on 7th Indian Infantry Brigade at Sidi Omar from the south-east.

Rommel's reckless dispersal of his dwindling resources was heavily paid for by 5th Panzer Regiment, starting with the loss of Colonel Stephan, one of *Afrika Korps'* best panzer commanders. He was killed by strafing British fighters as 5th Panzer Regiment moved off for the first of two abortive attacks, Major Mildebrath taking command of the regiment. Rommel's impulsiveness had effectively brought him back to where he had been at the end of April, squandering irreplaceable panzer resources against troops in fixed defences and enjoying adequate artillery support. The first of Mildebrath's attacks was beaten off by 1st Field Regiment, Royal Artillery. The second, in the afternoon, was repelled by the combined fire of 25th Field Regiment, Royal Artillery, 68th Medium Regiment, Royal Artillery, a troop of 57th Light Anti-Aircraft Battery, Royal Artillery, and a battery of 2nd South African Anti-Tank Regiment. This furious counter-fire by the gunners defending 7th Indian Infantry Brigade included 'everything but the kitchen sink': 25-pounders, 5.5-inch howitzers, 40mm Bofors AA guns and 2-pounder anti-tank guns. It was signal punishment for the unit which only 48 hours before had been savaging 5th South African Brigade in the *Totensonntag* attack. Nightfall on 25 November found 7th Indian Infantry Brigade still secure within the Sidi Omar defences, with 5th Panzer Regiment licking its wounds to the south, now reduced to only ten fit tanks.

Neumann-Silkow had meanwhile advanced on the Libyan side of the Frontier, pushing towards Sidi Azeiz in obedience to Rommel's delusion that the New Zealand Division was ripe for destruction from the east. Instead 15th Panzer Division began by blundering into the repair section area of 1st Army Tank Brigade, north-west of Sidi Omar. Thanks to a most gallant last stand by the crews of sixteen crippled Matildas which had been awaiting repair, 15th Panzer wasted the entire morning and lowered its already critical ammunition stocks still further for little appreciable result. By the afternoon of the 25th 15th Panzer was almost in as great a state of disarray as it had been on the 24th, its only dubious gain being to overrun the headquarters of 5th New Zealand Infantry Brigade at Sidi Azeiz. So far from gathering in the fruits of final victory, Neumann-Silkow had therefore found that the cupboard was bare; his intended victims were about their own business, preparing to reopen the battle for Tobruk 40 miles to the west. The depressing fortunes of the 25th left Neumann-Silkow with no option but to head for Bardia on the following day to replenish his division.

Rommel's orders for Ravenstein's 21st Panzer Division (deprived as it was of its vital 5th Panzer Regiment) were to execute a north-westerly sweep from the northern exit of Halfaya Pass, destroying the last of Eighth Army's forces east of the Frontier while 33rd Reconnaissance Unit drove east to Habata to sever Eighth Army's link with its railhead at Misheifa. Instead, hammered by British air attacks throughout the day, 21st Panzer never got moving at all. By nightfall on the 25th Ravenstein was still south of Halfaya, hoping to get 5th Panzer Regiment back on the morrow. The medium bombers of the Desert Air Force had wrought particular havoc on the already-depleted 33rd Reconnaissance Unit, destroying about twenty vehicles and thereby frustrating the only element in Rommel's gaseous planning which might have done serious damage to Eighth Army.

25 November, 1941, is therefore an admirable candidate for the honour of being the worst day's performance in Rommel's entire career. His persistent squandering of *Afrika Korps'* strictly limited resources, stubbornly ignoring the commonsense pleas of his highly competent subordinates, had, in Carver's words, 'succeeded in reducing Crüwell's command to complete ineffectiveness'.[21] To make matters worse, Rommel's self-delusion was not yet spent: he believed that he could still win the battle on the Frontier sector, resuming on the 26th. He persisted in this belief despite a message from Westphal at *Panzergruppe* headquarters at 1630 that 90th Light Division, left to hold the fort in the Belhamed/Sidi Rezegh area, had come under heavy attack from the New Zealanders. Though a second message from Westphal around midnight on 25/26 November reported that all was now quiet at

Belhamed, the opening chord of the resumed battle for Tobruk had been sounded, and Rommel had closed his ears to it.

Eighth Army: XXX Corps

While 4th Indian Division and the Desert Air Force were frustrating Rommel's disjointed assaults on the Frontier, Norrie's major worry on the 25th was *Afrika Korps'* most recent acquisition: 'Ariete'. By the 25th Gambara's armoured division was easily the most up-to-strength unit of *Afrika Korps*, having suffered least of all during *Totensonntag* and its aftermath. On 25 November, however, Gambara's half-hearted attempts to push 'Ariete' along the Trigh el Abd to the Frontier were frustrated by Pienaar's 1st South African Brigade – not in a stand-up fight, but rather in stand-off inaction.

It was one of the oddest interludes of the whole CRUSADER battle: an encounter between two hostile units, each of which simultaneously chose to do nothing as the least dangerous option. There were excuses for each side's inactivity. Gambara, a realist, was painfully aware of the inadequacies of Italian armour; he knew that on *Totensonntag* the lion's share of the work, and all the damage done, had been shouldered by the professionalism and technical excellence of the two panzer divisions. These had vanished to the east by the 25th, leaving 'Ariete' painfully isolated. For his part, Pienaar was not unreasonably hag-ridden by what had happened to 5th South African Brigade on *Totensonntag*. Now, less than 48 hours later, he was up against one of the three victorious armoured divisions which had carried out the *Totensonntag* attack. No more unreasonably, Pienaar besought Norrie for tank support for 1st South African Brigade.

With no clear idea about the whereabouts or intentions of Rommel's armour, Norrie refused to commit his re-forming tank battalions to what could well turn out to be another 'half-cock' action. He advised Pienaar to consider disengaging and moving south to join 22nd Guards Brigade; but Pienaar recoiled from the idea of being caught on the move by 'Ariete'. So 'Ariete' and Pienaar's brigade stayed where they were and 4th Armoured Brigade took no action against 'Ariete' – with the exception of Crisp's patrolling tank troop, which suffered the utter frustration of locating 'Ariete' while the Italians were refuelling. Throughout the five hours which it took 'Ariete' to refuel, Crisp kept up a running commentary on what an ideal target lay at XXX Corps' mercy. 'Every gun in the area, plus a couple of visits from the RAF,' lamented Crisp later, 'followed up by a tank attack, would have knocked "Ariete" right out of the war. . . . For five hours the 4th Armoured Brigade did nothing, the 7th Armoured Division did nothing, the South African Brigade a mile or two to the south did nothing. At half-past four, their refuelling completed, the Italian tanks broke off in groups of eight or ten and moved off to the north-east.'[22]

Eighth Army: XIII Corps

In contrast to the tragi-comic overtones of XXX Corps' inertia, 25 November found XIII Corps moving up to its start-line for the break-in to Tobruk. In the early morning 4th New Zealand Infantry Brigade closed up to Zaafran, 5 miles east of Belhamed, while the 6th Brigade gained the ridges east of Sidi Rezegh and recovered the airfield. Ten miles to the north-west the 70th Division's breakout advance was resumed for the first time since the 21st, deepening the Tobruk salient by another 2 miles. As with the first relief attempt by XXX Corps, Godwin-Austen had ordered that the capture of Belhamed, Sidi Rezegh and El Duda by the New Zealanders was to precede Scobie's final breakout. Freyberg planned to accomplish this by the unusual expedient of a night attack timed to go in at 2100 on 25/26 November, with the 4th Brigade attacking Belhamed and the 6th Brigade pushing through Sidi Rezegh to El Duda.

The mood of confidence underlying XIII Corps' coming attack was not merely the result of the comfortable distance separating the New Zealanders from the uproar on the Frontier. It was helped by an excellently timed and worded message to the men of Eighth Army from Auchinleck, as he prepared to fly back to Cairo from Cunningham's headquarters:

> During three days at your Adv.HQ I have seen and heard enough to convince me, though I did not need convincing, that the determination to beat the enemy of your commanders and troops could NOT be greater, and I have no doubt whatever that he will be beaten. His position is desperate, and he is trying by lashing out in all directions to distract us from our object which is to destroy him utterly. We will NOT be distracted and he WILL be destroyed. You have got your teeth into him. Hang on and bite deeper and deeper and hang on until he is finished. Give him NO rest. The general situation in North Africa is EXCELLENT. There is only one order, ATTACK AND PURSUE. ALL OUT EVERYONE.

C. AUCHINLECK
General C-in-C

141

This message has been unkindly dismissed as a bald pep-talk, evoking the vainglory of Foch in the First World War: 'My centre is pierced; my flanks are turned; the situation is excellent – I attack!' But remember that this was the first real situation report 'from the top' which Eighth Army had had since crossing the Frontier on the 18th. After the panic of the 24th, it was badly needed. Nor was Auchinleck's message mere bravado, a desperate piece of 'picture-making'. It was drafted after the first encouraging reports had come in of the dispersed condition of Rommel's armour; after the failure of the first attack on Sidi Omar, where Messervy's infantry and artillery were holding their ground; after confirmation of XIII Corps' continued exploitation towards Belhamed and El Duda.

But Auchinleck was not prompted solely by the imminence of XIII Corps' attack and by the need to reassure the troops after their discomfiture on the 24th. Auchinleck had come to a painful but momentous decision, one which, without careful preparation, could have a catastrophic effect on the troops' morale. This was the absolute need to remove Cunningham from command of Eighth Army, in the midst of the battle, and replace him with a comparative unknown enjoying Auchinleck's complete trust.

Though the responsibility could only be Auchinleck's, his decision was taken neither impulsively nor entirely alone. It followed discussions between Auchinleck and his RAF commanders, Tedder and Coningham, and, after returning to Cairo on the 25th, with Minister of State Oliver Lyttelton. It was born of an unease with Cunningham's growing defensive-mindedness which Auchinleck had detected from the evening of the 22nd. Having obtained Lyttelton's agreement, Auchinleck signalled his decision to the Chief of Imperial General Staff in London, General Brooke. This was followed four days later by a telegram from Auchinleck to Churchill in which the imperative need to replace Cunningham was carefully spelled out. The confidence and simplicity of Auchinleck's phraseology was admirably calculated to ensure Churchill's approval:

The enemy is trying desperately to regain the initiative. In this he has succeeded in part, but locally and temporarily only. So long as we can maintain our pressure towards Tobruk, the real initiative is ours and we can disregard diversions towards Sollum or Maddalena or even farther east, temporarily inconvenient and unpleasant as these may be. Every effort is being devoted to the forwarding of the offensive by the New Zealand Division and other groups of XIII Corps towards Tobruk and I believe it is going well. While in the forward area I heard of no one who was not sure that we are going to win. There may be disquieting episodes but the general situation should remain greatly in our favour.

I have telegraphed DCGS to say that I have decided to replace General Cunningham temporarily by General Ritchie, my present DCGS. This is not on account of any misgiving as to present situation in my mind but because I have reluctantly concluded that Cunningham, admirable as he has been up to date, has now begun to think defensively instead of offensively, mainly because of our large tank losses. Before taking this drastic step I gave matter prolonged and anxious consideration and consulted Minister of State on my return here this afternoon. I am convinced I am right though I realize undesirability of such a step at present moment on general grounds. I will try and minimize publicity as much as possible.

Meanwhile we are making every effort to replace losses of tanks and armoured cars and Eighth Army are organizing defences against enemy raids in our back areas such as Sidi Omar, Maddalena and railhead.[23]

Auchinleck's decision to sack Cunningham was all the harder because of Cunningham's fine record in Ethiopia and his undoubted success in preparing Eighth Army for the CRUSADER offensive. Nor was Cunningham dismissed for any tangible error made during the first eight days of the battle; Auchinleck was fair-minded enough to recognize that Cunningham's sudden pessimism was entirely correct according to all military logic. But this was a battle for which more was needed than stock British Army 'Staff solutions'. Cunningham had to go for not having the mental resilience to cope with the built-in crises of Desert warfare, and Auchinleck accepted the likelihood (given stock War Office reactions to such dismissals) that Cunningham's many fine qualities would no longer be put to full use. Sadly, so it turned out; Cunningham was not given subsequent employment at corps level, a more fitting ceiling (as happened with his successor Ritchie). The rest of his war was spent as Commandant of the Staff College at Camberley, as GOC Northern Ireland, and as GOC Eastern Command.

No time was lost in effecting the take-over. Cunningham received the devastating news of his supercession in a letter from Auchinleck delivered to Maddalena on the 26th by Auchinleck's Chief of Staff, General Sir Arthur Smith, a few hours before Ritchie flew up from Cairo to take over. Nothing became Cunningham more than his departure from Eighth Army. 'General Cunningham, though he could not bring himself to agree with the Commander-in-Chief's reasons,

143

took the heavy unexpected blow with complete loyalty and selfless-ness.'[24]

Two decisions, taken within 48 hours by the rival theatre comman-ders, had now been made, and they were to transform the development of the CRUSADER battle. Rommel's decision to stake all on the 'Dash to the Wire' had enabled Eighth Army to regain the initiative outside Tobruk; Auchinleck's decision to replace Cunningham signified that the battle would be fought out to the bitter end. Events on 26 November were swiftly to show the extremes of validity between the thinking of the German and British commanders, as Eighth Army snatched the initiative again.

Day 9 – 26 November

Eighth Army: XIII Corps

By the night of 25/26 November the CRUSADER schedule was over 48 hours behind, disrupted as it had been by the mauling suffered by XXX Corps in the first four days; but the major initial objective of CRUSADER, the relief of Tobruk, was at last within the grasp of XIII Corps. The efforts of Freyberg's New Zealanders were about to restore the initiative to Eighth Army, but it was rapidly becoming clear that the link-up with Scobie would only bring fresh problems in its train. How could the link-up be most effectively exploited, and what would its immediate sequel be?

There had been no detailed planning for this sequel, for the simple reason that none was possible; subsequent operations would depend very much on the resources still left to Rommel at the moment of Tobruk's relief. The original CRUSADER plan had aimed at the virtual destruction of *Afrika Korps* as the essential preliminary to the link-up with Scobie, but that had gone out of the window. By the 25th the relief was only still 'on' because the 'Dash to the Wire' had carried the hitherto victorious *Afrika Korps* out of the way. It was hoped that Rommel's gamble had seriously depleted the tank strength of *Afrika Korps*, but the latter was still a force to be reckoned with. Rommel's reaction to the New Zealanders' breakthrough would be crucial. Godwin-Austen could therefore plan for nothing more ambitious than punching through 90th Light to join forces with Scobie, and then levering the Axis forces westward to the Tobruk – El Adem road. After that . . . it would be a question of wait and see.

Freyberg, however, saw the situation very differently. He only had

144

two brigades (the 5th New Zealand Brigade was still back east in the Bardia/Sidi Azeiz region), and these were very much out on a limb, short on artillery support and beset with logistic problems. By the night of 24 November he was thinking of getting *into* Tobruk, rather than extending a hand to join Scobie in a further advance to the west. 'If we had petrol and ammunition,' he signalled to Godwin-Austen just before midnight on 24/25 November, 'we might have been in Tobruk early tomorrow. As it is we hope to get there tomorrow night but impossible to be definite.' Carver also quotes Freyberg's words to Colonel W. Gentry, New Zealand Division's GSO1: 'We have to get in and join Tobruk. I have no doubts whatever that we have to go in, but we may have to go in tomorrow night' (ie the night of 26/27 November).

As it turned out this was too optimistic a forecast, despite a useful diversionary attack ordered by Scobie which narrowed the gap between 70th Division and Belhamed to 3 miles. Dawn on the 26th found Inglis' 4th New Zealand Infantry Brigade in possession of Belhamed after a night of confused marching and unexpectedly tough fighting. El Duda, however, had proved too ambitious an objective for Barrowclough's 6th Brigade, which was in no little disorder after the night's operations. The situation was further confused when daylight on the 26th enabled the German gunners around Belhamed to bombard 4th Brigade. Inglis interpreted this fire as coming from El Duda and asked for an air attack there to silence the guns.

Though Freyberg had mistakenly reported that both Belhamed and Sidi Rezegh had been captured, it was clear to Godwin-Austen that fighting was continuing at both places and that the impetus on the 26th must be sustained by 70th Division. Scobie's attack went in at 1210, carried by Willison's massed surviving 'I' tanks and 1st Essex Regiment. Only two 'I' tanks were lost in the capture of El Duda but the Essex Regiment, following up, suffered forty casualties in the bombing attack which Inglis had requested. This prompted a tart signal from Scobie to Freyberg at 1515: 'We are at El Duda – ensure NOT bombed'. But, when it came to deciding how to exploit this vital news, Freyberg had to accept that his 6th Brigade still had its hands full north of Sidi Rezegh airfield while 4th Brigade's most important task must be to ensure the retention of Belhamed.

Freyberg in fact only had one uncommitted battalion: Lieutenant-Colonel S. F. Hartnell's 19th, at Zaafran. Hartnell's battalion was therefore ordered to undertake yet another night march, aided by a squadron of 'I' tanks from 44th Royal Tank Regiment, ducking round Belhamed to the south to join up with Willison. The 6-mile march began at 2130 on the 26th and first contact with the Essex Regiment came 75 minutes later, after surprisingly little resistance had been encountered en route. By 0100 on 27 November, the 19th Battalion had closed up to come under Willison's command, 'adopted' by 70th Division as a reserve force posted between El Duda and Belhamed.

Godwin-Austen had hoped that the link-up, when it came, could be immediately exploited by a joint advance west to El Adem. This, however, was rendered impossible by the desperate late-night battle fought by 6th New Zealand Brigade to clear the escarpments north of Sidi Rezegh. Some of the toughest resistance encountered by the New Zealanders came not from Sümmermann's Germans but from the Italians of 9th Bersaglieri Regiment. The Axis defenders hit back with everything they had, turning even the solid shot of their anti-tank guns against the attacking New Zealanders:

> These projectiles had torn large portions of flesh from the bodies of their unfortunate victims and it would be hard to imagine a more unpleasant sight or a more heavily contested battlefield. The Bersaglieri Regt fought with much greater determination than is usually found among the Italian troops, and the numbers of their dead and the positions in which they lay showed that they had kept their guns in action to the last. Indeed it was reported from several of our men that the first to break under our onslaught were the German troops and that the Bersaglieri had been the last to yield. It was against such opposition as this that the exhausted and sadly depleted ranks of 24 and 26 Bns had fought their way to victory and their victory was complete.[25]

Freyberg's New Zealanders had therefore momentarily exhausted themselves in succeeding where the tank men of XXX Corps had failed during the first five days of CRUSADER. But the fact that a corridor had at last been opened into Tobruk had barely time to sink in before all was imperilled by the return of *Afrika Korps* from the Frontier.

Eighth Army: XXX Corps

Twenty miles to the south XXX Corps passed 26 November in a day of total contrast to the grim fighting being endured by the New Zealanders north of Sidi Rezegh. It was the second day of recuperation for Norrie's tank men, as the planners of XXX Corps struggled to rebuild a fighting force from the chaos wrought by the first week's fighting.

The easiest decision to make was that 7th Armoured Brigade was out of the battle, impossible to reconstitute from the resources available. Davy's survivors were therefore pulled out and sent east to railhead, en route for rest and reconstruction in the Delta. By nightfall on the 26th the first of the replacement tanks was beginning to trickle through, but, even after their arrival, 22nd Armoured Brigade still only had forty-four Crusaders, while 4th Armoured Brigade had no more than seventy-seven fit Honeys. This total of 121 tanks was in depressing contrast to the 600-odd tanks with which XXX Corps had begun the CRUSADER battle.

For the men, the day's respite was the first chance in eight days to shed foul and tacky clothing, the hardier spirits steeling themselves to shave. As Crisp put it, 'It was almost impossible to produce a lather, and shaving was a matter of hacking through the undergrowth with a succession of blades. Our skin, too, was cracked and tender from the dry, bitter winds and the extremes of temperature fluctuating between midday's heat and midnight's freeze.' But XXX Corps' day of rest was relative; there were those who barely recognized it as such:

> Always last to enjoy any of the rare relaxations that came our way were the tank drivers. At night, when the tanks stood in their mute rows and the crews were silent in sleep and exhaustion, grimy drivers would be seen going over the engines and tracks. In the morning's darkness they would be the first up to get their Honeys ready for the move. Their personal battle consisted in keeping their tanks mobile. An immobile tank could mean death for all. It was reasonable, no doubt, that they should have last access to the water and soap and towels; they were always covered in grease and oil and an abrasive amalgam of sand.[26]

The effect of XXX Corps' regrouping on November 25–6 was to maintain the equivalent of a two-brigade armoured division with which to continue operations against the three armoured divisions of *Afrika Korps*. It would soon become apparent that XXX Corps' aggregate tank strength was still greatly superior to that of *Afrika Korps*, even after the tremendous initial British losses. But this advantage was cancelled by the persistent dispersion of the British armoured effort. Even when reduced to mere handfuls of fit tanks, the Axis armoured divisions continued to function *as* divisions, with their full complement of supporting arms – and, consequently, greatly enhanced effect.

The most painful lesson of the first four days' action for the British was the failure to keep adequate anti-tank support close up with the armoured brigades, making it easy for the Germans to draw the British tanks onto anti-tank screens which advanced with the panzers. But the fundamental difference in 'all-arms' tank mentality between the two armies is typified by the effective break-up of 7th Support Group after *Totensonntag*. Instead of re-forming the Support Group into two groupings, and assigning these to each of the armoured brigades, the Support Group was broken up into individual raiding forces. The day of the 'Jock Column' had arrived.

Named for the redoutable 'Jock' Campbell VC, Eighth Army's most celebrated hero, the 'Jock Column' idea seemed at the time to be the ideal use of Eighth Army's most effective individualists. The idea of these roaming columns, vanishing into the Desert to strike at the enemy's rear where least expected, was a natural favourite with the journalists who, so far from querying its soundness, generally united to praise it to the skies. This had the interesting effect of enshrining a legend at birth, very much as the British Press had already done with Rommel himself. This is how Moorehead described the birth of the 'Jock Columns':

> In this hour of great crisis Auchinleck cast about for any expedient that would delay the enemy until we could return to organized attack. He found it in the Jock Column. Brigadier Jock Campbell had previously spent some time in the desert organizing small fighting patrols. Each was just a handful of vehicles – perhaps a troop of armoured cars, two or three troops of guns and a company of lorried infantry. They were provisioned for a few days or a week or more and the command handed over to a young lieutenant who knew the Desert. Each commander's orders were simply these – 'Get out and behind the enemy. Attack everything you see.' It was an order that had a peculiar attraction to a certain type of young Englishman. The elements of the Drake and Raleigh tradition were in it. Piracy on the high sands. Where the British Army still bungled hopelessly in massed fighting, there were still the individuals who fought brilliantly in small guerrilla groups, who had the inspiration of feeling free and the taste for quick and daring movement.'

Not a word, be it noted, that the main reason why the British Army 'bungled hopelessly' in its tank battles was its pernicious habit of scattering its resources and denying the tank units proper support. That being the undoubted case, 'piracy on the high sands', though doubtless a natural journalist's 'story', was nevertheless a recipe for more of the same. But Moorehead's enthusiasm was not spent:

> So the partisans of the desert were born. As fast as they could be put together Auchinleck rushed them out into the desert. Within a few days he had twenty or more groups behind the enemy lines, burning, looting, shooting, cutting in and running away, laying ambushes in the *wadis*, destroying enemy tanks, breaking signal wires, laying false trails, breaking up convoys, raiding airfields, getting information.

148

14. Panzer Mk II tanks

15. Panzer Mk III

16. Panzer Mk IV. Note the *Afrika Korps* symbol on the side.

17. German 88mm gun

It was a make-shift while the Eighth Army worked desperately to reorganize itself but it began taking immediate and heavy effect.[27]

As Sir David Hunt has commented, 'It is always interesting for the amateur writer to see how the professional does it.' There were grains of substance in all this, but not many. To take just one example, it was largely fallacious – though a pat journalist's phrase – to think in terms of 'the enemy lines' during CRUSADER. In the bewildering fluidity of the campaign there were few such 'lines', except after dark when the defensive leaguers were formed for the night. It was true that Auchinleck prescribed ad hoc mobile columns to harass any Axis forces making a push towards Eighth Army's railhead. But no man knew better that the decisive battle still rested with the tank brigades, and he grudged every gun and platoon drawn off from the main battle area. And it was certainly not true that the 'Jock Columns' went into action with 'immediate and heavy effect'.

On 26 November the main efforts of the dismembered Support Group were directed towards finding and harassing 'Ariete', which after its stand-off encounter with the South Africans on the 25th had vanished north-eastwards 'into the blue' north of the Trigh el Abd. Without the least embarrassment from the newly-formed 'Jock Columns', which never came near it, 'Ariete' wandered uncertainly onwards to fetch up for the night 15 miles west of Capuzzo. Had there been any cohesion to the dying Axis effort on the Frontier, 'Ariete's' belated arrival could have been put to good effect by Rommel, still rummaging for a victory which was not there for the winning.

The Panzergruppe: *end of the Frontier gamble*

By the morning of 26 November Rommel had accepted that *Afrika Korps* must head back west to counter the latest advance by Freyberg's New Zealanders to the threshold of Tobruk. But he was still chasing the mirage of a decisive, pincer-movement victory over XIII Corps on the Frontier, despite Crüwell's efforts to get him to see reason; and the result was another day of squandered effort and resources on the German side. The day also saw Rommel's subordinates, struggling to reconcile harsh reality with the decreasing reason of their commander's requirements, stretch the interpretation of their orders to the limit.

Neumann-Silkow, for instance, was ordered to attack Capuzzo and Sidi Azeiz, then rush south and help Mildebrath take Sidi Omar. East of the Frontier Ravenstein (still bereft of 5th Panzer Regiment) was to attack northwards from Halfaya to Sollum, then face about and tackle

11th Indian Brigade blocking the Sollum-Sidi Barrani road. But instead Mildebrath turned the Sidi Omar attack over to 33rd Reconnaissance Unit – which failed, as Mildebrath had already failed twice – and spent the 26th protecting Crüwell's makeshift headquarters from the attentions of Campbell's 'Jock Columns' from the south-west. Obsessed with the paramount need to replenish 15th Panzer Division in Bardia, Neumann-Silkow narrowly missed the headquarters both of 5th New Zealand Brigade and XIII Corps in his advance past Sidi Azeiz to the Bardia perimeter. Further north an ad hoc battle group from 15th Panzer Division, commanded by Colonel Briel with four or five patched-up tanks gleaned from 15th Panzer's field workshops, tried to open the Via Balbia at Menastir, 5 miles west of Bardia. But Briel's attack also failed in the teeth of spirited resistance by the 22nd New Zealand Battalion, which held on to Menastir and continued to deny the *Panzergruppe* a direct road link between Bardia and the Tobruk perimeter.

Neumann-Silkow therefore achieved nothing on the 26th other than his aim of commencing his division's replenishment in Bardia. Meanwhile, as the situation continued to deteriorate on the Tobruk sector, Westphal at *Panzergruppe* headquarters had taken a momentous step. Unable to contact either Rommel or Crüwell but still in touch with Ravenstein, Westphal on his own responsibility recalled Ravenstein west of the Frontier, with a direct order to break through to Bardia via Capuzzo/Sollum. From Bardia Ravenstein was to make his best speed westward to re-enter the fight at Tobruk. By his intervention, Westphal intended that at least one of the panzer divisions should be extricated from the wasteful chaos on the Frontier and speedily returned to the decisive sector on the Tobruk approaches. What he actually achieved was the reunification of *Afrika Korps* at least 24 hours earlier than would have been possible if Rommel had had his way.

Ravenstein's efforts to comply with Westphal's order were complicated by his mistaken belief that 15th Panzer was in full control of the Capuzzo/Sollum sector. Instead of linking hands with 15th Panzer between Capuzzo and Musaid, 21st Panzer, lacking its tanks, came off decidedly the worst. The fight continued until after dark and cost 21st Panzer seventy-six dead; Maori casualties were two dead, four wounded and two missing. Here, in miniature, was a perfect example of the needless attrition which Rommel's wasteful orders had inflicted on his own forces in the 'Dash to the Wire'. Indeed, Ravenstein only managed to resume his advance and break through to Bardia because the Maori Battalion's defence area was so wide. By midnight on 26/27 November, however, the two panzer divisions were back together at Bardia, reunited for the first time in three days.

As Ravenstein has testified, a stormy encounter took place when he reported to Rommel at Bardia. In fairness, Rommel's explosive reaction was probably the result of being jerked from sleep (of which Rommel had had all too little since the morning of the 24th) by Ravenstein's unexpected arrival. But, even when all allowances are made for Rommel's fury, the incident nevertheless shows how far from reality Rommel had distanced himself by the 'Dash to the Wire' and its failure:

'General,' said von Ravenstein, 'I am happy to tell you that I am here with my division!' Rommel exploded. 'What do you mean, you are here?' he demanded. 'What are you doing here? Did I not give you an order to be ready to attack from Halfaya in the direction of Egypt?' Von Ravenstein produced his copy of the countermanding wireless message. Rommel exploded again. 'A fake!' he shouted. 'This is an order from the British; they must have our code!'[28]

Even when Rommel had been convinced that Ravenstein's recall order was genuine, his anger was only diverted to enraged denunciation of 'that damned Westphal'; but the storm soon passed. It had almost certainly been prompted by Rommel's inner consternation that his plans had gone badly awry, and that his own subordinates seemed to be more in control of the situation than he was. This explanation is reinforced by Rommel's later apology to Westphal and generous acknowledgment that Westphal's action had been fully justified. For so it was. Thanks mainly to Westphal, *Afrika Korps* was, by the morning of 27 November, at last able to revert to counterstrokes in full, concentrated strength, for the first time since *Totensonntag*. Nor could there be any doubts as to what the next move of *Afrika Korps* must be: an immediate westward drive against Freyberg's rear to defeat the New Zealanders and reimpose the investment of Tobruk.

Day 10 – 27 November

The Panzergruppe: Afrika Korps' *return to Tobruk*

Though Rommel had certainly accepted that the time had come for *Afrika Korps* to restore the status quo ante on the Tobruk sector, his orders for the 27th gave no sign of urgency. He did not order Mildebrath to rush 5th Panzer Regiment north from Sidi Omar to complete the reunification of *Afrika Korps*. Nor did he order his two panzer divisions to drive westward in close contact. Rommel's orders amounted, rather, to a vague description for a final tidying-up in the Frontier area before the return to the west got under way. Only Ravenstein was to head directly for Tobruk along the Via Balbia (without waiting for 5th Panzer

Regiment to rejoin); Neumann-Silkow was to take 15th Panzer Division off at right-angles to 21st Panzer Division's advance, south to Sidi Azeiz. There Neumann-Silkow was anxious to complete the replenishment of his division by looting what he believed to be the New Zealanders' forward supply dump. While all this was going on, Mildebrath was to retake Sidi Omar and hand it back to the 'Savona' Division before setting off to rejoin Ravenstein. All this added up to a second dispersal of *Afrika Korps* before its reunification had been fully achieved.

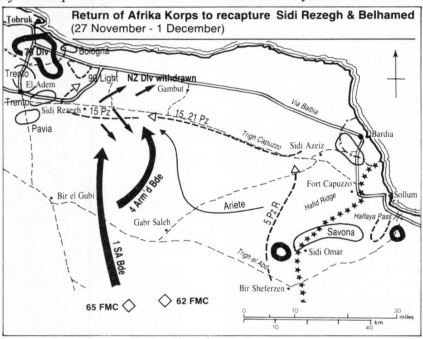

Piecemeal though they were, the operations of *Afrika Korps* on the 27th opened with a heartening success when 15th Panzer Division rolled clean over the headquarters area of 5th New Zealand Brigade at Sidi Azeiz. With 23rd and 28th Brigades 15 miles to the south-east at Capuzzo and Sollum, the only forces at Brigadier Hargest's disposal were B Company, 22nd Battalion and E Troop, 5th New Zealand Artillery Regiment. They nevertheless put up a most gallant if hopeless fight for their Brigade headquarters: four exposed 2-pounder *portés* against the forty-odd tanks of Cramer's 8th Panzer Regiment. The upshot was forty-four New Zealanders dead, forty-nine wounded and 696 officers and men captured and marched off to Bardia. Rommel himself, who had watched the whole engagement, congratulated Hargest on the gallantry of his resistance.

152

The capture of 5th New Zealand Brigade HQ had direct and fateful consequences for Hargest's countrymen at Sidi Rezegh. It had the effect of persuading Rommel that there was no more useful work for 15th Panzer Division in the Frontier area. He therefore ordered Neumann-Silkow to set off at once for Sidi Rezegh along the Trigh Capuzzo, but held back 33rd Engineer Battalion to mop up Capuzzo. This latest change of plan completed the ruin of Rommel's original hopes for the 'Dash to the Wire', because it left 23rd and 28th Battalions in possession of Capuzzo and Sollum. Rommel stayed behind to watch Neumann-Silkow's engineers take out Capuzzo but the attack was another costly failure: only one company area secured by nightfall, 100 German casualties, the New Zealanders still holding their main positions, and 15th Panzer Division denied the services of an important unit on its decisive westward advance.

Having committed 33rd Engineer Battalion to this fruitless and costly attack, Rommel rushed off in the opposite direction to join 15th Panzer Division's advance along the Trigh Capuzzo. This made excellent progress and by noon was approaching Gasr el Arid, 20 miles from Sidi Azeiz and roughly halfway to Sidi Rezegh. But Ravenstein and 21st Panzer were not keeping pace along the Via Balbia, 10 miles to the north. Instead the advance of 21st Panzer was halted in short order by the resistance of 22nd New Zealand Battalion at Menastir, which beat off Ravenstein's attacks for the whole of the afternoon. By 1600 Ravenstein had decided that he had no choice but to give up, head south and follow Neumann-Silkow along the Trigh Capuzzo. Here was a telling comment on the reduced strength of *Afrika Korps* by the tenth day of CRUSADER: a panzer division fought to a standstill by a lone battalion. Ravenstein's enforced change of plan at least enabled him to retrieve 5th Panzer Regiment, which came north from Sidi Omar to rejoin Ravenstein's command at Sidi Azeiz. But the setback at Menastir put Ravenstein a whole day behind Neumann-Silkow and left 15th Panzer Division out on its own, as the two armoured brigades of XXX Corps re-entered the armoured battle on the afternoon of the 27th.

Eighth Army: XXX Corps

The 27th was a depressing day for XXX Corps, one which could well have squandered all the gains in reconstituted tank strength made over the past two days. In brief, the tenth day of CRUSADER was a day of British muddle at the top and uncoordinated failure on the battlefield, a wasted opportunity to exploit the mistakes made by Rommel since 24 November.

This was not because Rommel's errors had escaped diagnosis 'on the other side of the hill'. It must be stressed that the German 'Dash to the Wire' had been correctly assessed at all levels, from tank troop commander to Auchinleck himself, as a cardinal blunder. It had allowed XIII Corps to crack the Tobruk siege perimeter and join hands with 70th Division; it had allowed 4th and 22nd Armoured Brigades to reassemble a joint strength of 119 tanks. By the 27th, therefore, XXX Corps was well placed to counter-attack and block Neumann-Silkow's attempt to reopen the Tobruk battle with the lone westward advance of 15th Panzer Division. But the reconstituted British armour, despite all the painful lessons of the previous ten days, failed to prevent the return of 15th Panzer and sustained another humiliating reverse in the process.

By 1300 *Panzergruppe* HQ's urgent messages to hasten *Afrika Korps'* return had been intercepted by British Intelligence, and it was clear that a strong panzer force was complying by moving west along the Trigh Capuzzo. At Eighth Army HQ the instant, 'knee-jerk' interpretation was hopelessly wrong: the familiar wishful thinking that at last the remnants of the German armour were retreating. But that did not matter. Comfortably deluded though he was as to Rommel's intentions, Ritchie still gave the correct order for the German armour to be counter-attacked. Norrie had meanwhile withdrawn 22nd Armoured Brigade from the task of protecting Freyberg's rear, putting it back under Gott's command. That did not matter either, for Gott also correctly ordered 22nd Armoured Brigade to straddle the Trigh Capuzzo and block the German line of advance. But the missing link was the failure to bring 4th Armoured Brigade 20 miles north, to a position from which it could simultaneously attack the German armour from the flank. Neither Norrie nor Gott modified the complacent, bet-hedging orders to 4th Armoured Brigade: to be ready to advance north-west to El Adem, or attack northwards towards the Trigh Capuzzo, according to circumstances. It was therefore hardly surprising that the reaction of 4th Armoured Brigade when it came, was belated, disjointed and a total failure.

The armoured battle got under way at 1345, with Scott-Cockburn's 22nd Armoured Brigade meeting 8th Panzer Regiment head-on 3 miles east of Bir Chleta. This confrontation pitted forty-five British cruisers against thirty-seven German mediums and thirteen light tanks – the tank strength to which 15th Panzer Division had been reduced since *Totensonntag*. Given the built-in superiority of the 50mm tank gun over the British 2-pounder, and Scott-Cockburn's chronic lack of artillery support, the odds were very much in the Germans' favour; the panzer professionals were adept at using their light tanks to draw the British fire, leaving their mediums 'unfired on'. Scott-Cockburn's crews

154

nevertheless fought magnificently and gave their all for two hours, trying to win time for Gatehouse to bring 4th Armoured Brigade into action and engulf 8th Panzer Regiment from the south-east. But when Gatehouse's leading crews arrived on the Trigh Capuzzo they found it crawling with 15th Panzer's supply columns. With no German armour in sight, the German transport seemed easy meat and the Honey crews plunged in to attack, to be stopped dead by the expert speed with which the German anti-tank crews brought their guns into action. Unexpected German reinforcements in the form of nine more panzers, driving straight into battle from their field workshops north of the Trigh, stiffened the anti-tank defence and cost 4th Armoured Brigade nineteen tanks.

By the approach of nightfall on the 27th the two British armoured brigades had failed decisively in their first combined attack on an isolated portion of Rommel's armour. There could be no denying that the honours had gone to Scott-Cockburn's men, whose gallant delaying action had prevented 15th Panzer Division from striking into the New Zealand positions that day. Scott-Cockburn and Gatehouse ended the day well-placed to join forces, keeping the Trigh Capuzzo blocked and renewing the battle at first light on the 28th. But instead, in a disastrous miscalculation left uncorrected by either Gott or Norrie, 4th and 22nd Armoured Brigades went into the time-honoured Desert ritual of withdrawing separately to leaguer for the night – 4th Armoured Brigade to the south, 22nd Armoured Brigade to the south-west. The net effect was to keep the British armour dispersed and to leave the Trigh Capuzzo wide open for a resumed advance by 15th Panzer Division on the 28th. Unwittingly presented with a unique chance to give *Afrika Korps* a decisive piecemeal mauling, XXX Corps had 'dropped the catch', and it was the suddenly exposed New Zealanders who would have to pay the price.

Day 11 – 28 November

Eighth Army: XIII Corps

The events of the 27th did little to change the priorities of XIII Corps, which was still faced with the task of consolidating the 'Tobruk corridor'. Since the first day of the German 'Dash to the Wire', Godwin-Austen had communicated an admirable self-reliance to his front-line commanders. He had refused to be panicked by the uproar in the rear areas and the apparent loss of his line of communications. 'Yes, everyone tells me I have lost my L of C; but I say I have got my objective,' he cheerfully told Hunt on the afternoon of the 26th. 'I say that Godwin plus his objective and minus his L of C is much better than Godwin minus his objective and plus his L of C.'[29] But this buoyancy was about to take the form of a dangerous slowness, not helped by Ritchie's comfortable belief that Rommel was on the run, to appreciate the true danger of the returning German armour.

The failure of 22nd and 4th Armoured Brigades to stop 15th Panzer on the 27th did not prompt a XIII Corps regrouping on the 28th. Instead, XIII Corps attacked the position still held by Mickl Group (consisting mainly of 155th Infantry Regiment) between Belhamed, El Duda and Sidi Rezegh. This was taken out in decisive style on the afternoon of the 28th by 18th New Zealand Battalion, aided by Matildas from 44th Royal Tank Regiment. Their finely-executed attack ended with the capture of Lieutenant-Colonel Mickl and 637 men of the 155th. But the southern most New Zealand battalion, the 6th, was still being troubled by the Böttcher Group west of Sidi Rezegh when, at 1700, startling news came from the eastern sector. German forces had pushed along the escarpment to overrun the main New Zealand dressing station east of Point 175, capturing all the staff and a thousand patients. (As the latter included wounded from both armies, about 900 Germans were taken out of British care by their own side.) By last light of the 28th it at last became clear to the British commanders that a major threat to the New Zealand Division was boiling up to the east. This was not another isolated raid: panzer forces were massing in strength between Point 175 and Bir Sciafsciuf.

Neumann-Silkow did not know how close this latest advance by 15th Panzer Division had come to overrunning XIII Corps HQ as well. By nightfall on the 28th Godwin-Austen's HQ Staff were uneasily deployed in battle order to defend their position, unable to dig in because of the limestone outcrop. Rather than stand his ground and squander resources in a wasteful battle of position, Godwin-Austen decided that his best option was to shift his Corps HQ into the Tobruk perimeter for the time being. The move was accomplished with some difficulty (the minefields, wire and trenches of the Axis siege lines and British defences took a lot of negotiating) but XIII Corps HQ was in its new secure position by dawn on the 29th. In reporting his shift of position to Eighth Army HQ, Godwin-Austen signed off with a characteristically defiant flourish. 'The corridor to Tobruk is perfectly secure and open to the passage of our troops and will be kept so. Have arrived there without incident. Press may now be informed that Tobruk is as relieved as I am.'[30]

Godwin-Austen's confidence yielded good copy for the war correspondents, as well as coining one of the more memorable phrases of the Desert War; but it was not mere whistling in the dark. The XIII Corps commander firmly believed that the 'Tobruk corridor' *would* be kept secure – by the two armoured brigades of the reconstituted 7th

156

Armoured Division, backed by Pienaar's 1st South African Brigade coming up from the south.

Eighth Army: XXX Corps

By nightfall on 27 November, when Ritchie urged Norrie and Godwin-Austen to prevent the 'escape' of *Afrika Korps* to the west, 1st South African Brigade had developed a unique importance. After the travails of the past week, Pienaar's South Africans represented Eighth Army's last intact infantry reserve west of the Wire. The trouble was that Pienaar was painfully aware of the fact. Since the liquidation of 5th South African Brigade by *Afrika Korps* on *Totensonntag*, Pienaar had seen his paramount duty as keeping 1st South African Brigade in being for the decisive engagement. His reaction to the whirling shifts and changes of the CRUSADER campaign, and to the obvious fact that Eighth Army HQ was not in full control of the battle, was to attempt nothing which might lead to the premature and futile sacrificing of his brigade. To this end Pienaar was fully prepared to demand cover from the armoured brigades wherever he happened to be, rather than expose his infantry by following the tank men in their dashes about the Desert. The inevitable result was to deprive 7th Armoured Division of much of its mobility, and this was certainly the case by nightfall on the 28th. Pienaar's cautious advance during the day had carried 1st South African Brigade 12 miles south of Sidi Rezegh, halting for the night with the leaguers of 4th and 22nd Armoured Brigades between the South Africans and the nearest German forces. The move had therefore done nothing to reinforce either Freyberg's hard-pressed New Zealanders, or to restore a fully offensive role to 7th Armoured Division. When the Tobruk battle burst into renewed life on the 29th, the movements of 4th and 22nd Armoured Brigades would be severely restricted by concern for Pienaar's South Africans.

The Panzergruppe: 'Ariete' and 21st Panzer Division

The other piece of XXX Corps 'fumble' on 28 November was the failure of Campbell's Support Group columns to block 'Ariete' out of play. 'Ariete' had begun a hesitant return from the Frontier zone on the 27th, advancing some 10 miles south of 15th Panzer Division's drive along the Trigh Capuzzo. On the 28th 'Ariete' encountered the scouting forces of the Support Group, whose columns were now deployed in a wide arc between the Trigh el Abd and the Trigh Capuzzo. Conditioned by Ritchie's urgings not to let *Afrika Korps* 'escape' to the west, the Support Group was more than content to nudge 'Ariete' away to the north-west, standing its ground and keeping Pienaar's South Africans covered from the east. This the Support Group chose to interpret as a stand-off local victory, herding 'Ariete' back into what was fondly believed to be an enveloping Eighth Army net east of Sidi Rezegh. But what the Support Group had unwittingly done was to ensure a wholly unexpected Axis counterstroke on the 29th: the participation of 'Ariete' in a converging attack on Freyberg's New Zealanders by all three divisions of *Afrika Korps*, briefly reimposing the Axis siege of Tobruk.

As with every *Afrika Korps* counterstroke planned since the beginning of CRUSADER, Rommel and Crüwell had both spotted the same opportunity but were in disagreement on how to exploit it to fullest advantage. The opportunity was the isolation of the New Zealand Division, which the British were apparently content to leave without reinforcement outside Tobruk. By nightfall on the 28th Neumann-Silkow was already in position with 15th Panzer Division closed up to the easternmost New Zealand positions. Ravenstein with 21st Panzer Division had suffered chronic delays in their advance along the Trigh Capuzzo because of fuel shortages, but would be ready to support 15th Panzer's operations on the 29th. Finally, having disengaged from the Support Group columns, 'Ariete' was coming in from the south-east, heading for Point 175.

The disagreement between Crüwell and Rommel was over the objective of the planned attack. Taking account of the ever-waning panzer strengths, Crüwell was content to put the New Zealanders under such sudden pressure that they would pull back into Tobruk. But Rommel, as ever, was far more ambitious. Still seemingly oblivious to his savagely reduced resources, he wanted the New Zealanders cut off and annihilated where they stood. Both generals envisaged opening the attack with a deep wheel to the west by 15th Panzer Division, which would enable a hammer-and-anvil onslaught on the New Zealand positions: 15th Panzer from the west and south-west, 21st Panzer from the east and north-east, with 'Ariete' filling the gap from the south-east. In the end Rommel had his way and overruled Crüwell, but Rommel's plan proved to be beyond the strength of the panzer divisions on the 29th, and the main honours that day went unexpectedly to 'Ariete'.

Day 12 – 29 November

The New Zealanders at bay

By first light on 29 November Freyberg's battle-worn battalions had been fighting non-stop for the ridges and strongpoints of Sidi Rezegh and Belhamed for a week. They now occupied a stretched oval of terrain measuring roughly 9 miles by 4, with Freyberg's HQ north of the Trigh Capuzzo 3 miles south-east of Belhamed. Zaafran, the north-eastern extremity of the New Zealand position, was held by the 19th Battalion, Point 175, the south-eastern extremity, by the 21st Battalion. The 25th Battalion was strung out along the escarpment between Point 175 and Sidi Rezegh, the latter being held by the 26th and 24th Battalions. Belhamed, the north-western extremity, was held by the 18th and 20th Battalions. Four miles separated Belhamed from its twin eminence to the west, El Duda, held by 32nd Tank Brigade and the 1st Essex Regiment of 70th Division.

Though Freyberg had spread his forces thin on the ground, he had done so in the firm expectation of early reinforcement by Pienaar's South Africans coming up from the south. But, even if the South Africans had kept their expected rendezvous, the New Zealanders would still have been in desperate need of water, food and ammunition after their week's ordeal at Sidi Rezegh. These were delivered by one of the most extraordinary improvisations of the whole CRUSADER battle: a massed truck convoy 260 vehicles strong. It was assembled at Maddalena by Brigadier G. H. Clifton, Chief Engineer of XXX Corps, loaded from the dumps at No.62 FMC, then navigated by Clifton himself on a 40-mile night run across the Desert. On the final stage of its journey the convoy had to traverse territory occupied by 'Ariete' and the advance units of 21st Panzer Division, but reached the Trigh Capuzzo and ran safely westward to enter the New Zealand divisional area before dawn.

Arriving at the eleventh hour, Clifton's convoy gave the New Zealanders the strength to fight on for three more vital days: the Third Battle of Sidi Rezegh (29 November–1 December). It ended with the New Zealanders battered from their positions and withdrawn from the CRUSADER battle, incapable of giving more, with the *Panzergruppe*'s recapture of Point 175, Belhamed and Sidi Rezegh, and Tobruk once more sealed off by Axis forces. Yet the immolation of the New Zealanders had not been in vain. Their last stand wore down *Afrika Korps* to such an enfeebled degree that Rommel, counting the cost of a truly Pyrrhic victory, had finally to accept that the *Panzergruppe*'s only chance of survival was retreat. Rommel's last chance of fighting CRUSADER to a draw had depended on a quick and painless restoration of the status quo ante at Sidi Rezegh. That had been denied him by the last stand of the New Zealanders, which in turn would hardly have been possible without the running of Clifton's supply convoy on the night of 28/29 November. Never was it more true that, in Rommel's own words, 'Supply was the basis of the battle.'

The Panzergruppe

The first day of *Afrika Korps'* pincer movements against the New Zealand Division began disastrously, with the loss of the first German general captured in the Second World War. At first light on the 29th, as he set out for the conference at *Afrika Korps* HQ which Crüwell had ordered, Ravenstein drove straight into the positions of 21st New Zealand Battalion at Point 175. Only a couple of hours before, Ravenstein had chatted with Rommel's former ADC, Schmidt (now commanding a company in 15th Panzer Division) on the Trigh Capuzzo. This was probably why Ravenstein chose the name 'Schmidt' in an ill-fated attempt to foil his captors:

> It was terrible, because I had on me the Chief of Staff's map with all our dispositions and had not time to destroy it. When I saw that there was no way out, I determined to call myself 'Colonel Schmidt' and hoped that they would not notice my rank badges. But then I was taken up to General Freyberg. You know how we Germans mention our name when we are introduced? I clicked my heels and bowed and before I could stop myself I had blurted out, 'von Ravenstein, General!'[31]

Such was Ravenstein's unhappy personal delivery of the *Afrika Korps* attack plan into Freyberg's hands, but this invaluable look at the enemy's cards did the British little immediate good. It enabled the defenders of El Duda to be alerted that 15th Panzer would be setting about them that afternoon, but no decisive British counterstroke was possible as long as 7th Armoured Division was tied down by the need to protect Pienaar. The actual capture of Ravenstein was much more useful, effectively keeping 21st Panzer out of the action throughout the 29th. By the time that Crüwell had appointed Böttcher to take over 21st Panzer, and Mickl to take over Böttcher's group, and Böttcher had arrived at 21st Panzer divisional HQ, it was late afternoon and 21st Panzer was not even on its start-line for the planned attack on Zaafran. This left the main weight of *Afrika Korps* operations resting on 15th Panzer and 'Ariete' throughout the day.

The encircling advance of 15th Panzer Division got under way at 0815, sliding unimpeded south of Point 175 and the wreckage-strewn Sidi Rezegh airfield to pass *Afrika Korps* HQ, on the escarpment 4 miles south of El Duda, at 1100. By 1300 15th Panzer had wheeled north across the Trigh Capuzzo and was facing east, poised for its assault on El Duda. This raged for over six hours, with attack after attack repelled by

160

1st Essex and the 2/13th Australian Battalion. The latter troops were veterans of the long siege under Morshead, left behind in Tobruk after the evacuation of 9th Australian Division (see p.73). Despite energetic backing by the last twenty-four Matildas of 4th Royal Tank Regiment, the defenders of El Duda were briefly forced out of the positions at the tip of their salient, south of the *Achsenstrasse*; but the lost ground was recovered by the Australians in a storming night attack at 0130 on the 30th. It had been another day of frustration and attrition for 15th Panzer, which by the morning of the 30th was down to a strength of twenty-eight medium and eleven light tanks.

The failure of 15th Panzer Division to isolate the New Zealand Division from the main body of XIII Corps in Tobruk was offset by the wholly unexpected success of 'Ariete', in circumstances which would have been ludicrous if they had not required the New Zealanders to pay such a brutal price. At 1515 a lone South African armoured car entered the New Zealand lines, establishing the first direct radio link between Pienaar and Freyberg's HQ. Freyberg seized the opportunity to order Pienaar to waste no time in advancing to Point 175, but Pienaar again refused to hazard his brigade when the radio link subsequently broke down. This was naturally unknown to 21st New Zealand Battalion at Point 175, which was briefed to look out for the approaching South Africans. At 1700, with the light already fading, a column of vehicles was sighted approaching Point 175, headed by what seemed to be armoured cars – but it was not the South Africans. It was 'Ariete' advancing confidently in the belief that Point 175 had already fallen to 21st Panzer! The men of the 21st Battalion did not realize their mistake until the Italians were right on top of them; only 200 shaken New Zealanders managed to escape captivity as 'Ariete' occupied Point 175, virtually without a fight.

The freak victory of 'Ariete' at Point 175 coincided with 21st Panzer's sole gain of the day: a 2-mile push at last light to take Bir Sciuearat from 19th New Zealand Battalion. The 29 November therefore ended with 'Ariete' and 21st Panzer firmly lodged in the New Zealanders' eastern sector. Though 15th Panzer had fared ill against El Duda, it was still perfectly placed to attack Sidi Rezegh on the 30th, finally catching the New Zealanders between hammer and anvil.

Eighth Army: XXX Corps

For the tank men of 7th Armoured Division, 29 November was another baffling and frustrating day. Though patrols had detected the approach of 'Ariete' from the eastward, 4th and 22nd Armoured Brigades were not unleashed in a mass attack against the indifferent Italian armour – prey for which the British tank crews, only too aware of the panzers' material superiority, had lusted since the outset of CRUSADER. Instead, the British armour was again held back to cover the advance of Pienaar – an advance which failed to materialize. For Pienaar's fellow South African Bob Crisp, wearily soldiering on with 3rd Royal Tank Regiment in 4th Armoured Brigade, awareness of the growing fulmination against Pienaar's obsessive caution was naturally painful:

> I overheard a staff officer saying to our CO: 'Uncle George [Brink] is all right, and Uncle George's boys are all right; but Uncle George's nephew [Pienaar] is just bloody awkward. We can't get him to fight a battle, or even to move to a place where he might have to fight a battle.'

There is a distinct note of tense control in Crisp's attempt to reconcile his very real resentment with loyalty to his fellow countryman (and superior officer):

> Perhaps it is as well to leave what, at the time, was a contentious subject with the comment that Dan Pienaar may have overdone the interpretation of suggestions made to him not to risk any more disasters.[32]

As for the 'Jock' Columns of the Support Group, which on the 28th had so unfortunately patted 'Ariete' in the direction of Point 175, 29 November was a day of more effective operations. The Support Group worked its way north across the Trigh Capuzzo into the rear area of 21st Panzer Division and launched a number of nuisance attacks. While presenting no outright threat to 21st Panzer, these attacks certainly encouraged a readiness to 'look over the shoulder'. Added to the confusion caused by the loss of Ravenstein in the morning, they certainly helped prevent any energetic westward moves by 21st Panzer for most of the day.

Frustrating though their inactivity was to the British tank regiments of XXX Corps, it had one vitally important result. In what was rapidly becoming a crucial battle of attrition, *Afrika Korps* continued to fritter away its remaining tank strength while that of 7th Armoured Division continued to be reinforced. The time was fast approaching when the sheer quantity of British tank fire-power would at last outweigh the hitherto superior quality of the few remaining panzers.

Day 13 – 30 November
The Panzergruppe: *assault on Sidi Rezegh*

By the morning of 30 November Crüwell was contemplating the waning resources of *Africa Korps* with deepening pessimism. Two weeks before, on the eve of the British attack, *Afrika Korps* had numbered 133 tanks in 15th Panzer and 111 in 21st Panzer. Now, on CRUSADER's thirteenth day, 15th Panzer was down to thirty-nine tanks and 21st Panzer to twenty-one. Happily for Crüwell's peace of mind, he could not know that 7th Armoured Division's tank strength now stood at 120: a British advantage of tank numbers of exactly two to one. But Crüwell did know that his hopes of forcing the New Zealanders back into Tobruk with a single heavy attack – like driving a cork through the neck of a bottle – had failed. He also knew that Rommel was still intent on destroying the New Zealanders where they stood, seemingly oblivious to *Afrika Korps*' enfeebled plight – and to the continuing threat posed from the south by the British armour and the South Africans.

Rommel's seemingly insane disregard for hard realities and mulish persistence with the Sidi Rezegh battle can be explained (if not justified in full) on several counts. There was, first and foremost, the panzer specialist's instinctive pursuit of battles of encirclement and annihilation. This was how every German victory since September 1939 had been won and, as long as there was a chance of crushing the New Zealanders, Rommel was incapable of passing it up. Taking a wider view, from the tactical to the strategic, Rommel still believed that he could fight the British to a standstill, then punish or panic them into giving up. The fact that Eighth Army, over the past ten days, had survived both punishment and panic and seemed determined to fight it out to a finish, never dismayed Rommel. His fighting instinct told him that the army which still had one tank on the field at the end of the battle would win and he was determined that it would be his. And Rommel was encouraged by the speed with which XIII Corps had withdrawn towards Tobruk after *Afrika Korps*' return from the Frontier. Sustained pressure could well reduce the forces in Tobruk to a point when they could be overwhelmed by a sudden converging attack. If this could be achieved while Eighth Army still had no substantial forces between the New Zealanders and the Frontier, the *Panzergruppe* still had a chance of taking Tobruk and maintaining its positions on the Frontier.

For 30 November Rommel therefore named Sidi Rezegh as the main objective, with Belhamed to follow at the earliest opportunity. While 'Ariete' and 21st Panzer exerted all possible pressure from the eastward, the main attack was to be pressed by 15th Panzer, seconded by the artillery and infantry of Mickl Group and 90th Light Division south and north of the New Zealanders' western positions. Before this could be attempted, however, 15th Panzer's 8th Panzer Regiment had to be hastily retrieved from an errant westward move towards El Adem, made in response to a decoding error, another instance of the remarkably high percentage of human error which bedevilled the operations of both armies throughout CRUSADER.

The attack on Sidi Rezegh was entrusted to Crüwell and, as on *Totensonntag*, he executed it with cold professionalism. While 8th Panzer Regiment was brought back and replenished for the attack, the artillery of 15th Panzer Division began to bombard 24th New Zealand Battalion from the south-west. Mickl Group's artillery meanwhile opened fire on the 26th Battalion from the Bir Bu Creimisa Ridge, barely 2 miles south of the Sidi Rezegh escarpment to which the New Zealanders were clinging. The defenders of Sidi Rezegh represented all that was left of Barrowclough's 6th New Zealand Brigade after a week of non-stop fighting: twenty-six officers and 829 men. With immense gallantry, unsupported by counter-bombardment and with only fifteen surviving 'I' tanks at their backs, Barrowclough's men stood their ground under the mounting weight of German shellfire.

Their plight has been compared[33] to 'Waterloo without a Blücher'. Withdrawal was impossible: pulling out of Sidi Rezegh would only have permitted 15th Panzer to sweep through to Belhamed and complete the encirclement of the whole Division. Barrowclough's men stuck it out with one hope – that 4th Armoured Brigade and Pienaar's South Africans, on the move at last, would arrive in time. But no help had come by 1600, when 15th Panzer's attack finally rolled forward (delayed, among other problems, by an unusually timely and well-aimed Desert Air Force raid on *Afrika Korps* HQ). As the panzers crushed 24th Battalion in a merciless three-pronged envelopment from the north, north-west and west, Mickl Group's infantry drove north against 26th Battalion. Within ninety minutes all was over: Barrowclough's two battalions had virtually ceased to exist, with 600 of them captured as Sidi Rezegh passed yet again into German hands.

Eighth Army: XXX Corps

It had taken the loss of Point 175 to jolt Norrie into personally directing Pienaar's advance to the relief of Freyberg's Division. The relief march by the South Africans on the 30th was to be covered by 7th Armoured Division, which had undergone yet another reshuffle. All 120 British tanks were now concentrated under Gatehouse's command, but the change brought no easement to the crisis of the New Zealand Division. When the tentative advance of one of Pienaar's battalions towards Sidi Rezegh ran into vigorous artillery fire, it was hastily brought back. Deciding against a costly relief march direct 'to the sound of the guns' at Sidi Rezegh, Norrie decided to kill two birds with one stone: recover Point 175 from the Italians, then relieve the New Zealanders by driving westward along the escarpment.

The trouble with Norrie's plan was that it required Gatehouse's tanks to defeat the Italian armour first – but Gatehouse's tanks were already under firm orders to cover the South Africans as they advanced across the open Desert from surprise attack by 'Ariete', 21st Panzer, or both. As ever, it was a distracting and essentially defensive brief. In a series of indecisive encounters in the Desert south of Point 175, 4th Armoured Brigade inflicted no serious damage on 'Ariete', though the Honeys of 5th Royal Tank Regiment claimed sixteen M-3s destroyed that afternoon. 'Ariete' was still holding its ground at Point 175 when Pienaar's South Africans finally reached Bir Sciafsciuf shortly before 1600, 7 miles east of Point 175, and almost 13 miles from where Barrowclough's New Zealanders were fighting for their lives at Sidi Rezegh. Inevitably Pienaar insisted on securing his new position at Bir Sciafsciuf before launching a tentative probe towards Point 175 after dark. This was entrusted to a mere three companies, which were withdrawn instantly to Bir Sciafsciuf after running into opposition which inflicted twenty-four South African casualties. Small wonder, therefore, that Freyberg sent a bitter personal message to Pienaar that night: 'Sidi Rezegh was captured this afternoon. Our position is untenable unless you can recapture it before dawn on 1st December. You will therefore carry out this task at once.'

Though it is certainly true that Pienaar's refusal to advance in time meant that only desperate measures could have saved Sidi Rezegh on the 30th, the task set him on the night of 30 November/1 December was a stark impossibility. Between Bir Sciafsciuf and Sidi Rezegh lay not only 'Ariete' at Point 175 but the infantry of 21st Panzer Division, with 5th Panzer Regiment grouped at Bir Sciuearat, 1½ miles north of Point 175. The real damage had been done by the flank march ordered by Norrie, when he took Pienaar under his direct command on the 30th. An all-out smash at 'Ariete' that afternoon, with the South Africans in close support of Gatehouse's tanks, *might* have regained Point 175 and forced reinforcements through to Barrowclough in time (assuming, that is, that 5th Panzer Regiment remained inactive at Bir Sciuearat). But Norrie's decision to roll up the Axis forces by an attack along the escarpment from Bir Sciafsciuf was not only much too ambitious for the force at his disposal, it was too late anyway. Norrie ordered Pienaar to wait until first light on 1 December before complying with Freyberg's order. Away to the west, however, Norrie's opposite number, Crüwell, had already issued the orders destined to win *Afrika Korps'* last victory in CRUSADER, knocking the New Zealanders clean out of the battle.

Day 14 – 1 December

XIII Corps: the New Zealanders overwhelmed

By first light on 1 December Godwin-Austen was reflecting bitterly on the hubris which had prompted his cheery announcement 'Tobruk is as relieved as I am' only 48 hours before. On the evening of the 30th Godwin-Austen had turned down Barrowclough's request that the remnants of 6th Brigade, after their ordeal at Sidi Rezegh, should be permitted to withdraw into Tobruk. Still hoping for XXX Corps to come to the rescue, Godwin-Austen had ordered Barrowclough's survivors to rally on 4th Brigade for the defence of Belhamed. But the XIII Corps commander was painfully aware that Freyberg's men were down to their last throw and sent a gloomy signal to Ritchie at Eighth Army HQ spelling out the consequences. If Pienaar failed to recapture Point 175, and Gatehouse failed to keep 15th Panzer Division from launching further attacks on the New Zealanders, Godwin-Austen recommended that XIII Corps should waste no time in pulling back into the Tobruk perimeter. Any further attrition suffered outside Tobruk following the considerable expenditure of ammunition and fuel during 70th Division's break-out could well make it impossible for XIII Corps to guarantee the defence of Tobruk.

Confronted with this appalling prospect at the moment when he was planning to resume Eighth Army's offensive, Ritchie prepared to fly up to XIII Corps HQ. But with the coming of daylight on 1 December it was immediately apparent that Eighth Army was to be granted no respite. Neumann-Silkow was on the move again, intent on finishing off the New Zealanders at Belhamed before XXX Corps could come to the rescue.

At 0600 the leading panzers hove into view of the defenders of Belhamed and started an agonizing dispute over identification, prompted by the error which had carried 'Ariete' on to Point 175. Not only was 4th Armoured Brigade's relief advance expected at any moment, but the Germans added to the confusion by using a captured Matilda as their leading tank. It speaks volumes for the excellence of German battlefield salvage that there were several instances of British uncertainty caused by

German use of captured British tanks (nearly always the tough-skinned Matildas and Valentines). If there were any occasions when British crews successfully took captured panzers into battle, no evidence has come to light of Axis forces being even momentarily troubled by the fact. But as the German artillery began to range on Belhamed, the last doubts were soon dispelled. This was indeed the decisive *Afrika Korps* attack, coming up from the south-west against weary, confused troops and ill-prepared defences.

Freyberg had had neither the time, the resources, nor the manpower with which to convert the New Zealand divisional area into a grid of strongpoints, each sited for all-round defence. Belhamed in particular was exposed to possible attack from the north (90th Light Division), east (21st Panzer Division) and south (15th Panzer Division). To make matters worse, the 20th Battalion at Belhamed had had five commanding officers in the last 72 hours. As a result, there were few effective defences at Belhamed; only five of the eleven anti-tank 2-pounders at Belhamed were pointed in 15th Panzer's direction. The biggest error (again prompted by the hope of early succour from XXX Corps, and unwillingness to imperil the approach of Gatehouse's tanks) was the failure to lay three truckloads of anti-tank mines, brought up by Clifton's supply convoy two nights before. All these weaknesses were ruthlessly exploited by Neumann-Silkow, with panzers and lorried infantry following hard and fast on a perfectly-directed artillery bombardment.

The main blow of 15th Panzer fell with stunning effect on 20th New Zealand Battalion, catching many New Zealanders still engaged in the ritual morning 'brew-up' of tea; others were seen to run to their guns from a corpse-burial detail. Nearly all the New Zealand guns brought into action did so over open sights at point-blank range, getting off maybe one or two rounds before the panzers were on them; the overwhelming impression was the speed at which the defenders came under machine-gun fire. Nor did 15th Panzer halt on its main objective after overruning Belhamed: by 0740 the leading panzers were on the verge of overrunning Freyberg's Battle Headquarters. Freyberg himself was under machine-gun fire as he strove to establish radio contact with Norrie, only to hear that no help would be coming from the South Africans, but that 4th Armoured Brigade was on its way. Freyberg then signalled this news to Godwin-Austen in Tobruk, and only then, with the gunners already surrendering only 150 yards in front of his imperilled HQ, ordered his surviving troops to rally at 4th Brigade HQ, 2 miles to the east.

The fast-dissolving New Zealand Division was only saved from total liquidation by the inactivity of 'Ariete' and 21st Panzer, both of them

167

occupied by 1st South African Brigade out to the east. To this extent, at least, it can be said that Pienaar's South Africans did finally succeed in taking pressure off their Dominion comrades. But in general on the British side events that chaotic morning were notable for another near-total breakdown in the chain of command. As had happened amid similar fluid crises earlier in CRUSADER, the decisions that mattered did not come from army or even corps level. The decision that the surviving New Zealanders must be withdrawn before it was too late was not made by Ritchie, Godwin-Austen, Norrie – or even by Freyberg himself. It was made by Gott via Gatehouse, who sent 4th Armoured Brigade across Sidi Rezegh airfield and into the chaos of the pocket to block the German advance and cover the withdrawal of the New Zealanders.

XXX Corps: 4th Armoured Brigade to the rescue

Crisp, who took part in the relief operation with 3rd Royal Tanks, has claimed that 4th Armoured Brigade was alerted to its new task 'long before sunrise', before the German attack on Belhamed got under way, which suggests admirable shrewdness on Gott's part. To Crisp and his fellow tank men, 'It was a shock to us to discover that our complete ignorance of the course the battle was taking, except in our limited vicinity, was concealing a set-back of such magnitude.' It was certainly thanks to Gott that 4th Armoured got going in time. By 0730 Gatehouse's Honeys had reached the southern escarpment at Sidi Rezegh and were peering across the airfield at the opposite ridge alive with Axis troops. The order to make contact with the New Zealanders and cover their withdrawal came through at 0800, the final approach being made under heavy Axis shellfire from both flanks. Colonel Drew took 5th Royal Tanks forward to meet Barrowclough and the remnants of 6th Brigade, assuming that the New Zealanders would pull out to the south as the British armour withdrew; Barrowclough, however, opted to follow Freyberg and withdraw eastward. It was Crisp himself who came upon the indomitable figure of Freyberg amid the New Zealand rearguard, perched on the edge of a slit trench, and passed on Gatehouse's message to withdraw:

> Maegraith and I watched Freyberg as he summoned the last of his officers and men. Twelve or fifteen soldiers got up out of the scrub and sand, and clambered into and all over the staff car. There was the usual moment of doubt and then, with men festooned all over the bonnet, mudguards and boot, it wheeled about, sped past us and vanished down the Trigh Capuzzo. I felt a nudge from Harry.

Coming down the slope into the area that had just been occupied by the New Zealanders was a long column of dark-coated men, four abreast, that seemed to stretch back indefinitely. We could not see the end of it over the next escarpment. They threaded their way slowly, disinterestedly, through the abandoned transport, slit trenches and shell-holes. They were not more than 500 yards away from us and I looked at them, almost unbelieving, through my glasses. I have never seen such a jaded, dispirited lot of men.

Many of them were capless, and the slanting rays of the early sun revealed starkly the dirt and dishevelment, the weariness of the spirit reflected in those weary faces. They shuffled glumly down the slope, not once looking up towards our tanks or the departing New Zealand troops. They came to a shambling sort of halt, looking about for a place where they could conveniently go to ground. . . . As far as I could see they displayed no interest whatever in our presence or our movement. One thing was clear – if the enemy had just won another Sidi Rezegh battle, those blokes didn't know it.[34]

This impression of the bone-weariness of the victors was neither wishful thinking nor one man's adrenalin-charged recollection. It was later confirmed for Crisp by the New Zealand official historian, Murphy, captured with General Kippenberger with the wounded in the New Zealand Main Dressing Station overrun on 1 December. Murphy later wrote to Crisp, 'My firm impression, and also General Kippenberger's, was that the German troops who passed through or near the MDS at that time were practically sleepwalkers and certainly did not regard themselves as victorious. I think their morale was very near breaking point.' And General Kippenberger recorded the dazed words of the German officer who approached him in the captured dressing station, saying 'We have retaken Belhamed and our eastern and western forces have joined hands. But it is no use. We have lost the battle. Our losses are too heavy. We have lost the battle.'[35]

It was indeed true that *Afrika Korps* was, for the moment, spent. The men of 15th Panzer Division, wearily consolidating Belhamed, made no attempt to molest the New Zealand rearguard as it withdrew east to Zaafran. Nor did 21st Panzer and 'Ariete', which moved west to join 15th Panzer at Sidi Rezegh and Belhamed – helping to clear the way for the retreating New Zealanders. But on the British side there was no inclination to risk further losses by trying to reverse what was undoubtedly a major setback. Once again 70th Division was sealed off in Tobruk while XXX Corps withdrew into the open Desert, with 4th Armoured Brigade heading 20 miles south to leaguer at Bir Berraneb.

At 1400 on 1 December Freyberg finally accepted that he could ask no more of his men and that the New Zealand Division was, for the moment at least, out of the battle. His decision to withdraw to the Frontier was at once approved by Norrie. In Tobruk Godwin-Austen toyed with the idea of evacuating El Duda, until he was assured by Lieutenant-Colonel Nichols of the 1st Essex that this dangerously exposed salient could be held.

So passed the rest of 1 December, bringing the second week of CRUSADER to a close in mutual weariness and apparent stalemate. It now remained to be seen how Rommel and Crüwell would exploit their latest victory and how Auchinleck and Ritchie would react to this latest defeat of Eighth Army's offensive.

Day 15 – 2 December

Eighth Army: plans for a resumed offensive

Though General Ritchie had exercised little or no direct control over the third battle of Sidi Rezegh, the mauling and withdrawal of the New Zealand Division never dented his resolve to feed fresh troops and replacement weapons into a resumed Eighth Army offensive. His determination was reinforced on 1 December by Auchinleck's arrival at Eighth Army HQ to discuss which units should be sent forward and which objectives should be pursued.

For his part Auchinleck was equally determined to make fullest use of the one solid advantage he enjoyed over Rommel: the troop resources elsewhere in Middle East Command. By 1 December the bulk of 1st Armoured Division, of which 22nd Armoured Brigade had been the vanguard, had arrived in Egypt from the United Kingdom. Its 2nd Armoured Brigade, with 106 Crusaders and sixty Honeys, was now committed to intensive Desert training, while the divisional artillery and the armoured cars of the 12th Lancers were sent forward to join Ritchie's command. Other forces to hand included the armoured cars of the Royal Dragoons from Syria; the newly-formed 38th Indian Infantry Brigade from Egypt; the 150th Infantry Brigade from Cyprus; and 30th Divisional Reconnaissance Battalion from Palestine. All these units were now under orders to swell the reserve at Maaten Baggush.

The arrival of these resources from the Delta, transmitted up the line, now permitted General de Villiers' 2nd South African Division to take over the Frontier zone from Messervy's 4th Indian Division, releasing 4th Indian for field operations west of the Wire. To this end 11th Indian

170

Infantry Brigade had already been relieved on the Halfaya/Sollum Frontier sector and sent forward to join Norrie at Gabr Saleh. Sidi Omar had now been completely cleared of Axis troops by 7th Indian Brigade. The Sollum/Musaid/Sidi Azeiz sector was now held by 5th Indian Brigade, taking over from 5th New Zealand Brigade; the latter had been moved west of Bardia to keep the Via Balbia blocked. Thus, with 4th Indian Division coming forward to replace the New Zealanders, Ritchie held to his original plan for a powerful thrust by XXX Corps to El Adem. He was confident that such a move would draw *Afrika Korps* westward like a magnet, permitting an early reopening of the 'Tobruk corridor'.

Norrie's original calculation was that, after using 2 December as a day of replenishment and regrouping, the advance to El Adem could get under way on the 3rd. This, however, was soon modified by the location of an Italian strongpoint 6 miles north-west of Bir el Gubi, the scene of 22nd Armoured Brigade's discomfiture on the second day of CRUSADER. Norrie and Gott thereupon agreed that this position must be taken out before XXX Corps could move on El Adem, and the job was given to Brigadier Anderson's 11th Indian Brigade. But before even this deck-clearing operation could get under way the incredible had happened. Seemingly undeterred by the failure of his 'Dash to the Wire' the week before, Rommel had again sent *Afrika Korps* driving to the east, its mission to crack Eighth Army's stranglehold on the Axis Frontier garrisons.

The Panzergruppe: *Rommel's second Frontier gamble*

After recapturing Belhamed on 1 December, 15th Panzer had virtually collapsed exhausted where it stood, like a sorely-tested runner who has barely made it to the finishing line. By nightfall on the 1st Rommel was contemplating panzer losses on such a scale (142 destroyed out of the original 249, and less that fifty of the remaining 107 still operational) that he had no choice but to devote the following 48 hours to a massive tank retrieve-and-repair operation. And yet, despite the most energetic protests from Crüwell, Rommel absolutely refused to let *Afrika Korps* remain inactive on the ground it had retaken.

It may well be (for lack of any explicit admission in Rommel's surviving writings) that the innermost core of his confidence had never quite recovered from the initial shock, when nearly 48 hours had passed before Rommel had realized that he was facing a major British offensive. Such inner uneasiness would certainly go far to explain his irrational 'knee-jerk' decisions during CRUSADER, of which the 'Dash to the Wire'

171

was a classic instance: an urge to deprive the British of the initiative, seemingly at any cost. At the same time Rommel was certainly trying to pursue his own master-plan as tenaciously as Ritchie was pursuing his. In CRUSADER this master-plan was the Axis equivalent of the British efforts to open the 'Tobruk corridor' and keep it open – Rommel's constant concern with relieving his Frontier garrisons. Having sealed off Tobruk and driven off the New Zealanders, Rommel therefore spent 2 December in planning for an early relief operation by *Afrika Korps* to break through to the Axis forces around Bardia.

Crüwell found the whole idea appalling, an apparently insane refusal to profit from the painful lessons of the 'Dash to the Wire' which had squandered *Afrika Korps'* victory in the first Sidi Rezegh battle. The sorely-tried *Afrika Korps* commander had no hesitation in putting his misgivings in writing: 'We must not repeat the error of giving up to the enemy a battlefield on which *Afrika Korps* has won a victory and undertaking another operation some distance away, instead of destroying the enemy utterly.' Crüwell urged that, while the German armour recuperated, the infantry and artillery of *Afrika Korps* should concentrate on taking out the El Duda salient, thus deepening and strengthening the precarious Axis blockade which had been reimposed on Tobruk with such difficulty. (As we have seen, Godwin-Austen in Tobruk was pessimistically expecting just such an attack.) But Rommel would have none of this. He insisted that two 'reinforced regiments' should be formed from the two panzer divisions, to thrust along the Trigh Capuzzo and Via Balbia and, he hoped, frighten the British away from Bardia. Though it would be impossible to give these 'reinforced regiments' any substantial armoured support, they were to be ready to advance on 3 December.

The 2nd December was therefore a day of reappraisal and regrouping for both Eighth Army and the *Panzergruppe*, with the two armies preparing reciprocal thrusts for the morrow: Eighth Army towards Bir el Gubi, *Afrika Korps* towards Bardia. The vital difference was the confidence in the deployment of fresh units on the British side and the growing despair among Rommel's overridden staff officers on the German. In Mellenthin's words, 'Tobruk was again isolated and on paper we seemed to have won the CRUSADER battle. But the price paid was too heavy; the *Panzergruppe* had been worn down, and it soon became clear that only one course remained – a general retreat from Cyrenaica.'[36] The only man in the *Panzergruppe* who still showed no sign of accepting this hard fact was Rommel.

Day 16 – 3 December

The Panzergruppe: *failure of the last drive east*

Overriding Crüwell's protests, Rommel had his way and by first light on 3 December *Afrika Korps* had been regrouped for its twin drive east to the Frontier. This regrouping took the form of two ad hoc motorized battalions: 'Group Geissler' to advance along the Via Balbia, 'Group Knabe' along the Trigh Capuzzo, both under the overall command of Neumann-Silkow. Gambara's XX Corps provided a third column to act as a flanking rearguard on the Trigh Capuzzo against any untimely thrusts from the south by the British armour.

It was, from the start, a dismal and costly failure. Both columns were detected by Desert Air Force reconnaissance during their 40-mile advance, and the defenders on the ground, deployed some 10 miles west of Bardia, were ready and waiting. Group Geissler ran head-on into a finely contrived ambush laid by the 28th Maori Battalion of 5th New Zealand Brigade. The Maoris exacted a summary revenge for the losses of their comrades at Sidi Rezegh and Belhamed. German records admit to 240 casualties, though the Maoris claimed some 230 more; the Maoris' own losses were two men killed and nine wounded. Down on the Trigh Capuzzo, Group Knabe was also fought to a halt by 31st Field Regiment from 5th Indian Brigade, operating with the armoured cars of the Central India Horse; the Desert Air Force weighed in with damaging attacks by Blenheims and Hurricane fighter-bombers ('Hurri-bombers'). These coordinated attacks were an example of the growing proficiency of the Desert Air Force in pursuing the famed German integration of air and ground operations. Neumann-Silkow's reaction was to withdraw both columns halfway between Sidi Rezegh and Bardia, Group Geissler to Gambut and Group Knabe to Gasr el Arid, hoping for better luck in a resumed attack on the 4th.

XXX Corps: the British armour shifts west

The total failure of Rommel's hopes of inflicting a second panic on Eighth Army was signified by the unhurried preparations of XXX Corps for its forthcoming shift to the El Adem/Bir el Gubi axis. This began on the morning of 3 December with the 20-mile advance of 4th Armoured Brigade from Bir Berraneb, placing Gatehouse's tanks across the El Adem/Bir el Gubi track. The advance of 4th Armoured was ordered by Norrie as insurance against any Axis counter-attack from El Adem to support the two Italian strongpoints north-west of Bir el Gubi. Gatehouse's tank regiments were in position by noon. In the afternoon

Crisp, making an unauthorized 'swan' north to the Trigh Capuzzo, reported the tail of the *Afrika Korps* column moving east along the Trigh. He reported it as a 'soft' target for 4th Armoured Brigade but was sharply ordered to take no action and refrain from 'any of his bloody nonsense': the eastward move of the Axis forces had been detected and was under constant observation. The immediate role of 4th Armoured was to avoid any wasteful tank losses on the eve of the battle for the El Adem approaches.

After all the heartbreaks and failures of the past two weeks, Crisp can be excused his bitter feeling that yet another golden opportunity was being wasted. He was not to know that this time his superiors *were* fully 'in the picture'. Nightfall on the 3rd therefore found 4th Armoured Brigade lodged in its blocking position north of Bir el Gubi, while 11th Indian Brigade prepared for yet another of the eve-of-battle night marches for which 4th Indian Division was famed. This march was to bring 11th Indian Brigade into position to attack the Italian positions from the west on the morning of 4 December.

Day 17 – 4 December

The Panzergruppe: *Rommel faces reality at last*

Rommel's orders for 4 December gave his subordinates no reason to hope that he was any closer to accepting the reality of the situation. His determination to relieve Bardia while maintaining the siege of Tobruk had already split his flagging forces yet again, resulting in nothing but more casualties and the consumption of priceless fuel and ammunition reserves. Rommel now compounded his error by ordering Neumann-Silkow to resume the eastward advance on Bardia, while ordering Böttcher, Mickl and Sümmermann to take El Duda in the west, restoring the full length of the *Achksenstrasse* to the *Panzergruppe*'s control. With the balance of forces swinging further and further in Eighth Army's favour, this was a recipe for failure on both fronts and the further weakening of the *Panzergruppe*. If Rommel had shown the same persistence with it as he had done during the 'Dash to the Wire', he would almost certainly have met with a shattering and permanent defeat on the south-east approaches to Tobruk. From this he was saved by the bungling of the British attempt to outflank him south of El Adem, which awoke Rommel to the true peril of the situation and enabled him to withdraw *Afrika Korps* south of Tobruk in the nick of time.

This latest British failure to the south, against what had been expected to be a fairly easy objective, was brought about by another fine example (as usual forgotten, owing to the preference for regarding the Italian soldier as a figure of fun) of Italian gallantry. The two Italian positions north-west of Bir el Gubi were manned not by troops of the regular Italian Army, but by the Blackshirt* *Coorto* (battalion) originally attached to 'Ariete'. It had been left at Bir el Gubi to defend the fuel and supply dumps of the division when 'Ariete' moved east to join the 'Dash to the Wire' on 24 November. On paper there were 650 men to a *Coorto*, two of which made up a *Legion*, but, allowing for the invariable lack of full establishment, there were probably no more than 500 Blackshirt troops at Bir el Gubi on 4 December. They had been given a troop of Italian tanks and a section of anti-tank guns to help them defend their strongpoints at Point 174 (4 miles north-west of Bir el Gubi) and Point 182 (across the Trigh el Abd 3 miles further north). These Blackshirts had already been 'blooded' during 'Ariete's' defence of Bir el Gubi against 22nd Armoured Brigade on 19 November, and despite two weeks of inactivity they acquitted themselves admirably on 4 December.

The British paid the price for poor reconnaissance (which led XXX Corps to expect only token resistance at Bir el Gubi) and, again, the belief that Italian garrison troops were not to be taken seriously. This underestimate was all the less forgivable after the tough fight which 44th Indian Division had already had for Sidi Omar. Anderson's 11th Indian Brigade went into action on 4 December with no real idea of what opposition to expect, but with the confident belief (perhaps the last unfortunate legacy of the first COMPASS attacks back in December, 1940) that there was nothing much to worry about. On the night of 3/4 December 11th Indian completed an approach march of 47 miles in six hours and attacked at dawn – the 2/5th Mahrattas against the main dump at Point 182, the 2nd Camerons against Point 174. Because of his ignorance of the opposition, Anderson gave the Mahrattas thirteen 'I' tanks to support their attack but only three to the Camerons. With this help the Mahrattas took their objective with comparative ease; but the Camerons were smartly repulsed from Point 174, losing all three 'I' tanks to the Blackshirts' artillery.

While the Blackshirts were fending off Norrie's over-confident snatch at Bir el Gubi, the German attack on El Duda was making only nominal progress 20 miles to the north. By noon the first German attack on the El Duda salient had been beaten off to the west, though a later attack by Group Mickl managed to push the British back across the

---

*Doubtless influenced by the Nazi German 'Hitler Youth', British practice was to describe all Blackshirt units as 'Young Fascists'. In fact the 'youngest' age group in Blackshirt recruiting was 21–36.

175

Achsenstrasse. Meanwhile, out to the east, the resumed advance of Group Knabe along the Trigh Capuzzo had caught the defenders of Sidi Azeiz by surprise, but any further German advance towards Bardia was now vetoed by Rommel, who was seriously alarmed by the implications of the developing battle in the Bir el Gubi sector. The prospect of the British reinforcing their new advance to the El Adem/Bir el Gubi axis, deep in the rear of *Afrika Korps*, at last convinced Rommel that he must concentrate on wiping out this unforeseen threat to his southern flank.

Eighth Army: setbacks and distractions for XXX Corps

Rommel's decision to recall *Afrika Korps* from the east came just in time to prevent Ritchie from calling off Norrie's advance to the west. The halting of Neumann-Silkow's advance on the 3rd had been regarded with satisfaction at Eighth Army HQ, but the renewed *Afrika Korps* attacks on the 4th caused distinct alarm. If Gatehouse's mass of armour stayed on the El Adem/Bir el Gubi axis, there seemed every chance of Rommel taking an important trick by retrieving his Frontier garrisons, or at least that at Bardia. The Axis troops thus released would cancel the effect of the fresh British troops being fed into Libya and increase the chances of Rommel forcing a draw on Eighth Army. By noon on 4 December Ritchie was therefore pestering Norrie with orders to do something about the renewed threat to the Frontier, and in the afternoon Norrie was ordered to pull 4th Armoured Brigade back east to Bir Berraneb.

In all fairness Ritchie's sudden change of heart was nothing like Cunningham's crisis-induced belief that CRUSADER could not succeed. All he wanted Norrie to do was to call off operations on the El Adem/Bir el Gubi axis until *Afrika Korps* had been beaten, pinned down, or at least withdrawn again from the Frontier. But Ritchie's interference on the 4th could hardly have been worse timed. It had the effect of jogging Norrie's elbow while Norrie was striving to retrieve the setback at Bir el Gubi. As a result the overwhelming strength of XXX Corps was never brought to bear against the Blackshirts at Bir el Gubi, or against the tank reinforcements pushed south from El Adem by Gambara's XX Corps. By nightfall on the 4th the Blackshirts had repulsed a second attack on Point 174 by 11th Indian Brigade, while aggressively handled Italian armour on the El Adem/Bir el Gubi track had inflicted several losses on the dispersed and distracted units of 4th Armoured Brigade. Poor preparation, unexpected resistance and the failure to bring all arms to bear on the point of attack had enabled one Axis battalion to frustrate XXX Corps for a whole day.

Day 18 – 5 December

Unaware of Ritchie's hesitation and the return of 4th Armoured Brigade to Bir Berraneb, Rommel withdrew *Afrika Korps* to El Adem in the belief that the whole of the British XXX Corps now lay to the south. The fact that the *Panzergruppe* was in a perilous condition was now dawning on Rommel at last. On the afternoon of the 4th he had been told, in a visit to the front by Colonel Montezemolo of *Comando Supremo*, that there was no chance of the *Panzergruppe* receiving anything but minimum supplies until early January. This brought Rommel abruptly face to face with the supply problem which his restlessness and impulsiveness had hitherto caused him to push aside. He now planned to tackle the crisis with a concentrated southern blow to 'see off' XXX Corps from Bir el Gubi, then loot the British supply dumps by a raid along the Trigh el Abd. (No record has survived at the dismay he must have felt in reflecting on the failure to locate and capture those dumps during the 'Dash to the Wire'.) But this southern counter-move was his last chance. If it failed to force XXX Corps into a decisive recoil to the east, there would be nothing for it but to accept defeat and withdraw the *Panzergruppe* from Tobruk. The inevitable alternative would be the destruction of his army where it stood for want of fuel, ammunition, food and supplies.

The Panzergruppe: *no decision at Bir el Gubi*

Rommel had intended to commit all three Axis armoured divisions to the Bir el Gubi attack, but delays suffered by 'Ariete' in its westward withdrawal along the Trigh Capuzzo made this impossible. General Balotta's tanks were not only heavily bombed (by the *Luftwaffe* as well as the Desert Air Force) but had to fight off Campbell's Support Group columns to the south, then run the gauntlet of artillery fire from El Duda in the north. The delayed return of 'Ariete' therefore ruined Rommel's plan for a morning drive to the south and 15th and 21st Panzer Divisions did not move off until 1430.

The two panzer divisions advanced in battle order, keyed up for an early head-on clash with 4th Armoured Brigade. But Gatehouse's tanks, in response to Ritchie's order of the previous day, spent the whole of 5 December cooling their heels at Bir Berraneb, 20 miles away to the south-west. The result was that Rommel's punch fell on the hapless 11th Indian Brigade, left completely unsupported west of Bir el Gubi. Anderson's battalions came close to suffering the same fate as 5th South African Brigade on *Totensonntag*, and indeed were nearly overwhelmed as they hastily formed defensive leaguers as best they could. But the panzers rolled on to relieve the jubilant Blackshirts still holding Point 174. Fortunately for 11th Indian, Crüwell never realized that he was confronted merely by a lone isolated brigade, ripe for destruction. Uneasy at having made contact with XXX Corps without any of the expected armoured opposition, Crüwell therefore withdrew north-west to leaguer for the night, right in the middle of 11th Indian Brigade's concentration area. The German armour and Anderson's beleaguered units spent a tense night within earshot of each other, with those British officers still able to communicate by field telephone speaking Urdu to fool any Germans who overheard.

If Crüwell's reaction had been one of over-caution, that of the British commanders was, for once, one of over-confidence. With *Afrika Korps* now a shadow of its former self, the days were long gone when the appearance of German tanks prompted a British overestimate of their strength by 20 per cent or more. The truth was that *Afrika Korps* was not, at first, identified as such. Gott mistakenly informed Norrie that only ten panzers had been involved in the afternoon's attack and that there was therefore no need to change the planned advance of 22nd Guards Brigade to relieve 11th Indian. The failure of Rommel's last throw was therefore assisted by errors on both sides. But even if Crüwell had wiped 11th Indian Brigade off the face of the earth on 5 December, this would hardly have provoked the decisive XXX Corps withdrawal on which Rommel's last hopes of stalemate rested. There remained 22nd Guards Brigade south of Bir el Gubi, 1st South African Brigade to the south-west – and, still at Bir Berraneb, the mass of Gatehouse's armour, which in tank strength now dwarfed *Afrika Korps* by over three machines to one.

Day 19 – 6 December

The Panzergruppe: *Rommel's last gamble fails*

On 6 December there were no dramatic sweeps of armour across the Desert; there were no desperate struggles for key strongpoints; there were no arrivals of reinforcements in the nick of time to stave off defeat, or carry a vital objective. The 6th was a day of mutual tension and wariness, unrelieved by any decisive action. Yet for that very reason this was a day of decision, the decision in question ruling out Rommel's last hopes of holding on at Tobruk.

Throughout 6 December *Afrika Korps* lay in the Desert north of Bir el Gubi, with its line of communication back to El Adem constantly bombed by the Desert Air Force. Five miles to the south XXX Corps also remained largely immobile in a wide arc: 11th Indian Brigade, 22nd Guards Brigade, 1st South African Brigade, and, from mid-morning, 4th Armoured Brigade, brought forward 10 miles from Bir Berraneb. Crüwell waited in vain for the arrival of 'Ariete' and the rest of Gambara's XX Corps, the day slipping by amid constant patrolling and long-range shelling between the British and Axis forces. By mid-afternoon, deciding he could wait no longer, Crüwell sent *Afrika Korps* into its last attack of CRUSADER, against the 22nd Guards Brigade. By 1700, in less than two hours, this attack had been ground to a halt by intense British shellfire and Neumann-Silkow had called for a Stuka attack to help clear the way. But the German bombers had not yet arrived when Neumann-Silkow was mortally wounded. Under Crüwell's urging the attack was nevertheless continued at last light, petering out after dark and leaving Crüwell with the confused impression that at least a wedge had been forced into the centre of the British arc. But he was under no delusion of having won any kind of decisive victory. Crüwell therefore told Rommel that, fearing the encirclement of *Afrika Korps*, he wanted permission to withdraw. Reluctant as ever to accept defeat as long as he had a single panzer fit to run, Rommel ordered Crüwell to stay where he was and make one final effort on the following morning.

By nightfall on 6 December Rommel's hopes for the morrow rested solely on Eighth Army HQ undergoing another of its spasmodic fits of pessimism, but by now there were no grounds for pessimism on the British side. For the past 24 hours every air reconnaissance sortie had confirmed constant Axis troop withdrawals from the eastern face of the Tobruk salient in the direction of El Adem. Everything pointed to the imminence of further Axis withdrawals to the west, and for the first time since 18 November Eighth Army Intelligence had got it right. This was confirmed by the re-establishment of contact with XIII Corps in Tobruk, not by tanks or infantry, but by an armoured car patrol of the 11th Hussars. Ritchie thereupon ordered Norrie to prepare XXX Corps for the north-westerly advance, which only 48 hours before Ritchie had postponed. At the same time Godwin-Austen in Tobruk was ordered to prepare for an advance on El Adem from El Duda.

Day 20 – 7 December

The Panzergruppe: *Rommel abandons Tobruk*

At 0930 on 7 December Rommel arrived at Crüwell's HQ to spell out the situation – and effectively announce the hard decision to which he

179

had at last been driven. Rommel told Crüwell that 'If the enemy was not beaten today [which would require nothing short of a miracle, with only forty panzers still fit to run], we would have to abandon the Tobruk front and go back to the Gazala position. Preliminary measures for this had been taken the previous night – the heavy artillery had been withdrawn from the Tobruk front, and 90th Light Division and the Italian formations had been withdrawn. The Sollum front would also have to be abandoned.' None of this curiously elliptical wording, with its stress on the conditional tense, could disguise the real nature of the task which Rommel was now setting *Afrika Korps*. This was to hold its position and prevent XXX Corps from wrecking the disengagement of the Axis forces from the remaining southern and western sectors of the Tobruk siege perimeter. '*Afrika Korps* was to hold out today and keep the enemy off, and to counter-attack if the enemy pressed too hard. During the night it was to withdraw 30–35km [18–21 miles] north-west.'

In other words *Afrika Korps*, for the first time since its formation, was charged with covering the retreat of as much of the *Panzergruppe* as could be retrieved. One of the original ten Axis divisions had already gone – 'Bologna', effectively destroyed as a fighting unit during the first British relief of Tobruk in CRUSADER's second week. Another, 'Savona', was now to be abandoned on the Frontier, together with Bach's Germans at Halfaya. This left *Afrika Korps* responsible for the retreat of 90th Light, 'Ariete', 'Pavia', 'Trieste', 'Brescia' and 'Trento'. As the withdrawal of these divisions proceeded on the afternoon of the 7th, *Afrika Korps* stood its ground with such tenacity that Norrie decided against any immediate forward move by XXX Corps. Though Rommel had conceded defeat and the retreat of his army had begun, *Afrika Korps* thus retained the moral superiority over XXX Corps which it had exercised since the first week of CRUSADER. Ritchie therefore had no choice but to order XIII Corps to take up the running, with an attack on Rommel's rearguard from El Duda on the night of 7/8 December. The respite thus won enabled Rommel's retreat to proceed one vital step ahead of the British pursuit.

After twenty days, thirteen more than provided for in the original British planning, Eighth Army had gained the first objective of CRUSADER. The siege of Tobruk had been raised at last, eight months after its imposition at the end of Rommel's first offensive. It now remained to be seen whether Eighth Army could close with the retreating *Panzergruppe* and bring it to battle, or whether Rommel would succeed in escaping from the indefensible wastes of western Cyrenaica.

CHAPTER 4

THE PURSUIT

Phase 1: From Tobruk to Gazala – 8–13 December

If an acid test of supreme generalship is fighting a successful retreat, it was a test which Rommel was now about to pass with honours. This was, be it noted, the first time in his entire career that he had had to do so, and it was an art in which Rommel soon proved himself a master. With his long obsession with Tobruk over at last, shattered as much by his own mistakes as by the efforts of Eighth Army backed by Auchinleck's iron persistence, Rommel turned in his best military performance since BATTLEAXE back in June. All his talents for improvisation were now concentrated on withdrawing the *Panzergruppe* to a line on which it could turn and strike back at its pursuers. By 7 December, the first day of the retreat, he had already delineated its first objective: the 'Gazala position', 25 miles from the western Tobruk perimeter.

Though he planned to make Eighth Army fight for its subsequent gains, Rommel never intended to make a permanent stand at Gazala. The thing could not be done, if only because the so-called 'Gazala position' was little more than a line on the map, nothing like the chain of mined and wired defensive 'boxes' which Eighth Army would create in the following spring. It had first been drawn in May 1941, as a possible stop-line in the event of an Axis defeat on the Frontier followed by a British advance past Tobruk. The original 'Gazala position' was an extension of a defile running inland from the coast at Ain el Gazala, an arc of defensible high ground some 15 miles long, petering out in the open Desert at the south-eastern extremity of the Alam Hamza Ridge.

It did, however, offer the chance of stopping any pursuit relying too heavily on the Via Balbia. Of rather more importance at the outset of the *Panzergruppe*'s retreat, it offered a morale-boosting goal within the reach even of the slow-moving Italian infantry divisions.

Yet long before the *Panzergruppe* reached the 'Gazala position' Rommel had taken steps to speed the subsequent retreat which he knew would be necessary. His greatest fear was that Eighth Army would emulate the cross-Desert advance to Agedabia with which O'Connor had trapped the retreating Italians in January–February, 1941. The early advance of Oasis Force to Aujila and Jalo had been an early indication that Auchinleck was planning precisely such a move. Rommel therefore made his first priority the extrication of 90th Light Division and its immediate despatch to Agedabia. This was successfully accomplished despite heavy bombing by the Desert Air Force, one of whose raids killed General Sümmerman on 9 December.

The withdrawal of 90th Light had been prepared by its timely redeployment west of 'Pavia' Division, which bore the brunt of the British breakout attack from the El Duda salient on the night of 7/8 December. The weight of this attack was carried by the 1st Durham Light Infantry and it mauled 'Pavia' considerably, taking 130 Italian prisoners. These losses were mainly the fault of Gambara who, wearing his 'second hat' as Bastico's Chief of Staff, had countermanded Rommel's order withdrawing Navarrini's XXI Corps west to El Adem. And the incident was the prelude to a prolonged row between Rommel and Bastico, not over how the retreat from Cyrenaica should be conducted, but whether it should be conducted at all.

It all came down to the hard fact that once a decisive battle had been won east or west of the Jebel Akhdar, the beaten army had no choice but to abandon the whole of the Cyrenaican 'bulge' if it were to escape to fight again. This had been conclusively proved by O'Connor's triumphant knock-out of the retreating Italian Tenth Army at Beda Fomm in February, 1941. The British and Rommel were as one in accepting the essential defencelessness of the Jebel, but it was all very well for them: Libya was not their territory. From the Italian viewpoint, by 1940 Libya was a showcase for the beneficial effects of European colonization, most notably in the field of desert reclamation. To the Italian High Command Benghazi was not, as it was to the British and Germans, a minor objective impossible to defend. As the second city of Libya, it *deserved* defending. On the purely operational level there were natural fears that Rommel was planning to use the slower-moving Italian divisions (one of which he was already prepared to write off where it stood, on the Frontier) in order to safeguard the escape of the German forces. The result was a blazing row between Rommel and Bastico which lasted the best part of a week. Rommel did not help matters by furiously condemning Gambara's failure to reinforce Crüwell's advance to Bir el Gubi, and by threatening to withdraw all German forces to accept internment in French Tunisia. A grudging agreement was made possible by Bastico's fear that the Italian divisions would be left to their own devices and be cut off at Agedabia. Rommel was able to argue that the prompt withdrawal of 90th Light to Agedabia was the obvious insurance against such a fate, and so gain the reluctant approval of his Italian superiors for a fighting retreat to the Gazala position. He was, however, left in no doubt that the *Panzergruppe*'s retreat was to end at Gazala, with 90th Light standing by to repel any cross-Desert thrust at Agedabia.

Rommel's disengagement from the Tobruk/El Adem sector was made possible by a crucial decision on the part of Eighth Army's commander. This was prompted by Ritchie's desire to contain the Axis garrisons isolated on the Frontier and reduce them at the earliest opportunity, while at the same time pressing the pursuit of the retreating *Panzergruppe*. On 9 December, Ritchie therefore ordered that the pursuit was to be handed over to XIII Corps, while XXX Corps (less 7th Armoured Division and the two forward brigades of 4th Indian Division) returned to the Frontier area. Norrie protested that this was a total reversal of the original roles envisaged for XIII and XXX Corps, but Ritchie overruled him and was backed up by Auchinleck. As a result 10 December, the last day on which Gatehouse's tanks had a chance of engaging the retreating *Panzergruppe* east of Gazala, passed with the tank men of 4th Armoured Brigade kept in baffled inactivity while the change-over was completed. Ritchie's decision, added to the excellent rearguard performance of Crüwell with *Afrika Korps*, therefore enabled Rommel to withdraw the *Panzergruppe* to the Gazala position by nightfall on 11 December.

The British redeployment therefore granted Rommel an invaluable respite of 48 hours, for it was only on 11 December that 7th Armoured Division and 4th Indian Division passed to Godwin-Austen's command. The XIII Corps commander was now required to overtake and destroy the retreating *Panzergruppe* with the built-in disadvantage of a two-day handicap. His now motley collection of forces consisted of 5th New Zealand Brigade, the Polish Brigade from the former Tobruk garrison (eager to resume operations against its adversaries in the long siege), 5th and 7th Indian Brigades, Campbell's Support Group columns, and Gatehouse's 4th Armoured Brigade (now back down to about ninety tanks). It was therefore not before 13 December that XIII Corps closed up to the Gazala position. Mindful of the battle-worn state of his forces, and of the already parlous supply problem which was bound to deteriorate the further XIII Corps advanced from its forward bases, Godwin-Austen took the whole of the 14th in preparing for a battle which, he hoped, would trap the *Panzergruppe* and end the campaign at a stroke.

Battle of Alam Hamza, 15–16 December

What should logically be remembered as the 'First Battle of Gazala', but which is habitually styled the 'Battle of Alam Hamza', took place on 15–16 December, 1941. It was a punishing experience for Eighth Army, dispelling any lingering hopes that the *Panzergruppe*, though forced to retreat from Tobruk, was in any moral sense a beaten army.

One of the hoariest military maxims is that 'the order of march should be the order of battle'. The *Panzergruppe*'s battle order on the morning of 15 December certainly reflected its intended future continued retreat to the west. Rommel had stationed his three Italian infantry divisions – 'Brescia' 'Trento' and 'Pavia' – on the coastal sector, close to the Via Balbia on which their most rapid movement depended. The inland extremity of the Gazala position, the Alam Hamza Ridge, was entrusted to 'Trieste', with 'Ariete' covering its right flank. The two panzer divisions were widely deployed on a north-south line from Sidi Breghisc, 5 miles west of the Alam Hamza ridge, down to the Trigh Capuzzo, 10 miles east of Rotonda Segnali. Rommel knew that he could do nothing to prevent the British from exploiting the Desert flank, but with this deployment he hoped to make it as difficult as possible for them. Whatever happened, his vulnerable Italian divisions would be able to fall back and continue their fighting retreat down the Via Balbia while *Afrika Korps* covered their inland flank.

Godwin-Austen's attack plan reflected his determination to force Rommel into a decisive stand-up fight, but events soon proved it to have been over-ambitious. Godwin-Austen intended the New Zealanders and Poles to pin down the Italians on the coastal sector while 4th Indian turned the inland flank of the main Axis positions at Alam Hamza. The Desert flank of 4th Indian was entrusted to the Support Group columns, but the biggest weakness of Godwin-Austen's plan was the contradictory role entrusted to 4th Armoured Brigade. Rommel's maximum tank strength was reckoned at fifty, and the surviving panzers were the main objective outlined to Gott. But Gott was also ordered to send 4th Armoured Brigade on a deep encircling advance to Bir Halegh el Elaba, a sickle-cut at the *Panzergruppe*'s back. Gott was left to decide how to force a decisive tank battle on *Afrika Korps* while simultaneously bypassing the German armour and advancing into its rear. And the resultant indecision prevented Gatehouse's tanks from either severing the *Panzergruppe*'s line of retreat or from stopping *Afrika Korps* giving a bloody nose to the surprised infantry of XIII Corps.

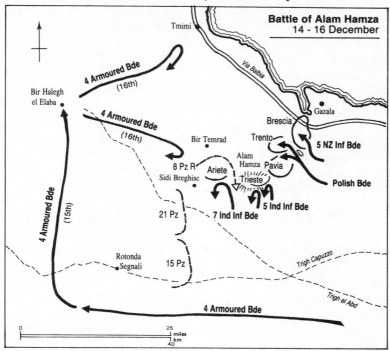

The prospects of Eighth Army were not helped by the over-ambitious programme allocated to 4th Indian Division under Messervy. He, too, was aiming at the remote objective of Bir Halegh el Elaba, in the belief that Rommel had put most of his eggs into the coastal sector. Messervy believed that his two brigades would be able to turn the inland flank of the Italians by breaking through at Alam Hamza with comparative ease. This would permit 4th Indian Division, driving on north-west towards Bir Halegh el Elaba, to act as anvil to the hammer of 4th Armoured Brigade. Yet again, however, the British planning was frustrated by the unexpectedly tough opposition put up by the Italian divisions.

The stand of Navarrini's corps was vastly encouraged by early German successes west of Alam Hamza on the 13th and 14th, which appeared to guarantee the security of the inland flank. Messervy had hoped that the final approach of 4th Indian to the Gazala position could be maintained without a halt, probing round the Desert flank of the main Axis positions. But deteriorating weather made it impossible for the

185

Desert Air Force to provide any clear reconnaissance picture of the German positions west of Alam Hamza, which 7th Indian Brigade was left to discover the hard way. Blissfully unaware that this was the headquarters area of *Afrika Korps*, Messervy had directed 7th Indian Brigade (Brigadier R. Briggs) to push on to Sidi Breghisc. On the morning of 13 December the 4/11th Sikhs, supported by the batteries of 25th Field Regiment RA and twelve Valentines of 8th Royal Tank Regiment, were smartly counter-attacked by thirty-nine panzers with lorried infantry and artillery in support. Briggs hastily withdrew the Sikhs to let the gunners and 'I' tanks fight a delaying action. Throughout the afternoon of the 13th the German armour continued to grind forward. After a tough fight it overran the 31st/58th Battery, leaving only 12th/25th Battery to hold what was developing into a dangerous thrust at XIII Corps' left centre. By last light, however, German losses were rising fast; Briggs's gunners had knocked out fourteen panzers and the remainder withdrew, content to have beaten back Messervy's incautious thrust at the Axis centre.

Messervy's only gain on the 13th was the capture of Point 204 by the 1st Buffs, but the 'Trieste' Division successfully defended Point 208 from the attack of 4th Rajputana Rifles (5th Brigade). This left the Buffs precariously lodged on Point 204, within striking range both of 'Ariete' and the German armour. On 14 December 5th Brigade again failed to carry Point 208, while the Buffs beat off a succession of probing attacks. Godwin-Austen therefore accepted that the only way to get the advance moving again was to order an all-out attack by XIII Corps on the Axis positions, while 4th Armoured Brigade carried out its deep encirclement of the Axis rear.

On 15 December Godwin-Austen did not win the decisive action which he had sought, and the real reason was the two-day delay (while Messervy tried in vain to turn the Axis centre on the 13th and 14th) in pushing 4th Armoured Brigade forward to the *Panzergruppe*'s inland flank. The idea was that Gatehouse's tanks should have advanced to Bir Halegh el Elaba by 1100 on the 15th, poised to strike at the Axis rear, while Messervy resumed his frontal attack. But the huge 70-mile advance over unfamiliar terrain, far outrunning the labouring petrol supply colums, presented 4th Armoured Brigade with too great a task. It was not before 1500 that 4th Armoured reached Bir Halegh el Elaba – four hours late, with evening fast approaching on an overcast day. Not only was 4th Armoured Brigade kept out of action throughout the whole of the 15th, it had no chance of preventing *Afrika Korps* from dealing a savage blow at XIII Corps' centre.

The right-flank attack of XIII Corps was carried by 5th New Zealand

Brigade and the Polish Brigade, charged with breaking and surrounding the three Italian divisions on the coastal sector – 'Brescia' and 'Pavia', with 'Trento' in close support. The Poles and New Zealanders made good initial progress, taking several hundred Italian prisoners; but the Italians rallied well, and by noon it was clear to Godwin-Austen that his two brigades lacked the weight to achieve a decision on the right flank. It was the same story in the centre, where the Italians of 'Trieste' continued to repulse 5th Indian Brigade's attacks on Point 208. By mid-afternoon the XIII Corps attack had been fought to a halt all along the line, from the Via Balbia on the coast to the Alam Hamza Ridge. And it was at this point, with 4th Armoured Brigade barely arrived at Bir Halegh el Elaba 25 miles away to the north-west, that Crüwell unleashed 8th Panzer Regiment in a devastating counter-attack against the Buffs on Point 204.

The attack on Point 204 was one of the most perfectly timed operations in Crüwell's career. He held it back until it was clear that there was no immediate threat of a pincer attack from the north or north-west by 4th Armoured Brigade. To guard against unexpected intervention by units of 4th Armoured Brigade, Crüwell deployed the nineteen 'runners' of 21st Panzer. The twenty-three tanks of 8th Panzer Regiment were given enough infantry and fire-power support – 105th Lorried Infantry Regiment and 2nd Machine-Gun Battalion – to surround the Buffs on Point 204 and crush them in converging attacks from 1400 to 1530. It was another hard-fought action in which the Buffs fought to the last round, effectively destroying 105th Lorried Infantry Regiment in the process, but nothing could stop the relentless advance of the *panzers* across the British position:

> Tom Rowe, Staff Capt. at 7th Bde, told us that the Buffs' Commanding Officer remained at his wireless transmitter until the very last moment, passing back information as to the progress of the battle and directing his own troops. Finally most of the Buffs and a Field Regt [the 31st] were overrun. The CO, through his transmitter, told the Bde HQ that he had three of our 'I' tanks about him in phalanx and that they were firing everything they had got; then he said; 'The Boche tanks are coming towards me now; I think this will probably be my last transmission.' There was a silence, followed by a loud crash as someone put a bullet through the transmitter so that it should not fall whole into enemy hands.[1]

The last stand of the Buffs on Point 204 cost them about a thousand prisoners and caused considerable shock when the news spread through XIII Corps. Viewed objectively, it was no more than a trade-off: a bloody nose for XIII Corps, but for Rommel the effective destruction of an irreplaceable motorized infantry unit for the gain of no decisive result. The undoubted defensive victory of the *Panzergruppe* on 15 December was the prelude to an immediate resumption of its retreat. Any hopes Rommel may have had of a prolonged stand at Gazala were dispelled by the location of 4th Armoured Brigade, overflown by a German reconnaissance aircraft on the late afternoon of the 15th at Bir Halegh el Elaba.

For his part. Godwin-Austen was undismayed by the immolation of the Buffs and swiftly changed his battle plan from the original pincer movement to a hammer-and-anvil operation, 4th Armoured Brigade acting as the hammer and the discomfited 4th Indian Division as the anvil. Even when he heard that the fuel crisis of 4th Armoured Brigade forbade any decisive move before nightfall on the 15th, Godwin-Austen still hoped that Gott and Gatehouse would pull it off on the 16th. But dawn on 16 December found 4th Armoured Brigade incapable of any operations in full strength; the vital fuel and supply column had not yet arrived. The most that Gatehouse could do was to send lightweight forces to demonstrate in the Axis rear areas: a squadron of the 5th Royals north-east towards Tmimi on the Via Balbia, another Squadron of the Royals and one of 3rd Royal Tanks south-east towards Bir Temrad and the rear of *Afrika Korps*. Even this modest contribution was only made possible by plundering fuel and ammunition from the whole Brigade, which was to head *south* from Bir Halegh el Elaba to hasten the rendezvous with the supply column.

Had he only known it, Godwin-Austen's urgings for Gatehouse to get into action ruined the last real chance of forcing Rommel to fight and lose a decisive armoured battle east of the Jebel. In his loyal attempts to comply with Godwin-Austen's order as best he could, Gatehouse only managed to re-open Rommel's route to safety. Though painfully and belatedly achieved, the advance of 4th Armoured Brigade to Bir Halegh el Elaba had been replete with promise. It blocked the Tmimi-Mechili track down which *Afrika Korps* would have to retreat to avoid being pinned down in the Jebel. It can certainly be claimed that Gatehouse's demonstration towards Bir Temrad dissuaded Crüwell from resuming the mauling of 4th Armoured Division on the 16th. But on balance, with the probe towards Tmimi, it only sharpened Rommel's determination to resume his retreat. And the 15-mile southerly withdrawal of 4th Armoured Brigade on the morning of the 16th left the track to Mechili, Msus and Agedabia wide open to the Axis armour.

Rommel's decision to pull out of the Gazala position on the night of 16/17 December prompted another row with the Italians. In an angry session at Giovanni Berta, Cavallero, Bastico and Gambara all opposed further withdrawal, and they found an unexpected ally in Field-Marshal Kesselring, who from now on was to play a crucial role in the North African campaign. Hitler had appointed Kesselring 'Commander-in-Chief, South' at the end of October. With increased air resources – II and X *Fliegerkorps* were to be placed under his immediate command – Kesselring was to suppress Malta and secure the Axis supply links to North Africa. At the same time twenty-five U-boats were to be withdrawn from the Atlantic battle to break British naval supremacy in the Mediterranean. Though a major strategic realignment, involving the withdrawal of II *Fliegerkorps* from the Russian Front, it brought no immediate benefit to Rommel during the CRUSADER fighting east of Tobruk. By the beginning of December, however, the transfer of II *Fliegerkorps* was nearly complete and the first U-boats into the Mediterranean had already begun the assault on the British Mediterranean Fleet, sinking the famous aircraft-carrier *Ark Royal* on 14 November and the battleship *Barham* on 25 November. As he prepared to support the North African forces by unleashing the air assault on Malta, Kesselring strongly opposed Rommel's plan to abandon the airfields east of the Jebel, particularly the key field at Derna. Rommel, however, insisted that if the *Panzergruppe* did not retreat, Kesselring would soon have nothing to support. In Rommel's own words,

I fully realized that this would mean the eventual loss of Cyrenaica and that political difficulties might result. But the choice I was faced with was either to stay where I was and thus sacrifice the *Panzergruppe* to destruction – thereby losing both Cyrenaica and Tripolitania – or to begin the retreat that night, fight my way back through Cyrenaica to the Agedabia area and at least defend Tripolitania. I could only choose the latter. Excellency Bastico and Gambara behaved so violently in my room that evening that I was finally obliged to ask Bastico how he, as Commander-in-Chief of the North African forces, proposed to handle the situation. Bastico evaded the question, and said that as Commander-in-Chief it was not his business; he could only say that we ought to keep our forces together. Finally, the delegation left my HQ, having accomplished nothing.[2]

The Italians vainly resumed the debate on the 17th, but by then Rommel's orders for the retreat had already been issued and there was clearly no time for further argument; the British 7th Support Group had already been spotted heading in the direction of Tengeder, south of the Jebel. By nightfall on the 17th the retreat had begun, with *Afrika Korps*

189

heading south of the Jebel for Msus and Antelat and the Italian infantry divisions heading west down the Via Balbia for Barce and Benghazi. Demolition parties were set to blowing appropriate sections of the coast road to delay the British pursuit. Rommel's greatest anxiety was that Eighth Army would manage to push enough armoured and mobile forces westward to cut the Italians' line of retreat before *Afrika Korps* could intervene.

That this threat never materialized was due mainly to Ritchie's mistaken belief that Rommel would fight a rearguard action for Derna and Mechili, and to the three-day delay in preparing a strong pursuing force to strike across the Desert south of the Jebel. This delay, assisted by the continued resistance of the Axis Frontier garrisons forcing wide detours on Eighth Army's struggling supply echelons, gave Rommel the respite he wanted, enabling the separated elements of the *Panzergruppe* to make good their escape to the west.

The Pursuit, 17–23 December

The execution of the British pursuit from Gazala was dogged by what can best be described as baffled improvisation. If it was not true that Eighth Army had been worn to a shadow by the CRUSADER battle for Tobruk, its original two-corps structure – the armour in XXX Corps and the infantry in XIII Corps – had become woefully disrupted. Over half of what had once been XXX Corps was pinned down between Tobruk and the Frontier, masking the Axis garrisons. Other units which had been in the front of the action since 18 November were in desperate need of a rest – most notably 4th Armoured Brigade. Now, with the need for sudden pursuit some of those units could not be relieved – the 3rd Royal Tank Regiment and the 7th Support Group were cases in point. Ritchie was denied the luxury of waiting until 1st Armoured Division had completed the long overland advance to the lengthening front from railhead at Misheifa. The best he could do was to send forward the reconstituted 22nd Armoured Brigade to relieve 4th Armoured Brigade at Mechili, and press 22nd Guards Brigade (now styled 'Bencol') into service as a synthetic armoured brigade. When 'Bencol' took up the pursuit on 20 December, its armoured strength consisted of the armoured cars of the 11th Hussars and fourteen Honeys from one squadron of the 2nd Royal Gloucestershire Hussars.

Having been denied a decisive victory over the concentrated *Panzergruppe* at Gazala/Alam Hamza, Ritchie planned a two-handed pounce on what he thought would be the next rearguard standing-points chosen

190

by Rommel. Ritchie therefore ordered Messervy to head into the eastern Jebel towards Lamluda, 30 miles west of Derna. Gott was ordered to head for Mechili with 7th Armoured Division. Brigadier Marriott was ordered to prepare 'Bencol' for a Desert crossing south of the Jebel, aimed at Benghazi. Within 24 hours, however, Ritchie ordered a fundamental revision of this plan as reports from 4th Indian Division confirmed that the *Panzergruppe* had no intention of holding either Mechili or Derna. Gott was now ordered to head through the Jebel for Benina and Benghazi, while Marriott took 'Bencol' across the Desert south of Tengeder in pursuit of the Axis armour.

Ritchie's advance from Gazala was therefore delayed at the outset by a crucial misreading of Rommel's true intentions. It was further afflicted by the conviction that the bulk of Rommel's forces were retreating on Benghazi – the classic mistake that what was a vital objective for the British had to be an equally vital objective for the enemy. Ritchie had no idea that by despatching 'Bencol' on the cross-Desert route he was in fact sending it straight for the Axis armour – not intercepting its retreat. And Bencol's advance was only made possible in the first place by stripping 7th Indian Infantry Brigade of most of its transport – thus inevitably delaying the pursuit along the Via Balbia, and taking the pressure off the retreating Italians. It was a depressing example of robbing Peter to pay Paul, and it was made worse by the number of objectives which Ritchie gave Marriott. To secure the Msus airstrip, push west to Ghemines, and cut the Via Balbia south-west of Antelat, Marriott would have no choice but to split 'Bencol', a dangerous weakening of his force.

These were avoidable errors and they were compounded by a run of coincidences all running in Rommel's favour. His retreat was assisted by the worsening weather of an abnormally foul Libyan winter, with low cloud and torrential rains hitherto unknown in the region. The most immediate effect of the bad weather was to prevent the Desert Air Force from operating at full strength from the former Axis airstrips gained by Eighth Army's westward advance. This not only deprived Ritchie's foremost ground forces of the air reconnaissance they should have had, but saved Rommel's withdrawing columns from the sustained bombing to which they would otherwise have been treated. At the same time the inexorable law of Desert warfare was now working ever more strongly on the *Panzergruppe*'s behalf. The retreating army's supply position steadily improved as it fell back up its own line of communication, while that of the pursuers steadily deteriorated. To this was added a startling development in the unremitting British naval attempts to block Rommel's flow of seaborne supplies. Rommel was about to receive the first-fruits of Kesselring's appointment as C-in-C, South, and they could not have been more timely.

The Royal Navy maintained its stranglehold on the Axis convoy routes until the second week of December, by which time the Italian Navy had resorted to making fast supply runs by warships as well as merchant ships. On the night of 12 December two cruisers, *Alberico da Barbiano* and *Alberto di Giussano*, sailed for Tripoli from Palermo, their decks crammed with cases of petrol. Heading straight across the Sicilian Narrows, they turned south-east down the Tunisian coast, intending to make a coast-hugging approach to Tripoli. Unluckily for the Italians, four destroyers, three British and one Free Dutch, were cruising even closer inshore, and at 0223 on 13 December they carried out a devastating surprise attack with torpedoes and gunfire. Doomed as much by their lethal deck cargo as by the well-timed ferocity of the attack, both *Giussano* and *Barbiano* were set ablaze and sunk. On the same day the disaster to the cruisers was crowned by the loss of two Italian freighters carrying tank reinforcements to Libya: *Carlo del Greco* with twenty-three tanks, and *Fabio Filzi* with twenty-two, both sunk by the submarine *Upright*.

Though the loss of these four ships deprived Rommel of the last tanks and fuel which could have reached him in time for the Alam Hamza battle, it was followed by the sailing of four Axis supply ships, three bound for Tripoli and one for Benghazi on the afternoon of 16 December. This was a major evolution, planned the week before, and it was covered by the entire Italian battle fleet, a prospect which plunged Foreign Minister Ciano into near despair. 'All the ships and all the admirals at sea,' he noted despondently on 8 December. 'May God help us!' Ciano's misgivings about the venture would have been even greater if he could have known that the British were coincidentally planning a similar venture; but in fact the Italian fleet fulfilled its mission, with results that transformed the armoured balance in Libya.

On 15 December the fast merchantman *Breconshire* sailed from Alexandria, bound for Malta with desperately needed supplies. As the tracks of the British and Italian ships converged on 17 December, the rival escorting forces clashed in the confused engagement known as the 'First Battle of Sirte' (a second action would be fought in the same waters in March, 1942). The net result of the action was that each side's supply run ended in success. *Breconshire* and her escorts won through safely to Malta on 18 December, but on the following day the German *Ankara* safely unloaded twenty-two tanks at Benghazi, while *Monginevro* delivered another twenty-three at Tripoli. Once again the inherent mechanical superiority of German armour came into play, for unlike

British tank reinforcements, panzers newly arrived in Africa did not require weeks of maintenance and conversions before they could be considered Desert-worthy. Within four days of their landing at Benghazi, the first of Rommel's new tank reinforcements had joined *Afrika Korps* and were ready to help Crüwell take full advantage of the dangerously dispersed British columns seeking to cut him off.

By 20 December, 4th Indian Division was doggedly pushing westward along the Via Balbia from Derna, wearily coping with a succession of shrewdly blown roadway sections and escarpments. Behind these obstructions the Italian infantry divisions were making good their escape through Barce, Tocra and Benghazi. Forty miles further south of 4th Indian, in the hill country of the southern Jebel, 7th Support Group made brief contact with the rearguards of 'Trieste' and 'Ariete' at Charruba, 60 miles west of Mechili. With both sides beset by foul weather and bad going, the scale was tipped by the British suffering far more than the Italians from fuel shortages, and the Italians got away on the 21st. Meanwhile the northern elements of 'Bencol' (11th Hussars, 3rd Coldstream and 2nd Scots Guards) were approaching Msus. The southern element of 'Bencol' (the Honey tanks of the Gloucestershire Hussars and 51st Field Regiment RA) was 20 miles further south, heading for Antelat.

Though the *Panzergruppe* was not yet wholly out of the woods, Rommel was watching the pieces of his plan falling one by one into place. He already had 15th Panzer stationed at Beda Fomm, reinforced from Benghazi by *Ankara*'s timely load of new tanks. From Ghemines, 40 miles north, 21st Panzer was speeding south to complete a concentration of German armour with which Rommel intended to cover the final stage of his army's retreat. Thirty miles east of Benghazi, 'Ariete', 'Trieste' and 'Pavia' were falling back from El Abiar. Up on the Via Balbia 'Trento' and 'Brescia' were already past Barce and retreating through Tocra on Benghazi. And at the southernmost end of Rommel's rapidly contracting front, at Agedabia, 90th Light and the remnants of 'Bologna' stood poised to repel any deep encircling move which the British might contrive from the south-east.

While the *Panzergruppe* was thus re-forming after its retreat through the Jebel, Ritchie and Godwin-Austen faced a hopeless task in seeking to cancel the time advantage which Rommel had won. The British supply problem was now assuming nightmare proportions, for the port of Tobruk had not provided the magic solution to Eighth Army's supply needs which had been envisaged during the planning of CRUSADER. Because of his lack of enough supply vessels and escorts, and the ever-present threat of Axis air and submarine attack, Admiral Cunningham was not able to run seaborne supplies into Tobruk until the Royal Air Force could guarantee fighter cover – and this guarantee was impossible before 13 December. As a result, by 25 December only 18,000 tons of supplies (over half of them petrol and aviation spirit) had been landed at Tobruk. This was insufficient to supply the troops moving westward to the front, and at the same time build up forward dumps to supply the planned advance into Tripolitania.

There was therefore no alternative but to tie up transport in running lorry convoys overland from the Misheifa railhead – transport which could otherwise have accelerated XIII Corps' build-up in Western Cyrenaica. The forward Field Maintenance Centres opened at Sidi Muftah south of Gazala (15 December), Tmimi (18 December) and Msus (24 December) filled all too slowly. And the time lost in running these land convoys went hand in hand with the fuel consumed by the vehicles in transit, and the continued appalling wastage from leaking tins. It took until 28 December before the Msus FMC received any petrol at all and then the shipment was only 28,000 tons, against a demand for 60,000 tons.

The ever-worsening British supply position was compounded by the continuing belief at Eighth Army HQ that the bulk of Rommel's forces were still in the Benghazi region, with next to no Axis forces in the Agedabia/Antelat area. This may be judged by the welter of tasks required of 'Bencol' from 21 December. By this date 'Bencol' was very much out on a limb. The all-important tank reinforcement of 22nd Armoured Brigade – eighty cruiser tanks and thirty Honeys – was still at Mechili, over 100 miles to the east. But on the 21st Marriott was ordered to advance on El Magrun airfield (20 miles north of Beda Fomm), then to turn in his tracks and advance south through Agedabia to El Agheila and send patrols in the direction of Marada Oasis. Happily, the fuel shortage made instant compliance an impossibility. To have accomplished this programme Marriott's motley and divided force would have had to defeat first 21st Panzer, then 15th Panzer, and finally 90th Light and the Italians at Agedabia!

Though it would take Ritchie and Godwin-Austen two more days to grasp the fact, all hopes of repeating O'Connor's decisive interception of February, 1941, had vanished by 23 December. By this day Rommel had completed the gathering-together of his armoured units, with 21st and 15th Panzer Divisions at Beda Fomm and 'Ariete' in close support, midway between Beda Fomm and Agedabia. 'Trieste' was already halfway between Benghazi and Beda Fomm, passing Ghemines to the east, while 'Brescia' had safely disengaged from Benghazi and was also on the 'home stretch' of its march to rejoin the rest of the *Panzergruppe*.

Looking to the morrow, the *Panzergruppe* was well placed to continue Rommel's planned withdrawal to the El Agheila bottleneck. For the moment it had all the strength it needed to beat off the fumbling British probes towards Antelat and Beda Fomm.

This was demonstrated on the 23rd when 15th Panzer struck at the lightweight 'Bencol' column – a company of the Coldstream supported by 3rd Royal Tanks – which had been moving cautiously on Beda Fomm. In a brutal little action the British were forced back into the Desert east of Antelat – an ominous setback, optimistically interpreted by both Ritchie and Godwin-Austen as an unlucky skirmish with the remnants of *Afrika Korps*. To shatter this kernel of German resistance Godwin-Austen, encouraged by the belated advance of 22nd Armoured Brigade from Mechili on the 23rd, ordered a converging attack by 22nd Guards Brigade and 22nd Armoured Brigade. But once again the increasingly filthy weather and fuel shortages combined to delay and enfeeble the British attempt to re-enact Beda Fomm. The 22nd Armoured Brigade, having struggled forward as far as Saunnu, remained stranded there with empty tanks for another 24 hours. And on the evening of the same day Rommel finally gathered in the last of his retreating Italian divisions, 'Brescia', whose rearguards pulled out of Benghazi that morning.

By Christmas Day, 1941, having coolly exploited every single problem and mistake which had bedevilled Eighth Army, Rommel had re-concentrated the *Panzergruppe* in the triangle Beda Fomm-Antelat-Agedabia after its vulnerable nine-day retreat from Gazala. And still the British generals persisted in the empty hope that the Axis forces were running away and that a conclusive encircling victory still lay within Eighth Army's grasp. Rommel's next move, redeploying *Afrika Korps* to the Agedabia sector, only encouraged this British delusion, prompting Godwin-Austen to order an attack on Agedabia for the 27th–28th.

This gave Crüwell the chance he had been looking for ever since the panzer reinforcements had reached Benghazi on the 19th. On the 28th, exploiting the wide gap between the oncoming leading formation of 22nd Guards Brigade and 22nd Armoured Brigade, Crüwell struck with forty-four concentrated Pzkw-IIIs and IVs against about thirty-five scattered Honeys and fifty-five Crusaders. The cold ferocity of the German attack showed that the long retreat had deprived *Afrika Korps* of none of its professionalism. This was an outright defeat for the British armour, which lost a total of thirty-seven tanks – most of them breakdowns – as Marriott's survivors fell back to the South, across Wadi Faregh. German tank losses came to no more than seven.

This successful tank battle on the 28th offered Rommel the respite he wanted to complete the *Panzergruppe*'s withdrawal to El Agheila, but before carrying it out he gave Crüwell permission to reinforce success and grind down the British armour as far as possible. On 30 December Crüwell attacked again. After the losses inflicted on the British on the 28th the panzers had an even easier time, destroying and damaging twenty-three out of the sixty-two British 'runners', again for the recorded loss of only seven panzers. The net effect of the tank battles of the 28th and 30th was to reduce 22nd Armoured Brigade to the dangerously weak state of 39 Honeys, and the brigade was subsequently withdrawn for refit. The armoured balance in western Cyrenaica was now squarely in Rommel's favour, but though he sensed the fact it prompted no return of the wild rashness which had brought *Afrika Korps* to grief in the Sidi Rezegh fighting. Rommel now completed his withdrawal to El Agheila and Mersa Brega (1–6 January, 1942). When *Afrika Korps* went into second line on 10 January it was, as Rommel noted in a letter to his wife, for the first time since 18 November.

The last act of the CRUSADER drama was played out where it had all begun – on the Frontier, where Norrie now pressed XXX Corps' attack on the doomed Axis garrisons. After heavy air and naval bombardments followed by a night tank attack across the perimeter, 8000 Italian and German troops under Major-General Schmitt surrendered at Bardia on 2 January. Initially under Italian command, the Halfaya-Sollum garrison (6300 Italians and Germans under Major-General de Giorgis) fought on until Sollum fell to 2nd South African Division on 12 January. Five days later the last of Rommel's Frontier garrisons, the Germans at Halfaya under the indomitable Major Bach, accepted the inevitable and surrendered in turn. When they staggered into captivity, they left the Eighth Army undisputed masters of the North African coast from the Nile Delta to the Gulf of Sirte.

CHAPTER 5

ASSESSMENT

So ended CRUSADER, the extraordinary story of Eighth Army's first Desert campaign. From the first crossing of the Frontier Wire to the last German surrender at Halfaya, it had lasted an incredible sixty-one days; a battle-studded campaign of attrition without parallel in the annals of the British and Imperial armed forces during the Second World War.

Of course it looked different at the time. The merciless rain and the mud it created, both on a scale unknown in the previous winter campaign, combined to drown out any immediate, concrete sense of victory. To the dispassionate observer it seemed that the elements were implacably determined that Eighth Army should be denied the logical reward for its efforts in battle: the onward advance to Tripoli.

> Rain fell. The people in Western Cyrenaica declared they had never seen such rain before. You might have expected them to say that, since the weather is always believed to be worse in wartime – probably because the people are more exposed to it. Even so this was exceptional. Day after day the heavy grey stormclouds hung over the Green Hills and drenched the countryside. Great hailstones came down, an almost unprecedented thing, and away to the south near Agedabia the front-line troops reported they had seen flakes of snow on the desert.
>
> The rain began in the neighbourhood of Derna and beyond Derna it engulfed one village after another – Giovanni Berta and Slonta, Cirene and Barce, Tocra and Benghazi. Everywhere the troops stood about huddled in their greatcoats and every spare bit of clothing they

could lay hands upon. Some protected their faces with woollen balaclava helmets; others draped captured bivouac tents about their shoulders and went foraging through the deserted houses in search of firewood. . . .

In the desert south of Benghazi it was far worse. Red mud stretched interminably across the dreary landscape. I went out to the airfields of Berka and Benina – those two key fields that were going to be the springboards of our next great air sweep through to Tripoli. Inch by inch the grounded enemy aircraft were sinking into the mud. There were scores of aircraft, all useless. Those which had not been wrecked or broken up at the last moment by the *Luftwaffe* were falling to pieces in the wind. The rain did the rest. . . .

It was the same at Barce and Maraua, at Magrun and Soluq. Only Msus was left as the one reliable field in the forward area that could be used. There was no question of supplying the troops by air, even if we had the transport planes, which we hadn't. . . .

Given Benghazi as a port the rest became fairly easy. But Benghazi could not be used as a port. Within an hour of my first going into the town on the heels of the leading patrols, it was being bombed and mined. When I came away it was still being bombed and mined. . . . The docks and the railways leading to the docks were a chaos of exploded stone and steel and concrete. There were no lighters to take off the cargoes, no cranes to lift the boxes of ammunition, no pumps to draw off the petrol from the tankers. A tangle of wrecked steamers blocked the channel through the bay. Benghazi was no use. Only the land route was left. And the land route was choked.

The Eighth Army was like a healthy plant that had suddenly been denied water. The young leaves at the top suffered first. Around Agedabia the troops first went short of tinned fruit and vegetables, then jam and cheese. Finally they had bully beef, biscuits and tea and not much else. Little by little all the supplies fell away. Petrol was the most serious. The men could keep going on bully and biscuits, but until the petrol came they were unable to move. All over the desert I saw parties out scouring for enemy fuel dumps. Squadrons of new tanks which had toiled all the way by train and road to the front found they could do nothing.

For hundreds of miles isolated groups of men were strung across the wet desert with no orders and no notion of what to do. The sap was being drained out of the Eighth Army, not by the enemy, for Rommel had withdrawn around the Gulf of Sirte, but by the desert and the weather and the distance.[1]

Yet despite the exhaustion and frustration which attended the expiry of CRUSADER, Eighth Army had won a genuine victory. It was a victory none the less real for being overturned by Rommel's surprise advance on 21 January, which recovered Benghazi and the 'bulge' of the Jebel Akhdar. Compared with the Allied disasters multiplying on the far side of the world as Japan's offensive continued, unbroken since 7 December, Rommel's second attack would inflict little more than a minor local setback to the British in North Africa. It would leave Tobruk still in British hands and Eighth Army substantially undamaged, recuperating in good heart for the resumption of the struggle along the Gazala Line. It was the enormity of Eighth Army's defeat at Gazala in June, 1942, the subsequent loss of Tobruk and the agonizing retreat to Alamein, that would eclipse the memories of CRUSADER and how much Eighth Army had achieved in its first battle.

The achievement is certainly still worth considering. On the eve of CRUSADER Rommel had commanded 65,000 Germans and 54,000 Italians. By 17 January, 1943, the *Panzergruppe* had lost a total of 38,000 casualties, or 32 per cent of its original strength: 1100 Germans and 2300 Italians killed, 3400 Germans and 2700 Italians wounded, and 10,100 Germans and 19,800 Italians missing (the latter category including the 13,800 Axis prisoners taken at Bardia and Halfaya). Out of Eighth Army's original strength of 118,000, British and Imperial losses came to 2900 killed, 7300 wounded and 7500 missing – total casualties of 17,700. Expressed in cold percentages, Eighth Army had therefore managed to inflict 32 per cent losses on a hitherto unbeaten enemy, in return for only 15 per cent losses to its own strength.

These cold figures are all the more remarkable when the nature of CRUSADER is taken into account. It was a battle of attrition, strategy at its most brutal, in which the defender (in this case the *Panzergruppe*) usually holds most of the cards. Rommel's ability to strike back on 21 January, 1942, owed little to having suffered less in the CRUSADER fighting. It derived rather from the unique circumstances of the latter phases of his retreat, which left the *Panzergruppe* concentrated and Eighth Army dispersed, and above all to the timely arrival of new tanks and fuel supplies in sufficient amounts at precisely the right time. And CRUSADER had not only been a battle of attrition: it had been a tank battle in which the master cards of fire-power and mechanical reliability had been held by Rommel.

If Eighth Army veterans of CRUSADER can still take a thoroughly justifiable pride in their achievement, the same can certainly be said of their opponents. For the Desert War was *clean*, in the sense of being atrocity-free, and for this the high professional standards and humanity of the rival armies can take the credit. One fact bears repetition; CRUSADER was arguably most creditable of all to the Italian forces which took part. From the casualty figures quoted above, it will be noted that the oft-despised Italians suffered nearly double the losses of their German allies – 43 per cent all told, against a German loss percentage of 22.5 per cent. Bearing in mind the humiliating record of the Italian Army in action since 10 June, 1940 (with the two notable exceptions of the Keren and Amba Alagi battles in Ethiopia), CRUSADER should also be remembered as the battle in which the Italian Army can claim to have recovered its self-respect.

Beyond doubt, CRUSADER stands out as the worst-handled of all Rommel's battles, the one of which he would comment least in his memoirs. The strange clouding of Rommel's judgment during the Sidi Rezegh fighting in November was not to lift until the Alam Hamza battle in mid-December, after which he suddenly recovered every facet of his tactical flair – first to extricate his army and then to lead it again to victory. It must be frankly admitted that Rommel's persistent mishandling of CRUSADER was an unexpected bonus to Eighth Army which went far to offset the *Panzergruppe*'s formidable material advantages. Yet in the final analysis nothing can detract from Eighth Army's achievement. Ill-equipped, with only one and a half armoured divisions to pit against three, amateurs contriving make-do tactics with which to tackle better-armed veterans, the men of Eighth Army endured and won their first battle against formidable odds. The first clear-cut British land victory since the outbreak of the war, CRUSADER was the harbinger of Allied victory in the West.

NOTES

Introduction: BATTLE TO EXHAUSTION

1 Mellenthin, Major-General. F. W. von. *Panzer Battles* (University of Oklahoma Press, Norman, Oklahoma, 1956). p. 56

1 – THE BATTLEFIELD

1 From 'Landscape near Tobruk' by Jocelyn Brooke; published in full in *Alamein and the Desert War* (Sphere Books & Times Newspapers Ltd, London, 1967)
2 Moorehead, Alan, *The Desert War* (Hamish Hamilton, London, 1965), p. 9
3 Hunt, Sir David, *A Don at War* (William Kimber, London, 1966), pp. 22–3
4 Ciano, Count Galeazzo, *Ciano's Diaries*, ed. Malcolm Muggeridge (Heinemann, London, 1947), for 21.6.40, p. 268
5 Balbo to Badoglio, 20.6.40
6 Ciano, *op. cit.*, for 2.10.40, p. 295
7 Quoted in Moorehead, *op. cit.*, p. 27
8 Quoted in full in *Hitler's War Directives 1939–45*, ed. H. R. Trevor-Roper (Sidgwick & Jackson, London, 1964)
9 Moorehead, *op.cit.*, p. 23
10 Rommel, Erwin, *The Rommel Papers*, ed. B. H. Liddel Hart (Collins, London, 1953)
11 *Ibid.*
12 *Ibid.*
13 Young, Brigadier Desmond, *Rommel* (Collins, London, 1950), p. 25
14 Schmidt, Heinz Werner, *Rommel in the Desert* (Harrap, London, 1953)
15 *Ibid.*
16 Hunt, Sir David, *op.cit.*, pp. 59–60

17 Lewin, Ronald, *Rommel as Military Commander* (Batsford/Van Nostrand, London, 1968), p. 22

18 Crisp, Robert, DSO MC, *Brazen Chariots* (Frederick Muller, London, 1959), 'The Days Before'

19 Hunt, Sir David, *op.cit.*, pp. 61–2

20 Crisp, Robert, *op.cit.*

21 Moorehead, *op.cit.*, p. 80

2 – THE ARMIES

1 Mellenthin, *op.cit.*, p. 44

2 Schmidt, *op.cit.*, 'Front-Line Day'

3 Churchill, Winston, *The Second World War*: Vol. 1, 'The Gathering Storm' (Cassell, London, 1948)

4 Montgomery of Alamein, Field Marshal Viscount, *Memoirs* (Collins, London, 1958), 'Eighth Army: My thoughts during the flight to Egypt', p. 92

5 Crisp, Robert, *op.cit.*

6 Churchill, Winston, *The Second World War*: Vol. 3, 'The Grand Alliance' (Cassell, London, 1950)

7 Hunt, Sir David, *op.cit.*, 'The Relief of Tobruk', p. 63

8 Crisp, Robert, *op.cit.*

9 *Ibid.*

10 Schmidt, *op.cit.*, 'Rommel on a raid: stranded in No Man's Land'

11 Mellenthin, *op.cit.*, 'Sidi Rezegh', p. 59

12 Quoted in Young, Brigadier. Desmond, *op.cit.*, 'Desert Ups and Downs', p. 102

13 Ciano, *op.cit.*, for 17.11.41, pp. 398–9

14 Hunt, Sir David, *op.cit.*, 'A view of Alamein from GHQ', p. 134

15 Crisp, Robert, *op.cit.*

16 Mellenthin, *op.cit.*, 'Sidi Rezegh: The Armoured Clash', p. 61

3 – THE BATTLE

1 Crisp, Robert, *op.cit.*, 'First Day'

2 *Ibid.*

3 cf. Hunt, Sir David, *op.cit.*, p. 73

4 Mellenthin, *op.cit.*, p. 63

5 Playfair, Major-General I.S.O., *The Mediterranean and Middle East*, Vol. III (Her Majesty's Stationery Office, London, 1960), fn. P. 40

6 Moorehead, *op.cit.*, p. 92

7 Schmidt, *op.cit.*, 'Crusader'

8 Crisp, Robert, *op.cit.*, 'Third Day'

9 Hunt is of this opinion – *op.cit.*, p. 76 – though he places the broadcast one day too early. Mellenthin, on the other hand, does not mention it at all; nor does Schmidt, by 20 November commanding a company in 15th Panzer

Division. On the whole it would seem that the more scarifying one's experience on the 21st, the day the battle broke loose, the deeper one's conviction that it took the BBC broadcast to wake Rommel up. This is the frame of mind emphatically stated by Crisp.

10 To the Gallic Wars and Alesia (52 BC) when Julius Caesar, besieging Vercingetorix, had to cope with a simultaneous relief attack and attempted breakout
11 Playfair, *op.cit.*, Vol. III, p. 46
12 Crisp, Robert, *op.cit.*, 'Fifth Day'
13 Lewin, Ronald *op.cit.*, 'Crusader: the Winter Battle, 1941', p. 73
14 Mellenthin, *op.cit.*, p. 76
15 *Ibid*, p. 77
16 Young, Brigadier Desmond, *op.cit.*, 'Desert Ups and Downs', p. 109
17 Moorehead, *op.cit.*, p. 96–7
18 Crisp, *op.cit.*, 'Seventh Day'
19 Carver, Lieutenant-General Michael, *Tobruk* (Batsford, 1961), 'Cunningham's Crisis'
20 Crisp, *op.cit.*, 'Seventh Day'
21 Carver, *op.cit.*, 'Cunningham's Crisis'
22 Crisp, *op.cit.*, 'Eighth Day'
23 Auchinleck to Churchill, 29.11.41
24 Playfair, *op.cit.*, Vol III, p. 61
25 Murphy, W. E., *The Relief of Tobruk*, New Zealand War History Branch, Department of Internal Affairs, Wellington, NZ
26 Crisp, *op.cit.*, 'Ninth Day'
27 Moorehead, *op.cit.*, pp. 99–100
28 Quoted in Young, *op.cit.*, 'Desert Ups and Downs', p. 112
29 Hunt, *op.cit.*, 'The Relief of Tobruk', p. 83
30 *Ibid*, p. 85
31 Quoted in Young, *op.cit.*, 'Desert Ups and Downs', p. 91
32 Crisp, *op.cit.*, 'Twelfth and Thirteenth Days'
33 Lewin, *op.cit.*, 'Advance and Retreat, 1941–2', p. 86
34 Crisp, *op.cit.*, 'Fourteenth Day'
35 cf. Crisp, *op.cit.*, 'Fifteenth and Sixteenth Days'
36 Mellenthin, *op.cit.*, p. 84

4 – THE PURSUIT

1 Fielding, Captain Sean, *They Sought Out Rommel: A Diary of The Libyan Campaign*, 16 November–31 December 1941 (HMSO, London, 1942), 'A Ferocious Encounter', pp. 53–4
2 Quoted in Lewin, *op.cit.*, pp. 93–4

5 – ASSESSMENT

1 Moorehead, *op.cit.*, pp. 114–16

SELECT BIBLIOGRAPHY

Barnett, Correlli, *The Desert Generals*, William Kimber, London, 1960
Carver, Lieutenant-General Michael, *Tobruk*, Batsford, London, 1964
Ciano, Count Galeazzo, *Ciano's Diaries* (ed. Malcolm Muggeridge), Heinemann, London, 1947
Connell, John, *Auchinleck*, Cassell, London, 1959
Crisp, Robert, *Brazen Chariots*, Frederick Muller, London, 1959
Fielding, Captain Sean, *They Sought Out Rommel* ('The Army At War'), HMSO, London, 1942
Hunt, Sir David, *A Don At War*, William Kimber, London, 1966
Joly, Cyril, *Take These Men*, Constable, London, 1955
Kennedy Shaw, W. B., *Long Range Desert Group*, Collins, London, 1945
Lewin, Ronald, *Rommel as Military Commander*, Batsford/Van Nostrand, London, 1968
Macksey, Major Kenneth, *Afrika Korps*, Pan/Ballantine, London/New York, 1968
Mellenthin, Major-General F. W. von, *Panzer Battles*, University of Oklahoma Press, Norman, Oklahoma, 1956
Moorehead, Alan, *The Desert War*, Hamish Hamilton, London, 1965
Playfair, Major-General I.S.O., *The Mediterranean and Middle East*, Vol III, HMSO, London, 1960
Rommel, Erwin, *The Rommel Papers* (ed. B. H. Liddel Hart), Collins, London, 1953
Schmidt, Heinz Werner, *With Rommel in the Desert*, Harrap, London
Willison, Brigadier A. C., *The Relief of Tobruk*, The Leagrave Press
Young, Brigadier Desmond, *Rommel*, Collins, London, 1950

INDEX

206

125; and 'Dash to the Wire', 130–44; returns to Sidi Rezegh, 149–70; and decision to abandon Tobruk 170–80, 183; at Alam Hamza, 184–90; and retreat to Adegabia, 190–6

Cunningham, Adml. A. B.; comands British Mediterranean Fleet, 73 193–4

Cunningham, Gen. Sir Alan; commands Eighth Army, 68; and formation of CRUSADER plan, 74–5, 81, 88; and opening phase of CRUSADER, 93–4, 101; orders early relief of Tobruk, 103–5; false picture of Sidi Rezegh battle, 117; switches Tobruk relief to XIII Corps, 122; ordered to continue offensive by Auchinleck, 125–7; shaken by 'Dash to the Wire' and XXX Corps panic, 131; replaced by Ritchie, 141–4

Curtin, John, 70

Cyprus, 8, 71

Cyrenaica, geography of, 2–6; Italian forces in (1940), 8–10; O'Connor conquers (Dec 1940–Feb 1941), 21–4; Rommel reconquers, 29–40; Rommel's retreat from, after CRUSADER, 181–196

Cyrene, 88

DAK, see GERMAN FORCES: *Afrika Korps*

Dalmazzo, Gen., 19

'Dash to the Wire', (24–25 Nov), as turning-point of CRUSADER, 127–44

Davy, Brig. G.O.M., 92, 97, 102–3, 112–13, 118, 123, 125, 146

Derna, 6, 23–4, 26, 36, 99, 189–91, 193, 197

Desert Air Force, British, 78–9, 86–7, 89, 90, 99, 106, 115, 136–7, 139, 140, 164, 173, 177–8, 182, 186, 191

'Desert Rats', *see* BRITISH FORCES: 7th Armoured Division

Dodecanese Islands, 73

Drew, Lt. Col. Denham, 168

Egypt; Italian threat to (1940), 1–8; Italian invasion of, 14–15; secured by COMPASS, 16–21; importance of to Axis, after German invasion of Russia, 53; Eighth Army build-up in, for CRUSADER, 63–89

El Abiar, 193

El Adem, 11, 91, 92, 132, 144, 146, 171, 173, 176, 179

El Agheila, 5, 26, 30, 32, 34, 75, 194–6

El Alamein, 5–6

El Daba, 6

El Duda, 111–12, 117, 141–2, 145–6, 156, 159–61, 170, 172, 174–5, 177, 179, 182

El Faidia, 5

El Magrun, 194, 198

Er Regima, 5, 35

Erskine, Brig, I. D., 46

Escarpment, Great Libyan (Bardia/Sollum/Halfaya), 6–7, 17, 26

Ethiopia, 14, 20, 25, 45, 52, 63, 68

Euryalus, HMS, 95, 99

Fabio Filzi, 192

Fadden, Arthur, 70

Farouk, King, 2

Field Maintenance Centres (FMCs); and CRUSADER plan, 77–8; overlooked by Rommel, in 'Dash to the Wire', 129, 131–2, 135, 137; 159, 194

Field Supply Depots (FSDs), 21, 77

Fliegerführer Afrika, 33

'Force K' (Malta), 85

France, fall of (1940), 1–2

Free French, in Chad, 31

Freyberg, Maj. Gen. Bernard, VC; commands New Zealand Division, 70; demands more armoured protection for XIII Corps, 88; and XIII Corps advance, 94, 99, 106, 115; advances on Sidi Rezegh, 121, 135–6; achieves first relief of Tobruk, 141–55; and Third Battle of Sidi Rezegh, 156–70

Frölich, Gen. Stefan, 33

Frontier zone (Egypt/Libya), geography of, 6–8; 10–13; Rommel defends in BREVITY and BATTLEAXE, 40–50; 57–63, 81–9 and *passim*

Fuka, 77

Gabr Saleh, 82, 92, 96, 100, 102, 105, 108, 114, 137, 171

Gallina, Gen., 19

Gambara, Gen. Gastone, 56–7, 85, 96–7, 102, 122, 125, 140, 173, 176, 179, 182–3, 189

Gambier-Parry, Maj. Gen. M. D., 26, 34; captured, 36

Gambut; *Panzergruppe* HQ at, 87, 89, 95, 100, 109, 116, 136–7, 173

Gariboldi, Gen. Italo, 29, 34–5, 55

Gasr el Arid, 153, 173

Gatehouse, Brig. Alec; commands 4th Armoured Brigade, 69, 79–80, 93, 98–103, 105, 106, 113, 115, 118, 120, 135, 154–5, 164–8, 173, 178, 183, 184–90

de Gaulle, Gen., 31

Gause, Gen. Alfred, 56–7, 130

Gazala, 6, 26, 99, 180–1, 181–90

Geissler, Gen., 25, 29

Gentry, Col. W., 145

GERMAN FORCES: *Army/Corps*

Panzergruppe Afrika; formation of, after BATTLEAXE, 54–8; Rommel prepares for assault on Tobruk, 61–3, 81–9; slow reaction of, to CRUSADER offensive, 93–7; first countermoves of, 100–7; 'great opportunity missed' by (20 Nov), 108

Afrika Korps: 'birth certificate' of, 22; formation of, 27–8; early moral superiority of, 30–1; *materiel* advantages of, 33–4; first attack of, 34–7; halted at Tobruk, 39–40; and BREVITY/BATTLEAXE Frontier battles, 40–50; as 'cutting edge' of new *Panzergruppe Afrika*, 56–7; Rommel prepares for assault on Tobruk, 61–3, 81–9; reaction of to CRUSADER offensive, 93–97; first clashes with XXX Corps, 100–8; Rommel orders to retake Sidi Rezegh, 109; in 'multi-layer battle', 113–15; victory of, at Sidi Rezegh, 116–20; and *Totensonntag* battle, 123–125; disorganized by 'Dash to the Wire', 127–44; and Third Battle of Sidi Rezegh,

209

Nezuet Ghirba, 11
Nibeiwa, 18–19
Nichols, Lt. Col. J. S., 170
Nofilia, 5, 26, 30
Norrie, Maj. Gen. Willoughby; commands XXX Corps, 69; and opening phase of CRUSADER, 93, 101, 103; over-taxes 1st South African Div, 105; and 'multi-layer battle', 113; at Sidi Rezegh, 117, 121; supports XIII Corps, 126, 140, 146, 154–5, 164–6, 170–1, 173, 175, 176, 178–80, 183; and surrender of Axis Frontier garrisons, 196
Nuovo, Sidi Oman, *see* Sidi Oman

O'Connor, Maj. Gen. Richard; in Frontier raids (June, 1940), 10–13; and COMPASS, 17–20; takes Bardia and Tobruk, 22–3; completes conquest of Cyrenaica, 23–5; Neame replaces, 26; captured, 36, 74, 182
Oasis Force, 75, 102, 136, 182
OKH (*Oberkommando des Heeres* – German Army High Command), 25, 27–8, 32, 35, 39–40, 54, 54–6, 60–1
OKW (*Oberkommando der Wehrmacht* – German Armed Forces High Command), 35, 55, 85
Olbrich, Col., 35–6, 39
Omar, Libyan, and Sidi Omar Nuovo, *see* Sidi Omar
Otto, Major, 31

Palestine, 8, 68, 72, 175
Paulus, Lt. Gen. Friedrich, 39–40, 54
Pienaar, Brig. D. H., 105, 122, 124, 140, 157, 161, 162, 164–6, 168
Points 174, 182, (Bir El Gubi); defended by Blackshirt Coorto, 175, 176, 178
Point 175 (Sidi Rezegh), 156, 158–62, 164–5
Point 204 (Alam Hamza), 186–7, 208
Polish Carpathian Bde., 72–3, 111, 183, 184, 187
Ponath, Lt. Col. Gustav, 36
Pope, Lt. Gen. V. V., 69
Prittwitz, Gen. von, 39

Qattara Depression, 5

Rabia, 18–20
Ras el Madauar, 38
Ras et Tin, 6
Rashid Ali, 45
Ravenstein, Gen. Johann von; commands 5th Light, afterwards 21st Panzer Div., 44; in MIDSUMMER NIGHT'S DREAM, 84; on eve of CRUSADER, 85, 89; opening moves, 95–7, 100, 113; and Sidi Rezegh fighting (22 Nov), 118–20; and *Totensonntag* battle, 122–5; and 'Dash to the Wire', 127–44; and return to Sidi Rezegh, 149–53, 158; captured, 160, 162
Regia Aeronautica, 86
Reid, Brig. D. W., 102, 136
Revetria, Lt. Col. Mario, 95
Rintelen, Gen. von, 55, 85
Ritchie, Maj. Gen. Neil; replaces Cunningham as Eighth Army commander, 143; and crisis of CRUSADER, 154, 156–7; determination of, to

resume offensive, 170–1, 176–7, 179–80; hands pursuit of *Panzergruppe* to XIII Corps, 183; and pursuit to El Agheila, 190–6
ROMMEL, Gen. Erwin: commands embryo *Afrika Korps*, 27–8; first steps in Libya, 29–30; forbidden to take early offensive, 32; first attack of, 34–7; fails to take Tobruk, 37–40; and BREVITY/BATTLEAXE Frontier battles, 40–50; strengthens Axis positions with 88mm guns, 41–2; promoted General, 56; and new *Panzergruppe Afrika*, 56–8; reorganizes Frontier defences, 58–60; supply dilemma of, 60–62; misled by MIDSUMMER NIGHT'S DREAM, 83–4; disbelieves coming British offensive, 85–9; reaction of, to CRUSADER offensive, 93–7, 100, 104–5; orders recapture of Sidi Rezegh, 109; orders destruction of 7th Armoured Division and XXX Corps, 116, 122, 127; and 'Dash to the Wire', 127–44; and return to Sidi Rezegh, 148–70; and decision to abandon Tobruk, 170–80; and Alam Hamza battle, 181–90; withdraws *Panzergruppe* to El Agheila, 191–6; performance of, in CRUSADER campaign, 197–200
Roosevelt, President F. D., 65
Rotonda Segnali, 184–5
Royal Air Force, *see* Desert Air Force
Royal Navy, *see* Mediterranean Fleet, British

San Giorgio, 12
Saunnu, 195
Sceleidima, 24
Schmidt, Lt. Heinz; on life as Rommel's ADC, 38–9, 58–61, 83–4, 107; and capture of Ravenstein, 160
Schmitt, Maj. Gen., 196
Schmundt, Col. Rudolf, 29
Schwerin, Lt. Col. Graf von, 31–2, 35–6
Scobie, Maj. Gen. R. M.; commands Tobruk garrison, 73, 82; and breakout battles, 109–11, 117, 141, 144–5
Sebcha el Chebira, 5, 26, 31
Scott-Cockburn, Brig. J., 92, 97, 98, 113, 154–5
Selby, Brig. A. R., 18
Sheferzen, 92, 131
Sicily, 4, 29
Sidi Azeiz, 40–1, 92, 106, 115, 135, 137, 139, 145, 149–50, 171, 176
Sidi Barrani, 6, 14–16, 17–20, 46, 150
Sidi Breghisc, 184–6
Sidi Muftah, 194
Sidi Omar, 10–11, 47–50, 75, 83, 93, 95, 99, 106, 115–16, 128–9, 136, 142–3, 149–53, 171
Sidi Rafaa, *see* Beda Littoria
SIDI REZEGH; and British capture of Tobruk (Jan 1941), 22; Rommel overlooks importance of (April–May 1941), 38; 7th Armoured Div. captures, 92, 94, 97, 101–3, 105; *Afrika Korps* recovers (First Battle), 109, 111–15, 116–21; New Zealand Div. captures (Second Battle), 136, 139, 141, 146; *Afrika Korps* recovers (Third Battle), 156, 158–70, 173